"Balancing on an intricate edge between volume offers an excellent selection of 're uals, from slaves to kings, who populated t ....an of Europe in the centuries before and after the first Millennium. The expert authors provide a refreshing and instructive read to students of history and to anyone who has roots in this region or wishes to broaden her mental horizon."

Katalin Szende, Central European University, Budapest

PORTRAITS OF MEDIEVAL EASTERN EUROPE, 900–1400

Portraits of Medieval Eastern Europe provides imagined biographies of twenty different figures from all walks of life living in Eastern Europe from 900 to 1400. Moving beyond the usual boundaries of speculative history, the book presents innovative and creative interpretations of the people, places, and events of medieval Eastern Europe and provides an insight into medieval life from Scandinavia to Byzantium.

Each chapter explores a different figure and together they present snapshots of life across a wide range of different social backgrounds. Among the figures are both imagined and historical characters, including the Byzantine Princess Anna Porphyrogenita, a Jewish traveler, a slave, the Mongol general Sübedei, a woman from Novgorod, and a Rus' pilgrim. A range of different narrative styles are also used throughout the book, from omniscient third-person narrators to diary entries, letters, and travel accounts.

By using primary sources to construct the lives of, and give a voice to, the types of people who existed within medieval European history, *Portraits of Medieval Eastern Europe* provides a highly accessible introduction to the period. Accompanied by a new and interactive companion website, it is the perfect teaching aid to support and excite students of medieval Eastern Europe.

Donald Ostrowski is Research Advisor in the Social Sciences and Lecturer in History at the Harvard University Extension School. His previous publications include *Muscovy and the Mongols: Cross-Cultural Influences on the Steppe Frontier 1304–1589* (1998) and over 100 articles and review essays. He is also the editor of *The Povest' vremennykh let: An Interlinear Collation and Paradosis*, 3 vols. (2003), and a co-editor of four collections of studies.

Christian Raffensperger is Associate Professor of History at Wittenberg University, as well as an associate of the Harvard Ukrainian Research Institute. He has published multiple books including *Reimagining Europe: Kievan Rus' in the Medieval World* (2012) and *Ties of Kinship: Genealogy and Dynastic Marriage in Kyivan Rus'* (2016). He is also the series editor for *Beyond Medieval Europe*, a book series published by ARC Humanities Press.

PORTRAITS OF MEDIEVAL EASTERN EUROPE, 900–1400

Edited by Donald Ostrowski and
Christian Raffensperger

Routledge
Taylor & Francis Group

LONDON AND NEW YORK

First published 2018
by Routledge
2 Park Square, Milton Park, Abingdon, Oxon OX14 4RN

and by Routledge
711 Third Avenue, New York, NY 10017

Routledge is an imprint of the Taylor & Francis Group, an informa business

British Library Cataloguing-in-Publication Data
A catalogue record for this book is available from the British Library

Library of Congress Cataloging-in-Publication Data
A catalog record for this book has been requested

ISBN: 978-1-138-63704-7 (hbk)
ISBN: 978-1-138-70120-5 (pbk)
ISBN: 978-1-315-20417-8 (ebk)

Typeset in Bembo
by Apex CoVantage, LLC

Please visit the book's companion website at
http://www.routledge.com/cw/ostrowski

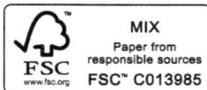

MIX
Paper from
responsible sources
FSC
www.fsc.org
FSC™ C013985

Printed in the United Kingdom
by Henry Ling Limited

To our predecessors, the trail-blazing scholars of medieval Eastern Europe . . .

CONTENTS

FIGURES

MAPS

Maps 1–5 were created by Ian Mladjov and reproduced with his permission.

CONTRIBUTORS

Neven Budak is Professor of medieval Croatian History at the University of Zagreb. As Associate Professor he was also teaching at the Central European University (Budapest). His main interests are early medieval history, urban history, history of identities, and cultural history.

Florin Curta is Professor of Medieval History and Archaeology at the University of Florida. His books include *The Making of the Slavs: History and Archaeology of the Lower Danube, ca. 500–700* (Cambridge, 2001), which has received the Herbert Baxter Adams Award of the American Historical Association; *Southeastern Europe in the Middle Ages, 500–1250* (Cambridge 2006); and the *Edinburgh History of the Greeks, c. 500 to 1050. The Early Middle Ages* (Edinburgh, 2011). Curta is the editor of five collections of studies and is the editor-in-chief of the Brill series "East Central and Eastern Europe in the Middle Ages, 450–1450."

Inés García de la Puente is Visiting Assistant Professor at Boston University and Assistant Professor at The Ohio State University. Her research focuses on different aspects of the culture of pre-Mongol Rus' and on Translation Studies.

David M. Goldfrank is Professor of History and Director of Medieval Studies at Georgetown University. Primarily a specialist in pre-modern Russian history, his books include *The Monastic Rule of Iosif Volotsky* (Kalamazoo, 1983; rev. ed., 2000); *The Origins of the Crimean War* (London, 1993); *A History of Russia: People, Legends, Events, Forces* (with Catherine Evtuhov, Lindsey Hughes, Richard Stites) (Boston/New York 2003); and *Nil Sorsky – The Authentic Writings* (Kalamazoo, 2008). He is currently working on a monograph on Iosif and a critical translation of his *Prosvetitel'*, as well as preparing for publication the late Andrei Pliguzov's collection of 268 documents,

The Archive of the Metropolitans of Kiev and all Rus'. His work on the Vojšelk convoy of texts goes back to the 1980s.

Isaiah Gruber is Research Associate at the Hebrew University of Jerusalem, Professor of Jewish History at the Israel Study Center, and co-founder of the academic services company Kol Hakatuv. He is the author of *Orthodox Russia in Crisis: Church and Nation in the Time of Troubles* as well as articles and translations related to art history and Jewish-Christian interaction in Eastern Europe.

Mari Isoaho is a docent in General History at the University of Helsinki. She received her PhD from the University of Oulu, where she wrote her dissertation, *The Image of Aleksandr Nevskiy in Medieval Russia: Warrior and Saint*, which was published by Brill in its series *The Northern World*, vol. 21, in 2006. Besides history, she has also experience in the field of archeology. She is an editor and co-author of the book *Past and Present in Medieval Chronicles*, published in the online series *COLLeGIUM, Studies Across Disciplines in the Humanities and Social Sciences*, vol. 17, 2015. Her recent research interests include the Kievan chronicle tradition and apocalyptic thinking in Kiev.

Eve Levin is Professor in the History Department at the University of Kansas, specializing in issues of gender, sexuality, religion, medicine, and popular culture in pre-modern Russia and Eastern Europe. She is also the Editor of *The Russian Review*.

Timothy May is Professor of Central Eurasian History at the University of North Georgia. He is also the author of *The Mongol Art of War* (2007), *The Mongol Conquests in World History* (2009), and the editor of *The Mongol Empire: A Historical Encyclopedia* (2016).

Paul Milliman is Associate Professor in the History Department at the University of Arizona. He is the author of *"The Slippery Memory of Men": The Place of Pomerania in the Medieval Kingdom of Poland* (Leiden and Boston: Brill, 2013) and teaches courses on the history of Europe in the global Middle Ages, including courses on games and food.

Balázs Nagy is Associate Professor of Medieval History at the Eötvös Loránd University and a visiting faculty member at the Department of Medieval Studies at the Central European University, Budapest. His main research interests are the medieval economic and urban history of Central Europe. He is co-editor of the Latin-English bilingual edition of the autobiography of Emperor Charles IV (ed. with Frank Schaer, CEU Press, 2001); has edited with Derek Keene and Katalin Szende, *Segregation – Integration – Assimilation: Religious and Ethnic Groups in the Medieval Towns of Central and Eastern Europe* (Ashgate, 2009) and *Medieval Buda in Context* with Martyn Rady, Katalin Szende, and András Vadas (Brill, 2016).

Leonora Neville is the John W. and Jeanne M. Rowe Professor of Byzantine History and Vilas Distinguished Achievement Professor at the University of Wisconsin–Madison. Her studies of authority and gender in Byzantium have led to *Anna Komnene: The Life and Work of a Medieval Historian* (Oxford, 2016), *Heroes and Romans in 12th Century Byzantium* (Cambridge, 2012), and *Authority in Byzantine Provincial Society, 950–1100* (Cambridge, 2004).

Donald Ostrowski is Research Advisor in the Social Science and Lecturer in History at the Harvard University Extension School. He is the author of *Muscovy and the Mongols: Cross-Cultural Influences on the Steppe Frontier 1304–1589* (Cambridge University Press, 1998) and the editor of *The Povest' vremennykh let: An Interlinear Collation and Paradosis*, 3 vols. (Cambridge, MA: Harvard Library of Early Ukrainian Literature, 2003), which received the Early Slavic Studies Association Award for Distinguished Scholarship. He has published over 100 articles and review essays and has been a co-editor of four collections of studies. He also chairs the Early Slavists Seminars at the Davis Center for Russian and Eurasian Studies at Harvard University.

Christian Raffensperger is Associate Professor of History at Wittenberg University, as well as an associate of the Harvard Ukrainian Research Institute. He has published multiple books including *Reimagining Europe: Kievan Rus' in the Medieval World* (Harvard UP, 2012) and *Ties of Kinship: Genealogy and Dynastic Marriage in Kyivan Rus'* (Harvard-HURI, 2016). He is also the series editor for *Beyond Medieval Europe*, a book series published by ARC Humanities Press.

Anti Selart is Professor of Medieval History at the University of Tartu, Estonia. He has published on several topics of Livonian and Russian history in the Middle Ages and in the sixteenth century.

Heidi Sherman-Lelis and Arnold Lelis[x] co-created Gorm and imagined his adventures throughout Eastern Europe together. Arnold and Heidi earned their doctoral degrees at the University of Minnesota, where they studied early medieval history and archaeology, each completing dissertations on differing aspects of trade and exchange in Northern Europe. They both love teaching, moving to Wisconsin for teaching positions at the University of Wisconsin–Stevens Point and the University of Wisconsin–Green Bay. Arnold died of cancer with Heidi at his side. We use the runic symbol Gebo (x) after his name to symbolize their gift of partnership.

Vlada Stanković is Professor of Byzantine Studies and Director of the Center for Cypriot Studies at the University of Belgrade. He is the editor of the series *Byzantium: A European Empire and Its Legacy* for Lexington Books.

Cameron Sutt received his PhD from the University of Cambridge, St. Catherine's College in 2008. He is currently Associate Professor at Austin Peay State University and Chair of the Department of History & Philosophy.

Susana Torres Prieto is Associate Professor of Humanities at IE University. Her main research interests are on medieval Russian literature and codicology.

Monica White is Assistant Professor of Russian and Slavonic Studies at the University of Nottingham. Her interests include the history of Byzantium and Rus, the Orthodox Church, and the religious aspects of warfare in the medieval Orthodox world. Her publications include *Military Saints in Byzantium and Rus, 900–1200* (Cambridge, 2013).

Lisa Wolverton, Professor of History at the University of Oregon, concentrates her research on the Czech Lands in the early and central Middle Ages. She is the author of several books, including a translation of Cosmas of Prague's *Chronicle of the Czechs* (Catholic University of America Press, 2009).

ACKNOWLEDGMENTS

Christian Raffensperger

This project would not exist without *Portraits of Old Russia* conceived of by Marshall Poe and set up and edited by Marshall Poe and Don Ostrowski. I had heard of that book when it was still in the early stages from my dissertation advisor, Richard Hellie, who was at first skeptical and then interested in the premise that Don and Marshall were advocating. Years later when the book came out from M. E. Sharpe I reviewed it for *Russian Review* and enjoyed it immensely. I wanted to teach with it, and subsequently began to do so, but another idea was percolating in my head.

The week after I submitted the review I was telling my wife, yet again, about the book, and how fascinated I was by it and how I wished I could do something like it for an earlier period. She made the extraordinarily logical suggestion that I should just do it, and email Don to see what he would say. I emailed Don later that same day and he liked the idea and wanted to participate in the new project! Thus, *Portraits of Medieval Eastern Europe* was born.

Admittedly, it took many years from that point to bring the book to fruition with Routledge, and along the way we incurred debts to a variety of people and groups. Don and I were able to arrange a panel to start off the Portraits process at the Association of Slavic, East European, and Eurasian Studies in Philadelphia in 2015. The participants and the audience were immensely helpful in providing positive feedback on the process which helped it grow and improve. We also hosted a conference at Harvard University in April 2016 to bring another group of Portraits contributors together. That conference was very generously supported by the Harvard Ukrainian Research Institute, the Medieval Studies Seminar, the Davis Center for Russian and Eurasian Studies, the Early Slavic Studies Seminar, and the Early Slavic Studies Association. That funding allowed us to bring in scholars from around the U.S. and Europe to participate in the conference. Getting so many contributors together in one room was an essential process to creating some of the basic synergy of the volume, and developing ideas for the companion digital humanities project.

The book would not have ever happened without the willingness of the contributors to devote their time and scholarly energy to a project that is largely devoted to undergraduates and is creative (with all of the opprobrium that brings to tenure and promotion committee). Their genuine interest and joy at talking about and writing these portraits convinced Don and me that we were onto something worthwhile. I hope that our students will agree and that these portraits will find a welcome place in the classroom.

Finally, I would not be able to do any of what I do without the support of my community and family. I want to thank Dar Brooks Hedstrom and the entire Wittenberg University History Department; Doug Lehman, Director of the Thomas Library at Wittenberg; and the Faculty Development Board who provided grants to assist me in the development of this project. Most importantly, I want to thank my family – Cara, Iris, and Malcolm – for their love and support amidst all of the work required to complete the various phases of this project.

Donald Ostrowski

My first expression of gratitude must, of course, go to Chris for coming up with this project and for his willingness to have me work with him on it. I saw it as an opportunity to introduce the Middle Ages both to students and the educated nonspecialists in a "user-friendly" way, but I also saw it as an opportunity to help change people's misconceptions about the Middle Ages.

Patricia Kolb, who was instrumental in getting *Portraits of Old Russia* published, has been a staunch supporter of the *Portraits of Medieval Eastern Europe* from the beginning.

The conference/workshop held at Harvard University in April 2016 would not have happened without a coalition of institutional co-sponsors that Chris mentioned. Institutions don't function without people, and their contributions need to be acknowledged. Dean Huntington Lambert III agreed to have the Extension School provide financial support and turned over his conference room for our workshop. Jeannette Binjour, financial associate, made that funding a reality. For the Davis Center, Professor Abdi Abdelal, Director of the Davis Center, approved funding, and Penelope Skalnik made it happen. For the Harvard Ukrainian Research Institute, Professor Serhii Plokhy, Director, approved funding, and Tymish Holowinsky, Executive Director, put it in operation. The President of the Early Slavic Studies Association approved funding from that organization, and Cynthia Vakareliyska, Treasurer, made it come true. For the Committee on Medieval Studies, Dr. Sean Gilsdorf, Program Administrator, both approved and enacted the Committee's support.

Finally, like Chris, my main academic and career consultant is my wife, Wren Collé. Although she is continually advising me to stop taking on more projects, she approved of my taking on this one. Her advice is unerring and much appreciated.

MAP 1 Medieval Europe

L. Onega
L. Ladoga
Beloe Ozero
Old Ladoga
L. Chud
Novgorod
Volga R.
Pskov
Rostov
Nizhnii
Novgorod
Kazan
Tver'
Suzdal'
Vladimir
Bulgar
Moscow
Murom
Kasimov
Polotsk
Riazan'
Smolensk
W. Dvina R.
KIEVAN RUS'
Briansk
Turov
Novgorod Severskii
Volynskii
Chernigov
Kiev
Pereiaslavl'
New Sarai
Dnieper R.
Don R.
Sarai
Dniester R.
POLOVTSY/CUMANS/QIPCHAKS
Tana
Astrakhan
Suceava
Sea of
Azov
CRIMEA
Caffa
Kherson
Caucasus Range
Derbent
Black Sea
Kutaisi
Tbilisi
Dristra
GEORGIA
Preslav
Sinope
Mesembria
Trebizond
Ani
Dvin
Adrianople
Heraclea
ARMENIA
Constantinople
Manzikert
Nicaea
Ancyra/Ankara
Sebasteia
Van
Tabriz
Gallipoli
Doryleum
EMPIRE
Caesarea
Ray
Smyrna
Acroenus
Iconium/Konya
Edessa
Mosul
Ephesus
Sis
Attaleia
Tarsus
Hamadan
Rhodes
Aleppo
Myra
Antioch
Tigris R.
Nicosia
Famagusta
Euphrates R.
Baghdad
Tripoli
Cyprus
Damascus
Acre
Nazareth
Basra
Jerusalem
Bethlehem
Alexandria
Nile R.
Cairo
Ural Range
Volga R.
Ural R.
Caspian Sea

Map by Ian Mladjov

MAP 1 (Continued)

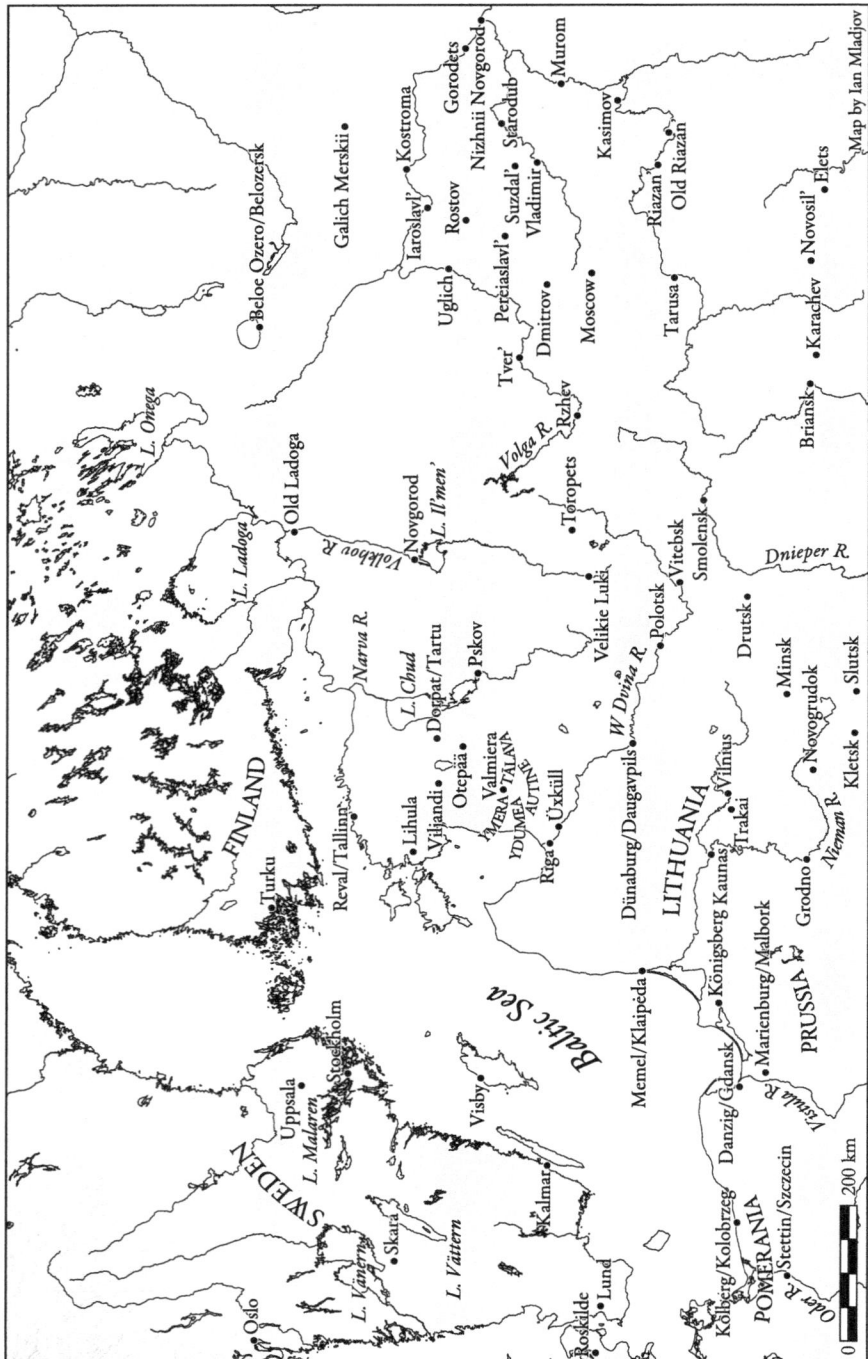

MAP 2 Northern Rus', the Baltics, and southern Scandinavia

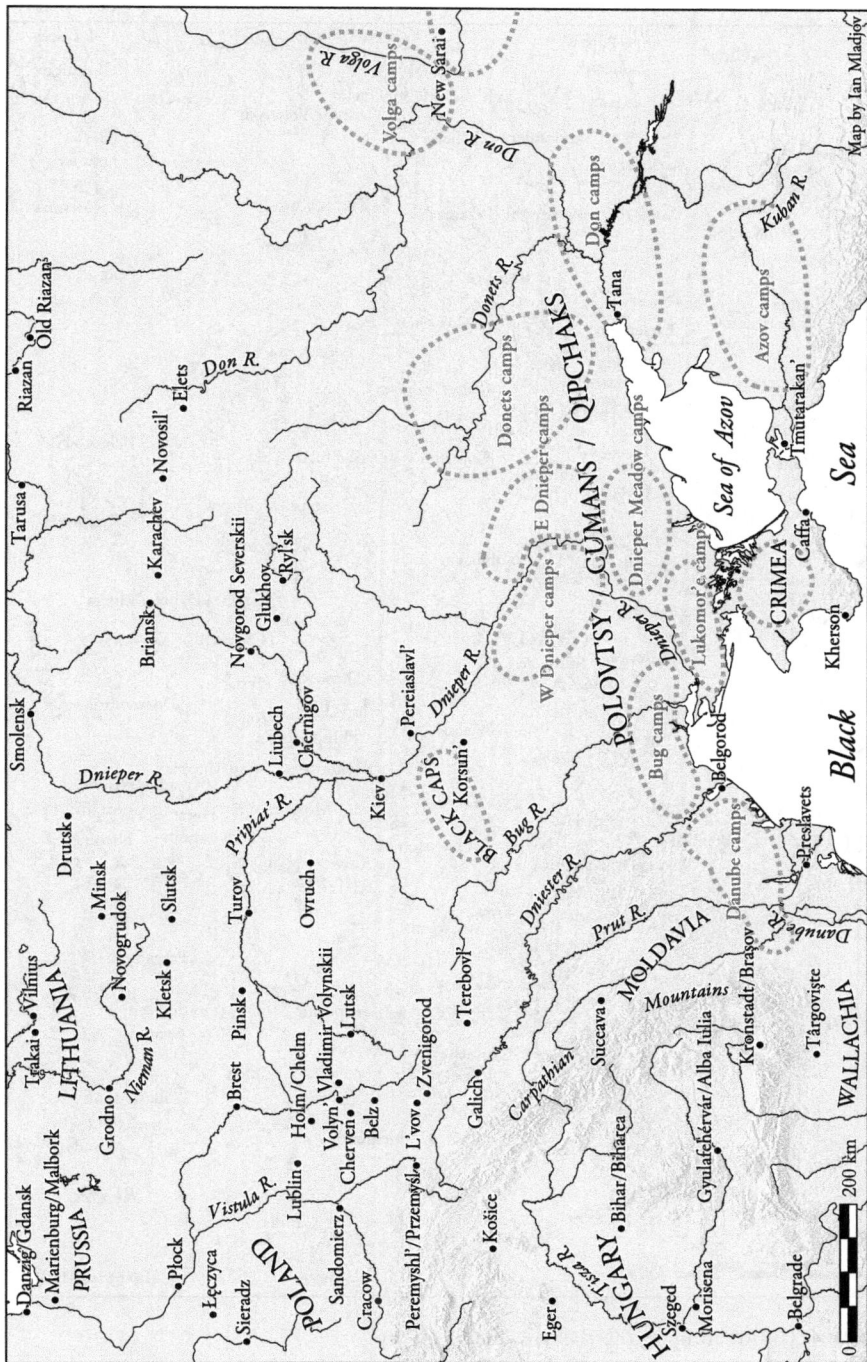

MAP 3 Southern Rus' and the western steppe

MAP 4 Constantinople, the Balkans, and Hungary

SWEDEN

Visby

Riga

LIVONIA

Kalmar

Baltic Sea

DENMARK

Aarhus

Memel/Klaipéda

LITHUANIA

Ribe

Roskilde

Lund

Königsberg

Kaunas

Schleswig

Hedeby

Starigrad/Oldenburg

Stralsund

Kolberg/Kolobrzeg

Danzig/Gdansk

PRUSSIA

Lübeck

Mecklenburg

Schwerin

Marienburg/Malbork

Grodno

Hamburg

POMERANIA

Vistula R.

Bremen

Verden

Oder R.

Elbe R.

Stettin/Szczecin

Brandenburg

Poznań

Gniezno

Płock

MAZOVIA

Brest

SAXONY

Minden

Hildesheim

Magdeburg

Łęczyca

Halberstadt

Wittenberg

LUSATIA

Głogów

Sieradz

POLAND

Lublin

Naumburg

Merseburg

Meissen

Wrocław

THURINGIA

Zeitz

Świdnica

Brzeg

SILESIA

Opole

Sandomierz

Fulda

Litoměřice

Eger

Prague

Racibórz

Cracow

Vistula R.

Przemyśl

Würzburg

Bamberg

Plzeň

Šternberk

Opava

Cieszyn

FRANCONIA

Nürnberg

BOHEMIA

Olomouc

Jihlava

Regensburg

Budějovice

Brno

MORAVIA

Velehrad

Košice

Eichstätt

BAVARIA

Znojmo

Sajó R.

Ulm

Freising

Passau

Linz

Melk

Nitra

Augsburg

Munich

Salzburg

Vienna

Bratislava

Visegrád

Eger

Tisza R.

Innsbruck

AUSTRIA

Győr

Esztergom

Vác

Danube R.

Buda

Pest

Alpine Range

STYRIA

Gurk

Graz

Veszprém

Székesfehérvár

Bihar/Biharea

TYROL

CARINTHIA

Klagenfurt

Marburg

HUNGARY

Somogyvár

Kalocsa

Maros R.

Trent

Laibach/Ljubljana

Pécs

Szeged

Morisena

Aquileia

Zagreb

Danube R.

Verona

Padua

Venice

Trieste

Drava R.

Po R.

Mantua

Sava R.

Parma

Ferrara

Adriatic Sea

CROATIA

Sirmium

Belgrade

Golubac

Modena

Bologna

Ravenna

Smederevo

Zara/Zadar

Jajce

BOSNIA

Knin

Sarajevo

0   250 km

Map by Ian Mladjov

MAP 5 East Central Europe

INTRODUCTION

Donald Ostrowski

Portraits of Medieval Eastern Europe is, in effect, a prequel to *Portraits of Old Russia* (Armonk, NY: M. E. Sharpe, 2011). In that book, Marshall Poe and I gathered together brief verbal portraits by noted scholars of imagined lives in Rus' from 1300 to 1725. In the current volume, Christian Raffensperger and I have done a similar gathering of depictions and expanded the geographical area to Eastern Europe as well as pushing back the date range of the depictions to the period from the 920s to 1401.

These imagined lives are not strictly speaking non-fiction history because in every case, the author has gone beyond the usual boundaries of speculative history. Nor are these depictions works of historical fiction, which are usually intended to entertain while maintaining a certain degree of correlation with the source evidence. In a sense, what we have here is a genre that falls in between the two, for the editors encouraged creative speculation on the part of the contributors (while of course respecting their natural inclination not to violate the testimony of the sources). In traditional works of history, the historian is not supposed to go beyond his or her sources.[1] Nonetheless, here we encouraged our historians to do so in order to present interpretations that could not otherwise be proposed. Additionally, the intent is not to entertain (although we hope these portraits are enjoyable to read), but to instruct. All the contributors are scholarly experts in the area of their subject's imagined life. Each has been trained to observe the boundaries of the source testimony. But here they venture into a gray area between historical non-fiction and historical fiction.

The genre is not new with these portraits in regard to medieval European history. Eileen Power's *Medieval People* (1924) and Norman Cantor's *Medieval Lives* (1994) each created a series of imagined biographies to allow readers to gain access to medieval lives of peasants, women, churchmen, and rulers who otherwise have little or no evidence about them. We followed in spirit Cantor's dictum: "This modest exercise of historical imagination preserves . . . medieval sense and sensibility that academic research has revealed."[2] One may be reminded of George Orwell's remark when he was told that a report he wrote for the *Partisan Review* was inaccurate: "It is essentially true."[3] Also one may be surprised to find out that Orwell's *Down and Out in Paris and London* (1946) is not strictly speaking a non-fiction memoir, for he "rearranged" the events and modified them in his description to make a better narrative. The problem in both cases is that he did not identify at the time that his *Partisan Review* report and his *Down and Out in Paris and London* were not completely "true" but only "essentially true." Here we openly signal that these portraits are "essentially true" with a heavy dose of historical imagination having been thrown in.

In a theoretical vein, Hayden White has warned historians about the shaping tendency that narrative emplotments and interpretations can have on the presentation of evidence.[4] The editors and contributors to this volume are consciously aware of that shaping tendency. In other words, we are not saying what we report is what happened and this is the way it happened (as many historical narratives seem to be at least implicitly asserting), but that this is a possibility of what happened (or something very similar to it in regard to composite characters) and this is possibly the way it could have happened. We have marked these depictions as "imagined" and as "creative speculation," and we hope the results will provide a user-friendly means of introducing medieval Eastern European history to students as well as the educated non-specialist. In the process we hope that specialists will also find something of interest in them.

The quotation from Norman Cantor above continues: "The innovation, if it may be called that, is in the way the narrative is told."[5] In the current volume the contributors have, likewise, been innovative in telling their respective narratives. The various narrative strategies they employ all derive from well-known narrative strategies for works of fiction.

Narrative strategies

Generally, there are basically three basic modes of narration – first person ("I/We did this."), second person ("You did this."), and third person ("He/She/It/They did this."). In third-person narration, one can have an omniscient narrator who knows, but does not necessarily tell, all. One can also have a subjective narrator, one who has a particular point of view. The subjective third-person narrator can make asides to the reader, as the narrator of Henry Fielding's *Tom Jones* (1749) does or even be a participant in the action, as are the narrators Nelly Dean and Lockwood in *Wuthering Heights* (1847) by Emily Brontë (Ellis Bell) or as is the narrator of the Sherlock Holmes stories – Dr. John H. Watson – who is involved in the story itself as it unfolds.

One can have an objective narrator. The strategy of the objective narrator was the basis of realist fiction of the nineteenth and twentieth centuries. Among the earliest and best examples of literary realism is Gustave Flaubert's *Madame Bovary* (1857), where the narrator tells the story in a way that is similar to a clinician's recording in the most objective and detached manner possible the unfolding of events as though they were part of an experiment.

In the present collection we have several examples of a first-person narrator. Susana Torres Prieto (IE University) adopts the diary form to tell the story of the arrival and first few years of the Byzantine Princess Anna Porphyrogenita's coming to Rus', her marriage to the King of Rus', Volodimir I (ca. 958–1015), and the misery of her longing for Constantinople where she had lived her whole life until then. One can imagine, as Torres Prieto does, what thoughts must have been going through the mind of this princess, who was raised in the lap of luxury only to find herself among those she considers barbarians.

Anti Selart (University of Tartu) provides another first-person narration in the form of a memoir written by Volodimir of Pskov (1170s–1230s) as he reflects toward the end of his life on his achievements and failures. As with any good memoirist, Volodimir passes judgments on those he discusses. He calls "greedy and jealous" the priest Henry, who is generally regarded as the author of the *Livonian Chronicle*, and tells us that "he lied." The people of Pskov are termed "fickle" because they twice voted for him to be their ruler and twice voted for him to leave off being their ruler. In this portrait, Selart personalizes a minor ruler who played a major role in events of his time.

Two more first-person narrations appear in the form of travel accounts. Isaiah Gruber (Hebrew University of Jerusalem) has his narrator, Yitshak ben Sirota, an imagined Jewish traveler and sometime slave of the eleventh century, tell his own life story as though it were one long peregrination. Gruber includes at the end a second first-person narrator in the form of Yitshak's grandson Shlomo who adds a postscript after he finishes copying the manuscript in which his grandfather's imagined life appears.

Monica White (University of Nottingham) provides an imagined travel account of the monk Fotii, a historical figure, who undertook a pilgrimage from Tver' to Constantinople in 1277. Fotii vividly describes what he sees on the way as well as his reactions to what he is seeing. In those descriptions, White intersperses the statements that historical Rus' travelers made in their own writings about their respective pilgrimages to Constantinople. Thus, she gives enhanced historical verisimilitude to Fotii's imagined travelogue.

Donald Ostrowski (Harvard University) employs a first-person account as reported by another person. The Rus' slave Vaska tells the story of Konchak, a Polovtsian leader, but in the process he tells us much of his own story. Vaska's narration is framed as a story that he related to Dusticello of Pisa, a friend of the family of a Genoese merchant who bought Vaska on the Black Sea slave market. Thus, we have a story within a story (*mise en abyme*) – Vaska's story within that of Dusticello's, and Konchak's story within that of Vaska's. Such a technique of the narrator's telling his own story as part of telling the story of another person was invoked by Robert Penn Warren in *All the King's Men* (1946), where the narrator, the historian Jack Burden, tells the story of the cynical populist Willie Stark in Louisiana of the 1930s but ends up telling as much if not more about himself.

The final first-person account is by Leonora Neville (University of Wisconsin) in her presentation of the eleventh-century Byzantine princess and historian Anna Komnene's response to criticism of her by modern-day historians. Neville refers to this technique by the Greek term *ethopoeia* (a rhetorical exercise). The same technique was used by the cultural historian Ihor Ševčenko (1922–2009) in 1992 to present the response of the tenth-century emperor Constantine VII Porphyrogenitus (905–959) to criticism of him, likewise by modern-day historians.[6]

Five of our contributors utilize omniscient third-person narratives that employ the past tense in the telling of the story. Inés García de la Puente (Ohio State University and Boston University) uses such a narrative strategy to advance an interpretation about Gleb Vseslavich's wife (1074–1158). We have little evidence about her; for example, we do not even know her name. But what evidence we do have is unusual for a woman in twelfth-century Rus', including a eulogy in the chronicle upon her death. She may have succeeded her husband as ruler of Minsk, and this portrait takes as its premise that she did so. It leads us through the princess's thought processes as she comes to grips with her husband's death and deals with concerns about her own situation and how she approached her new role.

Mari Isoaho (University of Helsinki) also employs an omniscient third-person narrative to describe a mother, Kuutamo Hyväneuvo, in an indigenous kinship group of Finns in the thirteenth century. Kuutamo is waiting for the return of her son from a long journey. Since we have no evidence about specific individuals among such Finnish kinship groups, the character of the mother is necessarily a fictive one. Isoaho draws extensively, however, on contextual historical and folkloric evidence for her depiction.

The portrait by Cameron Sutt (Austin Peay State University) of a thirteenth-century Hungarian slave, Zalava, is also told from the point of view of an omniscient third-person narrative. The narrator even knows what Zalava remembers and does not remember. The historian has little information about slaves in medieval Europe, let alone knowing many of them by name. Sutt is able to reconstruct events in Zalava's life using his imagination and from details found in official documents of the 1270s.

Vlada Stanković (University of Belgrade) also employs the historical past tense of an omniscient third-person narrator. He begins his portrait at a particular point in time – the early days of December 1282 when King Milutin of Serbia was expecting a military attack by the Byzantine Emperor Michael VIII. Stanković then uses that pivotal year to place Milutin's four marriages within the context of Serbia's relationship with the king of Sicily, the king of Hungary, the Byzantine Emperor, and the khan of the western part of the Ulus of Jochi (Qipchaq Khanate). In the process, the reader is provided an insight into the thinking, hopes and fears of Milutin, who was canonized within two years of his death.

Heidi Sherman-Lelis (University of Wisconsin–Green Bay) and Arnold Lelis (University of Wisconsin–Stevens Point) use a different form of omniscient third-person narrative, one that employs the historical present (*praesens historicum*) instead of the past tense. They tell the story of Gorm, a young Viking man of the tenth century and his trips to Gardariki (Rus'). Usually the historical present is associated with a first-person narrator, but William Gibson's novel *Pattern Recognition* (2003), among a few others, successfully employs the third-person historical present, as Sherman-Lelis and Lelis do here. Whether utilized through the first person or third person, the historical present serves to make the events described more immediate to the reader.

Paul Milliman (University of Arizona) chooses a non-omniscient third-person narrative to tell his story. He takes the multi-volume *History of Poland* by Jan Długosz (1415–1480) and adds an interpolation in the voice of Długosz. That imagined interpolation describes how the Master Chef of King Władysław Jagiełło of Poland invented a Polish national dish, *bigos*, a stew made with different kinds of game meat mixed together. Since the origin of Polish bigos is a matter of dispute, Milliman's interpolation provides an explanation of how it might have been invented. Another use of the non-omniscient third-person narrative is by Balázs Nagy (Eötvös Loránd University, Central European University, Budapest) in his portrait of Bela IV, king of Hungary from 1235 to 1270. Like Milliman's narrator, Nagy's is a historian. Instead of a fifteenth-century historian, however, Nagy's narrator is a present-day historian who has done his best to piece together biographical information about Bela IV based on the sources we have. The narrative strategy for presentation is an interview with the historian in which an interlocutor asks him to explain his understanding of significant aspects of Bela's reign as king of Hungary.

Four of the accounts herein use the epistolary form, made popular by Samuel Ricardson's novel *Pamela* (1740), but which ultimately derives from Diego de San Pedro's 1485 novel *Cárcel de amor* (*Prison of Love*). Each of two accounts utilizes a single letter written by a churchman.

Lisa Wolverton (University of Oregon) invokes an imaginary letter from an unnamed churchman in Prague to his uncle, another unnamed churchman in Olomouc, to tell the story of Bishop Henry Zdík, head of the church in Moravia, at a crucial moment in his career in 1140. It was also a key moment in the history of Moravia. The letter writer tells us that Soběslav, the ruler of Moravia, died two weeks earlier and the local dukes supported his nephew Vladislaus over Soběslav's son (also named Vladislaus) to succeed him. We learn of the impending crisis through the eyes of the young cleric in the city of Prague as Bishop Henry began to get involved in "worldly matters" – the politics of the succession struggle and potential civil war.

Florin Curta (University of Florida) creates an imaginary letter written in 1236 from a Bulgarian patriarch to a Bulgarian emperor to tell the story of St. Sava, a few months after his death. Sava was one of the most important figures of Serbian history and was canonized as the founder of the Serbian Orthodox Church. Curta utilizes as a source for his story a genuine biography written by the Serbian monk Domentijan, who traveled with Sava during the last few years of his life. In the process, Curta creates a portrait of Sava that is both secular and religious.

The two other narratives that use the epistolary form involve a series of letters written by a single secular individual. Christian Raffensperger (Wittenberg University) imagines two letters written by Evpraxia, daughter of Vsevolod (who ruled

Rus′ from 1078 to 1093), sister of Volodimir Monomakh (who ruled Rus′ from 1113 to 1125), and wife of Henry IV (Holy Roman Emperor from 1084 to 1105). As Raffensperger points out in the introduction, she was one of the most famous women of her time, took part in the Investiture Controversy, toured Europe giving speeches, and even addressed a papal council (Piacenza 1095). In these imagined letters dated 1093 and 1096, she writes to her family telling of her time at foreign courts and in foreign lands.

Timothy May (University of North Georgia) writes a series of four imagined letters from the Mongol general Sübedei, one of the great military commanders of all time.[7] The first letter is addressed to Chinggis Khan telling him of the Battle on the Kalka River in 1223 against the Rus′. The next two letters are to Qa'an Ögödei, the successor of Chinggis Khan, and the second of those takes the form of an "after-action" report on the campaign in Eastern Europe. The fourth letter is a letter of advice to Sübedei's son. The time span of the letters is twenty years.

Then there are the hybrid narratives, which combine two or more narrative strategies. Eve Levin (University of Kansas) uses an omniscient third-person narrator, who is able to report what the main character, Anna, is thinking and doing, interspersed with "letters" in the form of excerpts from genuine Novgorodian birch bark missives. Although it is unlikely the particular missives quoted were part of such a single story, given enough written birch bark documents, historians might be able one day to come close to constructing a story about a single individual based on them.

Neven Budak (University of Zagreb) begins his portrait of Paul I Bribir, the ban of Croatia, with a description in the historical present tense of his son Mladen entering the city of Zadar in March 1311. Mladen is about to receive the keys to the city for helping to oust the forces of Venice. Budak then switches to the historical past tense to describe the political and diplomatic circumstances, almost as a contemporary diplomat would, of Paul's rise to power that set the stage for Mladen's being honored in Zadar as well as his subsequent rule as ban of Croatia. The last paragraph of the portrait, however, is written in such a way as to evoke comparison with Percy Bysshe Shelley's poem *Ozymandias* on the decayed ruins and forgotten legacies of past mighty rulers.

Another hybrid can be seen in the discussion by David Goldfrank (Georgetown University) of Prince Vojšelk of Lithuania. Goldfrank employs an involved narrative style where he starts as a present-day historian who makes a few introductory remarks using the simple historical past tense. His historian then adopts the historical present to take the reader back to April 1267, describing Vojšelk's circumstances in a monastery. At that point, he puts the reader inside the mind of Vojšelk/Lavryš, who then recounts in the past tense his memory of how he became ruler of Lithuania and what happened when he was the ruler. In the coda of the account, the present-day historian returns adopting the historical past tense once again to make a few last comments. Thus, the narrative comes full circle: from historical past used by the historian–narrator to historical present used by the historian–narrator to historical past used by Vojšelk/Lavryš to historical present used by the historian–narrator and ending up by returning to historical past used by the historian–narrator.

Being mindful of the narrative strategy each contributor employs can increase the appreciation of that particular portrait. Other narrative strategies could have been used to present more or less the same story, but perhaps not so effectively.

Terms

Defining terms is an important component of any historical work, none more so than here. The contributors to this volume, of necessity, employ terms that are used and understood differently by different people. Perhaps there is no more elusive term to define than the one in the title of this book – "Eastern Europe." Definitions of it vary widely and some barely overlap.

The British scholar Dimitri Obolensky (1918–2001) defined *Eastern Europe* as that area occupied by people who are the "heirs of Byzantium." Obolensky's conception, which he acknowledged was "little more than a loose empirical category," combined geographical and cultural criteria. In his definition, *Eastern Europe* included Russia but excluded such Catholic countries as Poland, the Czech Republic, Slovakia, Hungary, Slovenia, and Croatia that are often included as part of Eastern Europe.[8] In contrast, Walter Kolarz defined *Eastern Europe* as that part of Europe after World War II where national boundaries were still in dispute. In that formulation, Kolarz encompassed Finland and Greece, as well as Poland, Czechoslovakia, Hungary, Romania, Yugoslavia, Albania, and Bulgaria, all of which had irredentist movements. He did not explicitly include the Soviet Union or Russia, but by implication included Ukraine and Belorussia.[9] Hugh Seton-Watson assumed *Eastern Europe* to be that area of Europe that came under Soviet domination after World War II.[10] This last definition included Poland, Czechoslovakia, East Germany, Hungary, Romania, and Bulgaria, but more or less excluded Albania, Yugoslavia, and the republics of the Soviet Union from *Eastern Europe*. Defining *Eastern Europe* for the time before the twentieth century based on political events after 1945, however, seems inherently faulty and anachronistic.

Indeed, the American historian Larry Wolff has argued that the term *Eastern Europe* developed during the eighteenth-century Enlightenment to relegate an area of Europe to the category of "other."[11] In this regard, Wolff saw a version of what in 1978 Edward Said called "Orientalism."[12] About the same time that Wolff published his book, the Serbian-American scholar Milica Bakić-Hayden began referring to *Eastern Europe* in the context of "nesting orientalisms" – in essence the further east an area is from Western Europe, the less civilized it is considered to be.[13] In the light of these ideas and of the changing geopolitical situation, a number of individuals such as the comparative literature scholar Steven Cassedy have questioned the usefulness of the term itself because of the tendency for its being given to misinterpretation.[14]

The American academic and journalist Sabrina Ramet has defined *Eastern Europe* as that area of Europe that has primarily Byzantine and Orthodox Christian, as well as some Turco-Muslim, influences.[15] If one were to adopt this definition, then presumably for that area that is neither Western nor Eastern Europe, the term *East Central Europe* would apply.

The Polish historian Oskar Halecki (1891–1973) divided Europe vertically into four zones: Western Europe, West Central Europe, East Central Europe, and Eastern Europe.[16] For Halecki, *East Central Europe* (or *Central-Eastern Europe*) comprised that area that between the two world wars existed east of Scandinavia, Germany, and Italy, and west of the Soviet Union. Thus, it would include the Baltic states, as well as Poland, Czechoslovakia, Hungary, Romania, Bulgaria, and Yugoslavia. *Eastern Europe* in his conceptualization is that area of Europe further east toward the Ural Mountains. While promising, this schema has the same drawback for medieval studies as Seton-Watson's schema, that is, anachronistic because it depends on later political events.

The United Nations Statistical Division divides Europe into four discrete geographic regions: Northern Europe, Western Europe, Eastern Europe, and Southern Europe. It defines *Eastern Europe* as comprising ten countries: Belarus, Bulgaria, Czech Republic, Hungary, Moldova, Poland, Romania, Russia, Slovakia, and Ukraine.[17] Thus, it excludes from *Eastern Europe* the Baltic countries – Estonia, Latvia, and Lithuania – which it places in *Northern Europe* along with Finland, Sweden, Norway, Denmark, Great Britain, Ireland, and Iceland. It also excludes from *Eastern Europe* Greece and the Balkan countries – Slovenia, Croatia, Serbia, Albania, Macedonia, Bosnia and Herzegovina, and Montenegro – which it places in *Southern Europe*.

For the purposes of this book, we can define *Eastern Europe* broadly and inclusively as the area of Europe east of a line drawn from Szczecin in the north at the mouth of the Oder River to Trieste in the south at the head of the Adriatic Sea.[18] But we also include the eastern part of the UN's *Northern Europe* – thus, Finland and the Baltic countries – as well as the eastern part of the UN's *Southern Europe* – thus, Greece and the Balkan countries. Whatever term one uses to describe this region, it is bound to provoke objection from one side or another. We can only provide our thinking for our choice in this matter.

Another term in the title also has provoked disagreement. The word *medieval* (or *mediaeval*) derives from the Latin *medium aevum*, which means "between ages." The ages being referred to are the Classical age of ancient Greece and Rome, on the one hand, and the Renaissance, on the other. The term was first used in the early nineteenth century as an adjectival form for *Middle Ages*, the period that Renaissance humanists had rejected in favor of the Classical age before it. *Middle Ages* is perhaps better than *Dark Ages*, whose first use has been ascribed to Petrarch but which was then used by humanists and historians to describe the period from the fall of the Western Roman Empire in the fifth century to the beginning of the Renaissance.[19] A secondary meaning of *medieval* is "too old to be useful or acceptable,"[20] and that is where the problem lies. The term *Middle Ages* was perceived as the least of the three ages – Classical, Middle Ages, Renaissance (or modern). Likewise, the adjectival form *medieval* exists within a context of denigration. So, both *Eastern Europe* and *medieval* have negative connotations.[21] Nonetheless, we persist in using them here in part because we would like, to some extent, to reverse those negativities and in part because we do not have better or more precise terms to replace them.

The term *Rus'* or *Rus* is one that has gained increasingly widespread usage during the course of the last forty years and is now being used to designate the area from the tenth through the seventeenth centuries where East Slavic dialectics were spoken. During this time period, the four East Slavic languages – Belarusian, Russian, Rusyn, and Ukrainian – had not yet clearly differentiated themselves from each other.[22] Formerly this area was referred to as "Old Russia," but that term gave priority to the Great Russian nationality, for then why not "Old Ukraine" or "Old Belarusia" instead? The term *Rus'/Rus* has the double advantage of being historically accurate – it was used to designate major parts of this area during that time – and of not privileging any one nationality.

The term *Kievan Rus'* is somewhat of a misnomer too. It is certainly better than *Kievan Russia*, the title of George Vernadsky's second volume of his *History of Russia* series. The point of it was to distinguish early Rus' (before the Mongol invasion) from later Rus' (Muscovy), but by juxtaposing *Kievan Russia* with *Muscovite Russia* it implied that both were the same kind of state, and that *Kievan Russia* with its capital at Kiev where the "grand prince" sat on his throne, covered all of Rus', just as Moscow was the capital of Muscovite Rus' where the grand prince, later tsar, sat on his throne and also covered all of Rus'. Instead, our sources present a significantly different picture of the early Rus' principalities, which contrasts with Muscovy. For one thing, for the ruler of Kiev, we have no evidence of a coronation ritual or regalia of power such as a crown, orb, or scepter. Beginning in 1018 the chronicles began referring to Galicia and Volynia as not being part of Rus'. By 1132, Novgorod was not part of Rus'. By 1140, Polotsk was not part of Rus'. By 1146, Rostov, Suzdal', and Vladimir-on-the-Kliazma were not part of Rus'. By 1147, Riazan' and Murom were not part of Rus'. By 1148, Smolensk was not part of Rus' (beginning 1148).[23] As the Swedish scholar John Lind proposed, the term *Rus'* was being equated here only with the towns whose princes were in the line of succession to the throne of Kiev.[24] As a result, insofar as there was a *Kievan Rus'*, it was limited to the province of Kiev and the two adjoining provinces, Chernigov and Pereiaslavl'.

The difference between the spelling *Rus'* and *Rus* (as well as the concomitant *Rus'ian* and *Rusian* is purely a spelling one). The Cyrillic spelling is *Русь* with the final letter being a soft sign. The soft sign has no phonetic value in itself but indicates how to pronounce the preceding consonant (i.e., in a soft rather than hard manner). Its function is somewhat similar to the final silent *e* in English in words like *tale* or *file*, which tell us to pronounce the antepenultimate letter, the vowel, in a long manner (ā, ī) rather than short (ă, ĭ), except in cases where it doesn't, such as in the verb *to live*. In transliterations to Cyrillic, such a final silent *e* is dropped or modified because it has no phonetic value in itself and can be confusing (тал/талэ, фил/филэ). On the other hand, the Library of Congress transliteration system does indicate the transliteration of each letter, including both soft signs and hard signs, be made. We have left the choice to each contributor to decide what they want to do with the final soft sign in *Rus'*/*Rus* and other proper names, such as *Igor'* or even the title *kniaz'*.

A third term that requires explanation is the word *kniaz'* (князь). Traditionally the term is translated as *prince*. Yet the position that the *kniaz'* often occupied in the early Rus' principalities was equivalent in many ways to that of *king* in medieval western Europe and Scandinavia.[25] We have allowed the contributors to decide for themselves how to translate, whether as *prince* or *king*, or leave the word *kniaz'* untranslated. The editors came to the conclusion that readers will not be confused by the apparent inconsistency between portraits as long as it has been explained in this Introduction, which it now has, and as long as each contribution is consistent internally.

We also have differences in the spelling of proper names. The Russians like to spell the name of the ruler who converted the Rus' people to Christianity as *Vladimir*. The Ukrainians prefer *Volodimer*, but the spelling *Volodimir* appears just as often as *Volodimer* (and more often than *Vladimir*) in the primary sources. Again, we have left it to the individual contributor to decide which spelling they prefer as long as they are being consistent within each sketch.

My co-editor picks up a number of these themes in the Conclusion to this volume and develops them further.

Notes

1 For a description of the types of generalizations that historians make, see Louis Gottschalk, "The Genealogy of Generalization of Historical Generalization," in *Generalization in the Writing of History: A Report*, ed. Louis Gottschalk (Chicago: University of Chicago Press, 1963), 113–129
2 Norman Cantor, *Medieval Lives: Eight Charismatic Men and Women* (Harper, 1994), xvi.
3 Quoted in Louis Menand, "Honest, Decent, Wrong: The Invention of George Orwell," *New Yorker* 78 (January 27, 2003): 87–88.
4 Hayden White, *Metahistory: The Historical Imagination in Nineteenth-Century Europe* (Baltimore: John Hopkins University Press, 1973).
5 Cantor, *Medieval Lives*, xvi.
6 Ihor Ševčenko, "Re-Reading Constantine Porphyrogenitus," in *Byzantine Diplomacy*, ed. Jonathan Shepard and Simon Franklin (Aldershot, Hampshire: Variorum, 1992), 167–195.
7 The military theorist and tactician B. H. Liddell-Hart (1895–1970) profiled him in his *Great Captains Unveiled* (Edinburgh: W. Blackwood and Sons, 1927), 1–17, along with Chinggis Khan.
8 Dimitri Obolensky, *The Byzantine Commonwealth: Eastern Europe, 500–1453* (Crestwood, NY: St. Vladimir's Seminary Press, 1971), 13–14.
9 Walter Kolarz, *Myths and Realities of Eastern Europe* (London: Drummond, 1946).
10 Hugh Seton-Watson, *The East European Revolution* (New York: Praeger, 1966).
11 Larry Wolff, *Inventing Eastern Europe: The Map of Civilization on the Mind of the Enlightenment* (Stanford: Stanford University Press, 1994).
12 Edward Said, *Orientalism* (New York: Pantheon Books, 1978).
13 Milica Bakić-Hayden, "Nesting Orientalisms: The Case of Former Yugoslavia," *Slavic Review* 54, no. 4 (Winter 1995): 917–931. The term *nesting orientalism* first appeared in the article Milica Bakić-Hayden and Robert Hayden, "Orientalist Variations on the Theme 'Balkans': Symbolic Geography in Recent Yugoslav Cultural Politics," *Slavic Review* 51, no. 1 (Spring 1992): 4.

14 Steven Cassedy, "Regions, Regionalism, and Eastern Europe," *New Dictionary of the History of Ideas*, 6 vols., ed. Maryanne Cline Horowitz (New York: Charles Scribner's Sons, 2005), 5: 2032–2035.

15 Sabrina P. Ramet, *Eastern Europe: Politics, Culture, and Society since 1939* (Bloomington: University of Indiana Press, 1998), 15.

16 Oscar Halecki, *The Limits and Divisions of European History* (New York: Sheed and Ward, 1950), 105–141.

17 United Nations Statistics Division, Methodology, "Standard Country or Area Codes for Statistical Use (M49)." <https://unstats.un.org/unsd/methodology/m49/>.

18 Winston Churchill had good historical and topographical, in addition to political, reasons for invoking this line as the boundary of the Iron Curtain in his Fulton, MO, speech of March 5, 1946.

19 Theodor Mommsen, "Petrarch's Conception of the 'Dark Ages,'" *Speculum* 17, no. 2 (1942): 226–242.

20 Merriam-Webster online dictionary.

21 For a recent attempt to meet head-on the negative perception that the Middle Ages have, see Regine Pernoud, *Those Terrible Middle Ages: Debunking the Myths*, trans. Anne Englund Nash (San Francisco: Ignatius Press, 2000).

22 As Roman Szporluk has written: "The Ukrainians of Russia and Austria did not become one nation because they spoke the same language; they came to speak the same language because they had first decided to be one nation." Roman Szporluk, "Ukraine: From an Imperial Periphery to a Sovereign State," in *A New Europe for the Old?* ed. Stephen R. Graubard (New Brunswick, NJ: Transaction, 1999), 111.

23 Henryk Paszkiewicz, *The Origin of Russia* (London: George Allen and Unwin, 1954), 7–10.

24 John Lind, "The 'Brotherhood' of Rus': A Pseudo-Problem Concerning the Origin of 'Rus'," *Slavica Othiniensia* 5 (1982): 71.

25 See Christian Raffensperger, *Kingdom of Rus* (Bradford: ARC-Humanities Press, 2017).

PART 1
Rus' and Northern Europe

1

THE WIDOW PRINCESS OF MINSK

Inés García de la Puente

The protagonist of this portrait is a twelfth-century Minsk princess whose name we do not know. Little was recorded in contemporary sources about the life of Rus' women, even of elite women like her. Compared to others, however, our Minsk princess is exceptional because the Kievan Chronicle (ca. 1200) devoted an encomium to her upon her death. Through it we learn many bits of precious information, like that she died at age eighty-four in the night of January 3, 1158, and that she had been a widow for forty years; it explains where she was buried and provides details of her donations to the monastery in her life and in her testament. The wording of the Kievan Chronicle allows for the interpretation that she may have actually ruled in Minsk during the decades of her widowhood. Other circumstances make this option a possibility: on the one hand, for most of the years of her widowhood, there seems to be no other prince of Minsk; on the other hand, also at around the same time, other princesses of Polotsk would take over leadership roles while the male members of their families were exiled in Constantinople.

The portrait that follows reconstructs how the Minsk princess could have come to rule; I try to provide a likely description of what the circumstances of her marriage, widowhood, and death were, and what her daily life and duties would have been like. Many details are based on actual information about her, Gleb, and Minsk in contemporary sources, and on archaeological studies; to the bone of historical evidence I add the flesh of some imagination and many an educated guess.

* * *

The princess of Minsk was worried. She had not heard from her husband, Prince Gleb Vseslavich, in months. He was being kept prisoner by their distant relative the Grand Prince Volodimir Monomakh in Kiev. The last envoys sent by Volodimir had not said what he had in store for Gleb, but had warned her that her husband was to be in Kiev for a long time. She had shortly thereafter sent her own envoys, but they came back with the same information. Alas, the princess could do nothing but wait. In the meanwhile, the principality of Minsk had to be kept running, so she temporarily took over its administration, something she had often done during the twenty-odd years of their marriage while her husband was away on his frequent campaigns.

Gleb was an ambitious and belligerent man. Not long after their wedding in the 1090s, he had received the well-populated although relatively humble principality of Minsk from his father, Vseslav Briacheslavich. Minsk was a town of secondary importance in the principality of Polotsk. Being the third son, Gleb could not aspire to more lucrative towns like the capital, Polotsk itself, so he had made the best of his appanage and taken on the task of strengthening it both symbolically and materially. He embellished Minsk with the building of the Church of the Holy Mother of God, a project never finished that nonetheless showed his love for his city as much as his ambitions. The Holy Mother of God was a stone church, something exceptional because building in stone was very expensive and technically difficult; the creation of this church demonstrated his wish to increase the visibility of Minsk. Indeed, in the whole principality of Polotsk only one stone church existed: the Church of St. Sophia, built by Gleb's father in his capital to emulate Kiev and Constantinople. From a more pragmatic point of view, Gleb strengthened Minsk through the addition of other towns that would bring in more income, like Drutsk. By conquering new territories, he had often clashed with his brothers and other Volodimirovichi princes, the dynasty that ruled Rus' and to which he also belonged. Yet Gleb was not the only one to ignite strife among his clan: regretfully, if one unspoken rule was followed by all, it was that personal interest came first; family and dynastic considerations, not to mention Christian morals, were subordinated to it. Thus treaties and friendship between brothers and cousins, even between fathers and sons, were sworn and broken with surprising ease, leading to armed conflicts that could and did raze entire towns to the ground.

In 1116, Gleb had attacked the territories of the Turov-Pinsk principality, provoking the rage of Volodimir Monomakh, who besieged him in Minsk. Gleb had first resisted. Yet as weeks passed, he started to run out of supplies at the same time as he realized that Volodimir had no intention of lifting the siege. In the end, he had bowed his head to Volodimir. Together with his family and retinue, Gleb had gone out to the gates of the besieged city and promised obedience to Monomakh.[1] On that occasion, the Grand Prince had been satisfied with Gleb's humiliation: although he deprived him of the towns he had recently conquered, he graciously left him Minsk, and so life had continued its regular pace. Gleb, however, was not satisfied, and in 1117 he once again attacked territories under Kievan influence, and Volodimir's son Mstislav successfully besieged him in Minsk. This time, however, a formal humiliation was not enough. Mstislav took Gleb to his father in Kiev, and ever since, the princess had been waiting in Minsk. Months passed and she feared for her husband and for herself.

November arrived and with it the end of her uncertainty. Volodimir sent news that Gleb had passed away. She did not know if he had died or been killed. She was angry at her husband for having behaved so provocatively – foolishly even, in her opinion – and then for having been unable to avoid his own imprisonment. At the same time, she was rancorous at Volodimir for having taken him away – from her point of view, Gleb's demise was caused by his imprisonment in Kiev, whether Volodimir had had him killed or not. In practical terms, however, the cause of his death did not make any difference. Even if he had been murdered, it had been the will of the Grand Prince, and there was nothing she could do to claim a justice different from that, even had she wanted to. The inescapable reality was that she had become a widow.

Now she had concrete reasons to be restless. Her fate was at stake. She may have to move and live with one of her sons, or she may easily be sent to a nunnery, forced to become a nun, like had happened and would happen to so many royal widows in Rus'. Grand Prince Volodimir could just command that she take the vows, and she would have to take them. She could not oppose his will, nobody would step up to her defense because, after all, what was left for a woman to do after the death of her husband? The veil, uncountable hours of praying and fasting and, eventually, a silent death, forgotten by all. She liked the liveliness of the princely estate, the constant coming and going of visitors, and she enjoyed the times when she was alone and free to decide over the administration of Minsk. The very idea of ending her days inside the quietness of the walls of a nunnery cast a shudder down her spine. Yet remarrying did not make any sense either. She was old, almost in her forties. She was past the age when women bring children to the world. Besides, neither did she have any personal interest in becoming a wife again nor was it politically advantageous from any point of view to have her wed again.

The loss of her husband was bad news, least of all because of her sorrow. As was common at that time and in her milieu, the personal match between the couple, not to mention love or personal compatibility, had had nothing to do with her engagement. Like many Rus' princesses, she was very young, just a teenager, when she married and moved to Minsk. Her role was clear to her: do what she was told to do. She was the daughter of Iaropolk Iziaslavich, Prince of Volodimir-Volynia, a wealthy southwestern principality; moreover, she was the grand-daughter of Gertrude, sister and daughter of Polish kings, and the niece of Sviatopolk Iziaslavich Mikhail, who was to rule Kiev for twenty years. The Princess was aware that she could have had better suitors, but her father had arranged her marriage when she was still a child and she had never had any say nor really understood why, of all options, she was given to Gleb, third son of Vseslav Briacheslavich. She knew that Gleb, by contrast, had immensely benefitted from their marriage. Hers had been a generous dowry consisting, among other items, of peasants and villages. She had seen part of that dowry evaporate in her husband's campaigns, and in his ambitious building projects to make Minsk more sumptuous.

She and her husband never became very close, but their marriage was a harmonious one. She had borne him girls and three boys who reached adulthood, thus fulfilling the role that was expected of her. In the princely palace in Minsk they had lived in separate quarters, as was common among the nobility of the time. They saw each other frequently when he was in Minsk, where each had her and his own business to attend to. He had only a few men he trusted, and so it was mostly she who took over the ruling of their lands while he was away trying to expand their territories. In that way he demonstrated his respect for her skills. But as soon as he was back, she relinquished those duties and he took over. He liked things his own way and she tried not to interfere. Had she been the prince, she would have never embarked on the, to her eyes, crazy project of the Church of the Holy Mother of God. Yet on the other hand, he had shown respect for her family when he followed her own father's and uncle's steps and sponsored the Monastery of the Caves in Kiev, a holy place she was fond of. In the years to come, she would grow to appreciate that gesture more and more: just as her dislike for the Grand Prince was starting to grow, hostilities between the abbot of the Caves and Volodimir were increasing, with the holy man constantly reprimanding the Monomakh for his policies. Although she would not acknowledge it even to her confessor, that antagonism pleased her tremendously.

A few weeks after she had received the news of her husband's death, Volodimir summoned her to Kiev. She started the journey in the darkest of moods. Her expectations were as somber as they were realistic: she would be told that Minsk was going to become the possession of one or another prince and she would be invited to move out. The conversation with the Grand Prince, however, surprised her. Volodimir was a proud man, self-righteous and confident in his power. In a tone that allowed no dissension, he said that for the time being, he expected her to keep administering Minsk. How she did it was her business as long as she did not allow any of her sons to take over. He demanded some tribute in gold and silver, but it was within reason. So long as he received the income yearly, he would not include Minsk in the pool of principalities he would be redistributing the next time a prince died. He had seen how Gleb had turned Minsk into a flourishing center, and he had heard about her administrative skills. She would be of more use to him and his successors in Minsk than as a nun or a widow in the house of any of her sons. Of course, she should not understand this arrangement as final, but she should prepare to operate as an administrator – in fact, as an unofficial ruler – for the next few years at least.

After paying her respects to the abbot of the Caves Monastery and seeing again the refectory that she and Gleb had sponsored a decade earlier, she headed back home. During the journey, the princess was busy thinking. Volodimir's decision meant that she had just become more independent than ever in her life. Although society sanctioned cases like her of widows who did not remarry because they had already produced heirs and had enough resources to live independently, she was lucky to be able to afford life out of marriage and as an administrator of her late husband's land. Her independence arrived at a point when she had lived and seen enough to take advantage of it wisely. She would not be a ruling princess of Minsk in her own right, and she knew better than to claim that. Yet she would be able to run the principality as she saw fit, keep on with her lifestyle, and take most decisions independently, at least as long as Volodimir, or whoever came after him on the Kievan throne, did not change his mind. Her situation was precarious, yes, but because she was a woman she had no option. What Volodimir had imposed on her he would not have imposed on any male member of his dynasty. Yet it was that or a silent retreat to a nunnery or to one of her sons' houses. She had nothing to lose.

Volodimir knew that his decision to have a widow administer – as he was careful to label it instead of rule – a principality was unprecedented, but he had good reasons for it. With the princess running Minsk, he did not have to worry about rebellious, too ambitious, princes like Gleb had been. Yet the princess would be powerless should he change his mind and grant Minsk to any other prince. He could use the principality as a joker if need arose to give some landless Rus' prince a town to rule. Unlike the princes who considered themselves entitled to rule, Gleb's widow would not be able to oppose him should she be left landless: she could be removed and reinstated at Volodimir's, or his successor's, will.

Once back in Minsk, the princess continued ruling it. The situation was not much different from the times when Gleb was away campaigning. A couple of her husband's men had remained in Minsk. They were reliable, loyal counselors, and they were willing to follow her commands. Collecting taxes from the peasants and storing the grain, exploiting the hunting in the forests and the fishing in the rivers and lakes, those were things she could manage well. She also organized the local trading posts efficiently, providing the Minsk treasury with considerable income from the exchange of goods that took place in certain villages. She insisted in providing advantageous regulations for trade in the yearly markets.

She had a taste for jewelry, but only she and some wealthy women could afford ornaments like bracelets made of glass beads, or jewels like *kolty* – earrings that were worn hanging not from the earlobes but from the headdress. They could buy them from Minsk or Kievan artisans. Trade with the Baltic was common, and so amber was one of the stones Minsk jewelers would process to make the jewelry that the princess liked to wear. Thanks to the exchange that happened along the long-distance routes, the princess would sometimes buy wine and olive oil, imported from the south in amphorae. She also liked walnuts and dried fruits, which had to be bought from traders from the Caucasus. Through commercial links to the West she could occasionally acquire a nice Frankish sword to be given as a gift to her advisors, or some beautifully crafted vessel for the feasts she now and then organized in the palace.

The palace where the princess lived was the largest of the homesteads inside of the wooden *detinets*, or fortified towns. The Minsk *detinets* had been built some decades earlier by her father-in-law, and Gleb had kept expanding it by adding new buildings and improving the defensive structure. The wall was made of tree trunks; the ramparts had been widened to avoid giving easy access to unwelcome visitors. The princely homestead was some 250 square meters (almost 2,700 square feet). It included a tower to watch the surrounding territories, barns to store the grain, as well as a hall that offered the men of the retinue a roof over their heads. The princess lived in the building designated for women, where female relatives and servants also slept.

As far as the layout went, a princely palace was not much different from the buildings where well-off non-princely families lived, which in turn were just larger versions of the semi-subterranean, one-story peasant dwellings. The dimensions of the palace, however, were much larger. The women's building consisted of a first floor semi-buried, divided into two rooms given its larger size, containing an oven large enough to keep it all warm. Through an external, covered stair passage women could reach the second floor, also divided into two rooms.

In the princely dwellings, the wood frames on the outside were carved and painted. The inside was also painted, and was much richer than other houses, as she possessed more than many due to her wealth and status: benches, chairs, and even armchairs, furs and carpets to decorate the walls and make the furniture more comfortable, numerous glass receptacles and pottery. The windows were small yet bigger and more numerous compared to those of other houses, making the interior a bit less gloomy. However, small openings were a wise and necessary option if one wanted to keep the palace warm in the winter. In the cold months the stove was on for many hours, as she could afford the firewood. However, like in all other houses, there was no chimney to extract the smoke, and so like the peasants, she and her family breathed a black, dark, heavy air that clogged their lungs and contributed to the low life expectancy in Rus'. At forty the princess was already among the oldest female members of her generation.

The palace where the Princess would live during her widowhood had only been built some ten years earlier, as a terrible fire had destroyed most of the previous one. She, like her contemporaries in Rus'ian towns, had had to witness fires ravaging their homes on more than one occasion. Cities were built of wood, and so fire was always a threat. The fire of the oven or the candles could easily catch on the logs of the buildings and spread quickly through the whole *detinets*. It was in that last fire that she had lost her youngest son, a four-year-old who had happened to be sick upstairs with a *kliuchennitsa*, a main woman servant; both had succumbed to the smoke as the fire that had started downstairs quickly propagated through the building, which became a burning trap. Yet death was such a present part of life that she had accepted it as one of the many calamities that one had to withstand.

Besides the men of the retinue, and a few noble people, the town dwellers were artisans: potters, smiths, jewelers, shoe-makers, bone and wood carvers, etc. Women made their own pottery and weaved the material for their clothes. Yet on the side everybody cultivated some land and raised animals, hunted, and fished.

The men of Gleb who had remained in Minsk knew that to continue their lives under the rule of his widow was an awkward but convenient arrangement. It was awkward because of the plain reason that she was a woman. Yet it was convenient because she was an intelligent and reasonable administrator, she was attached to her adoptive land, and had no reason or desire to move elsewhere. By contrast, outsider princes would have no incentive to take care of young, provincial Minsk. If Volodimir imposed a new prince in Minsk, he would come just to squeeze as much profit as possible from it while waiting to move over to the next town, hopefully richer and closer to Kiev in the ladder of Rus' principalities.

Minsk would enjoy peace and prosperity for the time of the princess's life, that is, the four decades following Gleb's death. Only at the beginning of the 1130s did events take an unpleasant turn for the princess. The Kievan prince of the moment, Iaropolk Volodimirovich, sent a new prince to Minsk, Iziaslav Mstislavich. That Iziaslav was there temporarily was clear to everybody – and indeed in 1135 he left for the more prized principality of Vladimir. Yet his arrival shook the tranquil life that Minsk had gotten used to in the previous years. The princess found herself in a very uncomfortable position, reviving the qualms she had gone through at the beginning of her widowhood. Luckily, Iziaslav proved to be a practical person. Soon after being allotted Minsk, he was also given Turov and Pinsk, and these two towns required more dedication than Minsk. He found it convenient to let the princess continue with the administration. During the time that he was in Minsk, he kept to his own devices. The princess could keep living in her part of the palace compound. Although she kept administering the principality, Iziaslav reaped a big part of the profit. Still, once again she had to lower her head and accept the situation: even if she could not profit from her land as before, she could decently live off of it and maintain her status as a widowed princess. Nevertheless, when Iziaslav left, she and all the inhabitants of Minsk celebrated with a feast that was to be remembered for years.

The princess outlived most of her contemporaries, enjoying full command of her faculties until a stroke took her when she was eighty-four in January 1158. A wrinkled, bony woman, she passed away in her sleep, quietly, with an expression of satisfaction in her face. She had had plenty of time on her hands to prepare her will. Her body was to be buried next to her husband in the Caves Monastery in Kiev. Also to the Caves Monastery she donated her dowry, or what was left of it – five villages and peasants she had been given when she married. That was her way of claiming what belonged to her by birth but which she had had to relinquish at marriage. On the other hand, with this donation she emulated those of her father, her uncle Sviatopolk Iziaslavich, the ruler of Kiev, and her husband. All her other personal possessions, amassed during the decades she administered Minsk alone, went also to the Caves Monastery. She had never forgotten the opposition of the Caves to Volodimir Monomakh around the time of Gleb's death; she had never allowed herself to forget the real reason why she had stayed in Minsk. These donations were her silent revenge, like her rule of Minsk had been silent. Bequeathing to the Caves Monastery the riches she had obtained as an unacknowledged ruler was a symbolic act. From the afterlife, she rewarded those who had opposed Volodimir Monomakh, the man who had killed her husband and treated her as a disposable princess.

Note

1 In fact, the *Kievan Chronicle* says that only Gleb "and his children and his druzhina" went out of the city, that is, his sons and men (PSRL 2, col. 282–283, year 6624/1116).

Source

The encomium about Gleb's widow appears in the Kievan Chronicle under the year 1158:

Shakhmatov, Aleksei A. (ed.) *Ipat'evskaia letopis', Polnoe Sobranie Russkikh Letopisej*, vol. 2. Saint Petersburg: Imperatorskaia Arkheograficheskaia Kommissiia tipografiia M. A. Aleksandrova, 1908 [1998].

A translation into English can be found in:

Heinrich, Lisa. *The Kievan Chronicle: A Translation and Commentary* [PhD Thesis, University of Vanderbilt, 1977, copyright 1978].

Suggestions for further reading

Alekseev, Leonid V. *Zapadnye zemli domongol'skoi Rusi: Ocherki istorii, arkheologii, kul'tury.* 2 vols. Moskva: Nauka, 2006.
Eck, Alexandre. "La situation juridique de la femme russe au Moyen Age." *Recueils de la societe Jean Bodin* 12, no. 2 (1962): 405–420.
García de la Puente, Inés . "Gleb of Minsk's Widow: Neglected Evidence on the Rule of a Woman in Rus'ian History?" *Russian History* 39 (2012): 347–378.
Goehrke, Carsten. *Russischer Alltag. Eine Geschichte in Zeitbildern. Vol. 1: Die Vormoderne.* Zurich: Chronos, 2003.
Levin, Eve. "Women and Property in Medieval Novgorod: Dependence and Independence." *Russian History* 10, no. 2 (1983): 154–169.
Pushkareva, Natal'ia L. *Women in Russian History: From the Tenth to the Twentieth Century.* Translated and edited by Eve Levin. Armonk, NY: M. E. Sharpe, 1997.
Weickhardt, George G. "Legal Rights of Women in Russia, 1100–1750." *Slavic Review* 55, no. 1 (1996): 1–23.

2

ANNA, A WOMAN
OF NOVGOROD

Eve Levin

The lives of non-elite people, particularly women, are not easily reconstructed from the best-known sources, which focus disproportionately on ruling families and high-ranking clergy. At most, normative sources such as laws and sermons describe how people ought to behave, rather than how they did. But archeological excavations in Novgorod and other places in Russia have uncovered hundreds of notes by men and women of all social orders. These notes are reminiscent of modern email or text messages and concern daily activities. Medieval people wrote on birchbark, which was plentiful, rather than parchment or paper, which were expensive. When the message had served its purpose, it was thrown away, to be uncovered centuries later. The birchbark documents usually preserve only one side of the dialogue, and make reference to unexplained circumstances and unidentified individuals. Holes and tears further obscure the meaning. Yet these are the unmediated voices of ordinary people, and as such, they provide rare insight into their thoughts.

The woman in this vignette, Anna; the members of her family; and her accuser, Konstantin, are composites of real people represented in birchbark documents. The material in bold type is excerpted from actual birchbark documents, with only the names of the authors and recipients changed, in order to weave them into a plausible but fictitious story. The other figures are all authentic, as are the locations and historical events. Because real surviving birchbark documents tell only fragments of the whole story, this vignette concludes with the situation yet unresolved, leaving readers to speculate on what ultimately happened to Anna. Anna's story takes place in 1216.

* * *

Anna stood praying before the icons in the refectory of the monastery of St. Barbara:

> **Virgin, all glory to you! I glorify you, who are the Mother of the Son of God, forgiving my sins.**

She winced as her hand, making the sign of the cross, brushed her left eye, swollen shut, her throbbing shoulder, her bruised ribs. The Mother of God would understand her predicament. After all, the Virgin's betrothed husband St. Joseph once berated her,

> **You have brought ridicule to me, shame in place of honor, and grief instead of joy![1]**

Yet the Mother of God was soon vindicated; Anna hoped that she would be too.

The abbess's arrival interrupted Anna's musings. "My lady," she bowed, trying to disguise her nervousness.

"I have consulted with the nuns," Abbess Varvara began. "Out of respect to your mother, of blessed memory, who took vows here after she was widowed, you may stay – for now. As for the future . . ."

"Please, my lady!" Anna burst out.

"Konstantin's allegations against you are serious. Your husband, Boris, will not be the only one to believe them," Varvara explained.

"I am innocent!"

The abbess waved a hand, both acknowledgment and dismissal. "Konstantin enjoys the favor of the mayor, and of Archbishop Antonii. And the archbishop has promised to build a new stone church here to honor St. Barbara."

Of course Abbess Varvara would think of such things; she was the daughter of Iurii Oleksinich, a prominent man in Novgorod and a leading supporter of Prince Mstislav. Anna sighed. "My brother is a clerk at the cathedral of St. Sophia. I will write to him for help."

"One way or another, your case will come to the archbishop's court of law," Varvara observed. "I will bring you birchbark and a stylus. Then our gatekeeper's boy can take your letter to him."

* * *

Anna held the iron stylus over the rectangle of birchbark. How could she explain to her brother what had happened to her?

It was Onfim who taught Anna how to read and write. He attended a school at the home of the widowed deacon from the Church of St. Blaise, located down Volosova Street in Liudin quarter, not far from their home. Onfim was an apt pupil,

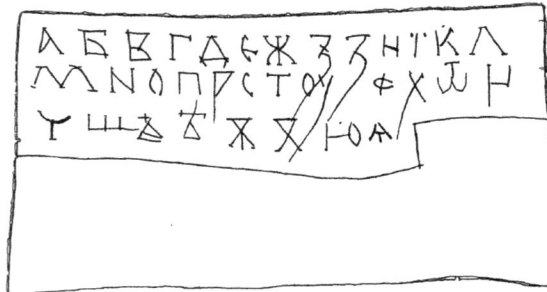

FIGURE 2.1 Alphabet on birchbark[2]

but when his teacher's back was turned, he preferred drawing pictures to copying the alphabet. Onfim had dreamed about becoming a great warrior, battling for St. Sophia, his city's patron, against invaders and forcing the wild Chud and Em and Iugra to pay the promised tribute.

And so he did for a few years, as a young man, until he was wounded, his left arm too weak to bear a shield. Then it was good that he had become adept at writing because he could make his living as a clerk instead.

Should she have sought refuge with Onfim instead of coming here to St. Barbara's? St. Barbara's was closer than her brother's quarters near the cathedral of St. Sophia in the Detinets, and he shared them with other men who served the archbishop. She did not want men to see her bareheaded, in torn clothing – shamed.[3]

FIGURE 2.2 Onfim's picture[4]

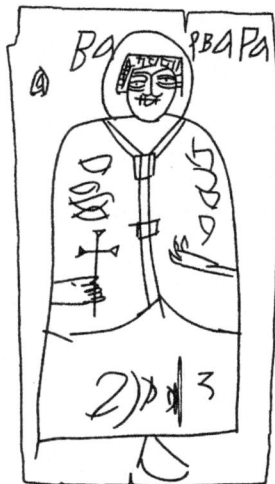

FIGURE 2.3 Birchbark icon of St. Barbara[5]

And St. Barbara had been her special protectress since she was a girl; she had even drawn herself a small birchbark icon of her.

That icon, and all of Anna's belongings, remained at her – Boris's – house on Riadiatina Street.

How many years had it been since she left Volosova Street? Twenty-five? Twenty-six?

Anna was in her thirteenth year when her parents presented her to an important visitor from Dobrynia Street, Milusha. That redoubtable lady scrutinized Anna, assessing her health and her demeanor. Several more visits followed, and Anna realized that her marriage was being arranged. Finally, her parents informed her: her husband-to-be was Milusha's nephew, Akim.

The betrothal was concluded at the bride's home, with great ceremony. A large cheese, symbolizing the bride's latent fertility, served as the centerpiece for the feast. Anna's father and Akim's father, Smen, slapped their hands together to confirm the joining of their families, and they then put Anna's hand in Akim's. The two eyed each other, curious. Nobody had asked either of them if they agreed to the marriage. Girls objected sometimes, and so did boys. The law stated that if a girl or boy committed suicide rather than marry the parents' choice of spouse, the parents bore the weight of that sin. But the parents usually won out in the end.

A flurry of preparations followed. Anna's father gave her a large trunk, and she and her mother began to fill it. Anna kept a list of the items:

A necklace, earrings, all the sheepskin coats, three embroidered ribbons with a headdress, six sponges, a featherbed and pillows, dresses – 5 dark-colored and three white – a pot of honey, a washstand, a chest.

On the wedding day, Anna bathed and dressed in new clothes: an embroidered linen shift, then layers of outer clothes made from expensive imported cloth: silk from Tsargrad; wool of exquisite fineness from England far to the west; cotton brought by the Volga Bulgars from lands far to the east. She wore her maiden's headdress for the last time that day.

The festivities stretched for days: the blessing in the church, the procession to Dobrynia Street, the feast, then the bedding. Milusha pronounced the ancient words of power:

May her womb drink of his penis!

Then Anna and Akim were left alone in the loft. Anna blushed, remembering how she and Akim kissed, shared sweet mead, kissed again – and again. The next day, the marriage covenant fulfilled, Anna's parents brought her trunk along with the rest of her dowry – silver bars called grivny and bundles of furs to use for smaller purchases.[6] "This is your share of your inheritance from us," they told her.[7]

Although Anna and Akim took a liking to each other, other aspects of married life were difficult. The ways Anna's mother had taught her, whether cooking, serving, spinning, sewing, or cleaning, did not satisfy Akim's mother. One day, soon after the wedding, all the older women of the family – Akim's mother, his two older brothers' wives, his uncle's widow, Milusha – went visiting, leaving her to prepare the evening meal. Anna could not remember where the necessary ingredients were stored. Not wanting to give her mother-in-law reason to scold, she instead wrote an urgent message to her father-in-law. He wrote back reassuringly:

Greetings from Smen to my daughter-in-law. If you have not already remembered, you have malt; the rye malt is in the cellar, and you can take it. For the bread, there is as much meal as you need; take it accordingly. And the meat is in the hayloft.

It was not only her mother-in-law who criticized. Anna's oldest sister-in-law, Marina, looked askance at everything everyone did. In the late winter in the first year of marriage, Marina cast a disapproving look at Anna's belly while they steamed in the bathhouse. "You know that it's a sin to engage in lust during Lent," she warned. "It is written in a book: any child you might conceive now will grow up to be a murderer, a thief, or a brigand." Anna was frightened enough by Marina's words to refuse Akim that night. But he asked his priest, who reassured him. "Such books ought to be burned," the priest said. "It is better to abstain during Lent, but if you are young and impatient" – and so we were, Anna remembered – "that is all right. There is no sin in your wife. But not during Holy Week!"[8] Still, Anna was relieved that their daughter, Olisava, was not born until a year later, during the summer.

If Akim had lived, would she be in these dire straits? Anna recalled the ill-omened invasion of Iugra land, just four years after her wedding. Of the hundreds of Novgorodian men who set out, only eighty returned home. Akim, his father, and Anna's own father perished; Onfim was badly wounded. Anna's mother took vows as a nun at St. Barbara's to pray for the soul of her husband, whose bones lay in a distant, pagan land. Anna, too, thought to take the veil, but she did not want to leave Olisava. She was not eager to remarry either – until she met Boris.

That happened four years after the tragedy that left her a widow. The civic and ecclesiastical leaders of Novgorod had chosen a new archbishop, Mitrofan, and the entire city – men, women, and children – gathered together to invest him in his office. Anna, with little Olisava, joined the crowd in the square in front of the cathedral of St. Sophia. She found herself next to Boris at the ceremony, and walking back to Liudin quarter afterwards.

Boris was from Riadiatina Street – and, as Anna soon learned from other women who shopped at the vegetable market, a widower without children. She began to notice him there, and at the cloth merchants' stalls. One day, he dropped a piece of birchbark at her feet:

May your heart and body and soul burn for me and for my body and for the sight of me . . .

Did she burn for Boris? There must have been power in the writing because Anna suddenly felt great yearning for him. Not too long after that, Boris's old Chud slave woman brought a note to her:

From Boris to Annitsa. Marry me. I want you and you want me.

The slave woman handed her a small packet containing a bracelet of yellow glass and a tiny copper pendant – a fecund, big-breasted bird, ready to lay. And so Anna and Boris were wed, and Anna moved into his house on Riadiatina Street.

At first things were good, Anna recalled. She liked being the mistress of the house, without a domineering mother-in-law and interfering sisters-in-law. If Boris drank too much and wasn't gentle with her, as Akim had been, Anna reminded herself of the priest's homily at church, "In the beginning, God said to Eve, 'You were taken from your husband, so he rules you. You must submit to him in silence.'"

And submit she did, for Boris was eager for a son, and Anna's healthy daughter had seemed to him promise of more to come. She conceived within a year. But after a difficult delivery, little Klimiata was a sickly baby. When he contracted a summer fever, Anna begged Onfim to write a prayer on birchbark to wrap around the ailing infant's head.

Three nines of angels, three nines of archangels, deliver the servant of God Kliment from the ague by the prayers of the holy Mother of God.

But to no effect. Boris's old slave woman offered another alternative. "There is a slave man who was a sorcerer among our Chud people. He can draw the fever spirit from the babe." Anna hesitated; hadn't the priest said that visiting sorcerers was forbidden? But the blessing hadn't worked, so Anna told the slave woman to bring the sorcerer. He whispered something over Klimiata in the savage Chud tongue. These ministrations did not help either, and Klimiata passed away. Anna berated herself for her sin that cost her son his life, but when she confessed it to the priest, he consoled her. Klimiata had been baptized and now found a place in Paradise. As for Anna's sin, the priest assigned her a penance of six weeks. Tears came to Anna's eyes at the memory of her lost baby.

Boris was gone then; he was away from home so much, collecting tribute from the half-wild people of the north or crop payments from the peasants outside the city, or transporting trade goods. When he traveled, Boris entrusted management of his business to Anna in his absence, occasionally sending her notes with instructions.

From Boris to Anna. As soon as this letter arrives, send a man on horseback to me, because I have much to do. And send my shirt, I forgot it.

Greetings from Boris to Anna. I mowed the meadow, and the villagers took my hay. Write out a copy from the purchase document and send it here. When the document explains, I'll be understood.

Truth be told, Anna was happier when he was gone. When Boris was at home, he joined in turmoil in the city. Anna recalled the uprising against Mayor Dmitrii Miroshkinich, then absent on campaign with the prince; it was the year that her granddaughter Nastasia was born. The men of Prusskaia Street called a veche – an assembly – to protest the imposts Mayor Dmitrii had levied. The

Miroshkinich family was the most prominent one of Liudin quarter, with a large compound stretching from Volosova Street to Dobrynia Street. Boris owed much to their patronage, so he joined the men of Liudin quarter who streamed to the veche meeting. If Anna had any thought of attending, Boris quashed it. "Stay inside," he ordered. The veche turned violent when the Prusskaia Street contingent brawled with their Liudin counterparts. Anna saw the flames to the north when the Prusskaia men pillaged the houses of Dmitrii and his brother, then burned them down. Where was Boris? Anna worried. He returned home late, bruised, dirty, and furious. When she asked him about what had happened, he slapped her.

Over the next years, the decline in the fortunes of Liudin quarter's leading family resulted in less wealth for most households, including Boris and Anna's. Fortunately, Anna had been frugal with her dowry, augmenting it when she could. Quite often she loaned out small amounts, keeping lists of debts owed to her:

> **From Negoshka twelve kuny. From Dedenia five kuny. From Chudka five kuny. From Dertka five kuny. From Nesdich's wife five kuny . . .**

Olisava, as her father, Akim's, sole heir, had much more money to invest. The year Novgorod heard the momentous news that the wicked Franks had sacked the fabled Tsargrad, Anna arranged a marriage for her. Stepan was older than Olisava, a widower, engaged in the importation of goods from abroad. They often cooperated in their business ventures.

> **From Olisava to Stepan. Look for my uncle. Is my debtor there? If he is there, get two grivny from him. If he isn't there, let me know.**

Onfim had helped his niece then; would he help Anna now?

Anna's current trouble had started a year earlier – a hungry one in Novgorod. An early autumn freeze destroyed the crops before harvest, although Torzhok, not too far away, had plenty. Prince Iaroslav, once again at odds with the Novgorodians, seized the stores of grain in Torzhok, and refused to allow them to be transported to Novgorod. Konstantin, an important man in town, had supplied Stepan with money and sent him south to buy grain, anticipating a sizeable return on his investment in the starving city. Stepan had written:

> **From Stepan to my wife Olisava. Sell the house, and come here to Smolensk, or to Kiev. Bread is cheaper. If you don't come, send me a letter saying you are well.**

But Olisava had not gone because the food crisis had passed. The Novgorodians held a veche to invite a different prince, Mstislav, to govern; both Anna and Olisava attended, taking the oath to him. Prince Mstislav and the Novgorodians launched an attack on Prince Iaroslav in Torzhok, defeating him and capturing the grain stores.[9]

Soon thereafter, Konstantin demanded that Olisava pay back the money he had advanced to her still-absent husband. His venture with Stepan could lose money, and he wanted to secure his own investment. Olisava did not have the cash to give him. She tried to call in a loan:

Stepan's wife said to Fima – either send the money or there will be a big penalty.

Olisava offered Konstantin the mortgage she had taken in exchange for the loan to Fima, and offered to name the witnesses to it. But Konstantin refused it, demanding a first installment of his reimbursement immediately. In desperation, Olisava wrote a note and sent him to her mother.

Respects to my mother. Give this person two grivny. Don't put me in the wrong, Mommy; if you don't have it, borrow it!

But Anna refused to pay Konstantin. She had not pledged surety for Stepan, and neither had Olisava; this was not their debt. Konstantin grew enraged: "I'll see you in court!" he bellowed. He left, railing against her and Olisava in a loud voice. Anna was sure that all the neighbors heard him. She was glad that Boris, with his hot temper, had not been at home at the time.

Konstantin did indeed summon Anna to the city's commercial court. Perhaps he thought that she would not dare to appear in public, with all the rumors about her, and he would win the suit by default. When Anna came, Konstantin walked out, threatening that he would send bailiffs to collect the money due him.

That night, Boris returned home. He had already heard about the dispute from Konstantin, and from many others. "How dare you dishonor me so!" Boris shouted, grabbing her by the arm, shaking her, punching her in the face, kicking her after she fell. He dragged her to the door of the house, and pushed her into the street, bedraggled and bleeding. Humiliated, Anna crept through the dark streets to the monastery of St. Barbara, hoping to find refuge there.

* * *

Anna read through the letter she had written to her brother:

From Anna greetings to Onfim. My lord brother, look after my case against Konstantin. Declare to him before witnesses: "Because you brought a claim against my sister and against her daughter, and called my sister a pimp and her daughter a whore, now Boris has returned, and hearing that accusation he drove my sister out and tried to kill her." Then, my lord brother, tell him this: "You brought this accusation and now you must prove it." If Konstantin says that I swore surety for my son-in-law, tell him this: "If there are witnesses against my sister who say that she swore surety for her son-in-law, I will be responsible

to you for this." So, brother, investigate any accusation or claim against me. And if there are witnesses to it, then I am not your sister, or my husband's wife. You, at least, help me, not regarding Boris.

How will this end? Anna thought to herself. Would Onfim help her? Would the court believe Konstantin, making her liable to pay him and branding her as an immoral woman? Or could she prove that he had defamed her? Then he would have to pay her compensation![10] And what would happen to Olisava? For now, she had taken refuge with her stern Aunt Marina, awaiting Stepan's return. Would Stepan see the situation in the same way as Boris? And what about Boris? He faced no penalty for beating her; she was his wife. If the rumors he heard about her behavior were upheld, the archbishop would authorize him to divorce her. But if she could prove that he expelled her without just cause, then the archbishop would order him to pay her for the insult.[11] In that case, where would she go? To live with Olisava, Stepan, and her granddaughter? Or would she take vows as a nun at St. Barbara's?
Anna rose, and stood once again before the icons.

Lord, hear my prayer.

Notes

1 The passage is from a well-known dialogue (play?) on the theme of the Annunciation.
2 By courtesy of V. L. Ianin.
3 Because proper married women always covered their hair when in public, a mature woman who appeared bareheaded was being immodest. Ripping off a woman's headcovering was a form of sexual assault.
4 By courtesy of V. L. Ianin.
5 By courtesy of V. L. Ianin.
6 Furs were used as currency.
7 Daughters were entitled to a share of their parents' property, usually given to them at the time of marriage.
8 Bishop Nifont of Novgorod recommended sexual abstinence during fasting periods as an act of virtue, but did not require it. Books circulated that attempted to frighten readers into strict abstinence by claiming that the parents' sin of sex at the wrong time would be visited upon the child. Nifont, however, condemned this idea.
9 The Novgorod chronicle notes specifically that the "all Novgorodians" took the oath to Mstislav, listing leading citizens "with their wives and children."
10 Iaroslav's Statute mandated that a man who expelled an innocent wife had to pay her a large sum of money, as well as pay a fine to the ecclesiastical court. The penalties were similar to those for kidnapping or raping a woman, and for defaming her.
11 See the provisions in Iaroslav's Statute on a man beating a woman other than his wife. While a husband was permitted to divorce his wife for suspected adultery on her part, a wife was permitted to divorce her husband if he attempted to kill her.

Further reading

Brisbane, Mark A., ed. *The Archaeology of Novgorod, Russia: Recent Results from the Town and its Hinterland.* Lincoln: Society for Medieval Archaeology, 1992.

Levin, Eve. "Novgorod Birchbark Documents: The Evidence for Literacy in Medieval Russia." In *Medieval Archaeology: Papers of the Seventeenth Annual Conference of the Center for Medieval and Early Renaissance Studies*, edited by Charles L. Redman, 127–137. Binghamton: State University of New York at Binghamton, 1989.

Pokrovskaya, Lyubov V. "Female Costume from Early Novgorod and Its Ethno-Cultural Background: An Essay on Reconstruction." In *Vers l'Orient et vers l'Occident: Regards croise sur les dynamiques et les transferts culturels des Vikings a la Rous ancienne*, edited by Pierre Bauduin and Alexander E. Musin, 101–112. Caen: Presses universitaires de Caen, 2014.

Pushkareva, Natalia. *Women in Russian History: From the Tenth to the Twentieth Century*, trans. and ed. Eve Levin. Armonk: M. E. Sharpe, 1997.

Pushkareva, Natalia L. and Eve Levin, "Women in Medieval Novgorod from the Eleventh to the Fifteenth Century." *Soviet Studies in History* 23, no. 4 (1985): 71–90.

3

PRINCE VLADIMIR OF PSKOV

Anti Selart

Vladimir of Pskov was a prince in the political arena in northwest Rus' and the Baltics in the first half of the thirteenth century. He is not among the top stars in the historical writing of the period and the region and is overshadowed in the history books by more influential and powerful contemporaries – or, most often, is not mentioned at all. However, what makes his person striking is the fact that he was able to validate himself as a ruling prince during this very complicated period when significant changes were underway in both Rus' and the Baltics. And he achieved this in a frontier region, where many different ethnicities, as well as religions and confessions, converged and intermingled – here connected the "East" and the "West" that are often seen as inflexible and intrinsically contentious units. However, the people of the thirteenth century living in this area stood much closer to each other – Christians and heathens, Catholics and Orthodox – than some contemporary polemic texts present it. And, certainly, they stood much closer to each other than several modern narratives about an immemorial "Russian-German" conflict try to convince their readers.

Of course, the fact that Vladimir has been overshadowed is also based on the sources. He appears on the pages of the Novgorod chronicle only when he is acting together with the Novgorod army. Pskov, as most of the smaller centers of Rus' at that time, lacked local chronicle writing. Therefore, it turns out that the most informative medieval text about Prince Vladimir is from neighbouring Livonia, rather than Rus' itself. This is the Latin Livonian Chronicle,[1] which is thought to have been authored by a priest named Henry (d. c. 1260). In the 1220s, Henry wrote a chronicle of the Riga camp of crusaders, which featured Bishop Albert of Riga (1199–1229) as the main hero and told the story of the conquest of the lands of the Livs and Estonians by the crusaders and the military order of the Brethren of the Sword (Swordbrothers). In this war, the rivals (and sometimes allies) of Riga's crusaders (most of whom came from Saxony) were the King of Denmark and the Rus' lands of Polotsk, Pskov, and Novgorod. In summary, there is significantly more that is unknown than known even in the most elementary data of Vladimir's biography. We even cannot be really sure about his father because his patronymic is not registered in the medieval sources.

To provide a brief biographical sketch, Vladimir was most likely born in the 1170s, or slightly earlier, as he had a daughter of marriageable age in c. 1210. Vladimir appeared on the political arena in 1208, when he participated in Novgorod's campaign against raiding Lithuanians. The next year he was already the prince of Pskov.[2] His career seemingly depended on the political success of Prince Mstislav Mstislavich the Bold, who was, probably, the younger brother of Vladimir and who became the prince of Novgorod in this time. Novgorod and Pskov were among the Rus' lands that lacked a local princely family with hereditary power – power belonged to the local community, which expressed its will at meetings of the veche (assembly) and invited a prince from another Rus' land to become its judge and military leader. Various branches of the princely dynasty of Rus' competed for princely power in these towns, but local powers also relied on foreign princely rulers. In 1209 Vladimir received Velikie Luki, on the southern border of the Novgorod lands, to rule, but he also remained the prince of Pskov until 1212 when according to the Novgorod chronicle "the people of Pskov at that time had driven out Prince Vladimir from amongst them."[3]

Vladimir then headed for neighbouring Livonia where revolutionary events were occurring in the thirteenth century. The east coast of the Baltic Sea, which was increasingly influenced by Christianity, both Western and Eastern Christians, in the twelfth century, still lacked ecclesiastical institutions and an episcopal system. The sporadic plundering raids that had gone on for centuries across the Baltic Sea between Scandinavia and the Baltics started to be reframed as a crusade against Baltic pagans in the second half of the twelfth century. The leading role in this process was played by nobles from Saxony. During the thirteenth century, the Finnic peoples (Livs and Estonians) and Baltic peoples (Letts, Curonians, Semgallians, and Selonians) were subjugated and Christianized. This resulted in the creation of medieval Livonia, a conglomerate of the holdings of the clerical states and the King of Denmark, which approximately corresponds to the territories of modern-day Estonia and Latvia.[4] The subjugation methods of the Crusaders were not limited to war and conquest. A patronage relationship was forced on some local leaders, while others collaborated with the crusaders in their own interests. The Livonian relations with the Rus' centres were also multifaceted. They included both wars and alliances. Around 1210, the bishop of Riga and prince of Pskov cooperated in order to conquer southeast Estonia. This cooperation was fixed around 1210 by the marriage between Vladimir's daughter (we do not know her name) and Bishop Albert's brother Theoderich. However, this collaboration later turned into a competition where Novgorod and occasionally some princes of northeastern Rus' interfered as well. Vladimir appears for the last time in the sources in 1225–26, when, together with his son Iaroslav, he was fighting against the Lithuanian invaders on Toropets land, his patrimonial possession. According to a later, perhaps apocryphal tradition, Vladimir's wife's name was Agrippina and they were both buried in Rzhev, a castle in the periphery of the Toropets principality. The prince may have died in the early 1230s.

The death of Vladimir did not end his family's relations with Livonia. Theoderich established the famous Baltic-German noble family of von der Ropp (although, it is true that, since the death date of Vladimir's daughter is not known, we cannot be totally sure that she was the family's forebear). In the 1230s, it is evident that cooperation existed between Vladimir's son Iaroslav and the Tartu bishopric where his in-law Hermann, another brother of Theoderich, was the bishop. At the time, many of those who were forced into political exile from Pskov and Novgorod sought refuge in Otepää castle in Tartu diocese. Finally, in cooperation with the bishopric, Iaroslav's claim to the Pskov throne led to the Livonians seizing power in Pskov in 1240, and this, in turn, resulted in the famous "Battle on the Ice" on Lake Peipus in 1242.

The following – fictional – text attempts to present the way in which Vladimir himself could have looked at his successes and failures at the end of his life around 1230.

* * *

Actually, the father[5] didn't leave us brothers almost anything besides our princely blood. To be a prince, ride on horseback in front of his retinue, to pass judgement over people – this requires power. It is wealth that can be shared to ensure that your men remain true and the people remain under the authority of the prince. In our patrimony in Toropets, there was not enough of all of this, at least not for all our brothers. There was nothing left to do but serve someone else. Mstislav [Mstislav Mstislavich the Bold] was fortunate, a skillful swordsman, courageous in battle, he knew how to befriend people. Already in his youth, he was close to mighty princes. He fought for them and achieved fame. And then he rose to be a ruler. The Novgorod boyars and people invited Mstislav to be their prince when they got into a fight with the Grand Prince of Vladimir [Vsevolod Iurevich the Big Nest] and deposed [1208/1209] his minor son [Sviatoslav] from their princely throne.

This was also my fortune. The people of Pskov also counted on Mstislav's bravery and art of military leadership, and alongside Novgorod, they had no other choice if they wanted to keep up with them. And they wanted to be ready for war. So they acclaimed me to be their prince. The Saxons, who had built fortresses, churches, and the city of Riga [1201] on the Livs' land on the banks of the Daugava River and installed their own bishop into office, were starting to form alliances with the Letts,[6] who paid tribute to Pskov. The Estonians in Otepää were demanding increasingly excessive duties from the merchants travelling the road from Pskov to Riga. They had to be reined in, just as in the old days when the people of Pskov and Novgorod had waged war with Otepää time and again and collected tribute there [in 1116, 1192]. The bishop's messengers came to see me and the men of Pskov. We made a treaty and I gave [c. 1209/1210] my daughter to the bishop's [Albert of Riga] brother [Theoderich of Buxhövden] as a wife. Mstislav and I went to Otepää, besieged them, and collected tribute [in 1210].

However, the people of Riga said that the Estonians and Letts and everyone else who did not pay tithes were heathens. Wherever they subjugated people they baptized everyone with their baptism and subjected them to their taxes and power. They have knights of God[7] who live like monks and fight in the name of God, and the knights from the entire land of the Saxons come to support them, in order to cleanse themselves before God by fighting the heathens and suffering tribulations. Our priests came home along with the warriors, but the Saxons sent theirs to Otepää and baptized the locals and said that this land now belongs to them. The knights of God did not listen to the advice of the bishop, who at that time was a friend of Pskov and Novgorod, and wanted to have Otepää by themselves, and they again pillaged it [in 1210].

Now the people of Pskov said that they no longer wanted me to be their prince because I have been the friend of the people of Riga and gave them my daughter, but they of Pskov have lost the tribute from Otepää. My brother [Davyd] ruled in Toropets, and the prince [Vladimir] of Polotsk also did not want me in his castles. With my son and my men, I rode down the Daugava River to stay with the bishop and my son-in-law. Wars often occur here, and my son [Iaroslav] stayed at the bishop's house in Riga because he was still young. Still, to be a bailiff [8] of the Letts and Livs somewhere in a castle – this is not really worthy of the dignity and status of a prince. But the bishop didn't have anything better to offer because he didn't have a large army, and time and again, he had to sail to the land of the Saxons and even go as far as Rome [in 1210, 1215, and 1220] to the see the Pope in order to procure aid and support against all of the adversaries of him and the Saxons.

Previously the bishop had ordered one of his priests in this place to mete out justice and the priest had kept the duties and fines he imposed. And when the sea ice melted in the spring [in 1213] and Bishop Albert and his brother Theoderich were supposed to travel across the sea to the land of Saxons again, and left another bishop [Philipp of Ratzeburg] in Riga to replace them, this priest [Alebrand] along with another priest named Henry[9] turned the bishop against me and my men. He incited the people, said that my justice was not fair, but actually he was greedy and jealous. He lied, saying that I was not a true Christian. The people wanted to withhold their dues because of this priest, while everything that I and my men needed had still to be taken from them. The castle[10] had to be reinforced alike. The priests from Pskov, who visited other Letts, never dared to administer justice and didn't think that the princely tribute belonged to them, which is proper for a cleric. We may have the same God, the same Saviour, and the same Mother of God as the Saxons, but their bishops and priests want to rule instead of the princes and boyars. Thus, Theoderich, the brave knight, always had to listen to what his brother the bishop said.

But then the people of Pskov could no longer cope without a prince and asked me to go back [in 1213 and 1215/1216]. When Mstislav and I, along with the men of Smolensk and Novgorod and everyone else, were in the great war [in 1216][11] to help Prince Constantine [of Novgorod] ascend to the throne of the Grand Prince of Vladimir, which his father [Vsevolod] had unjustly deprived him of,[12] the people of Pskov said that the people of Riga had taken Otepää away from them. Take it for yourself and don't let anyone else collect tribute there, they said to me. I went with the Pskov forces and took the Otepää castle [in 1216] and started collecting tribute throughout the land – if possible with good, if necessary by force. I collected tribute from the land of the Letts in the same way. But when we returned to Pskov, the people of Otepää started to resist again and said that they preferred to be taxed by the people of Riga, and started to rule the Otepää castle with the bishop and the knights of God. Together, they conducted campaigns to the lands of Novgorod and Pskov, where they pillaged and burned.

Then the Novgorodians came and wanted revenge. And again, a large force gathered, and the Chuds [Estonians] who had not yet been baptized came, as well as those who had, but did not want to pay tribute to Riga anymore. We besieged the Otepää castle [in 1217] for seventeen days and fought a fierce battle with the men of Otepää and Riga. It was winter and the horses did not have much to eat. What we could obtain from the villages was not enough for the men and they suffered shortages. But inside the castle real famine was in the shadows because there were too many people and horses in it. The horses were so hungry that they chewed off each other's tails, they told later on. Theoderich was also in the castle and because of the starvation we concluded an agreement and ended the war.

But when Theoderich came to me to agree and confirm the peace, the men of Novgorod forcibly took him into captivity and said that I was just serving them and they took Theoderich away and demanded that the bishop pay a good ransom for his brother, which he was forced to do some time later. They said they have been fighting and their lands have been pillaged and the spoils must belong to them. And, together with some Chuds [Estonians], Novgorodians started to contemplate a great war against the people of Riga. However, Mstislav left Novgorod at that time [1217], and the Saxons were able to defeat [in 1217] and subjugate the Estonians before the army of Novgorod and Pskov was assembled. Nevertheless, we fought on the lands of the Estonians, the Letts, and the Livs and gathered the spoils [in 1218]. And my son Iaroslav was now old enough to have his own unit. He fought at castles and took many prisoners, burned a great deal and demanded tribute, proving that he is ready to be prince. Then we arrived at our bailiwick in the land of Letts and Livs, where we gathered excellent spoils. That greedy and cheeky priest escaped our grasp, but nothing but charcoal and ashes remained of his church and house!

But thereafter, the men of Novgorod took most of the spoils and prisoners for themselves. And they said that Otepää belonged to them, and that the Novgorod princes had collected tribute from the Tartu castle since time immemorial [in 1134 and 1191/1192]. But the Saxons and Letts and Estonians still came and pillaged the Pskov lands again and again because they were close by. Then the boyars and people of Pskov did not want to wage war anymore because they had always sustained losses and their lands had been pillaged; but the men of Novgorod had always taken the fruits of war for themselves. However, the men of Novgorod now thought that they could make the land of the Chuds [Estonians] pay tribute to them without help from Pskov or me. They strongly manned the Tartu castle with their men and the Chuds [Estonians] [in 1223]. But the Riga bishop's men and the knights of God now took entire control of Otepää [in 1224]. They started to reinforce it and assigned their own men to rule it. Then they besieged the Tartu castle and conquered it [in 1224], killing everyone in it; and Albert assigned his other brother [Hermann] to be the bishop there. They started to build their own castles and churches and established their own tithe. Theoderich remained as the ruler of our bailiwick and Albert gave him also a part of Otepää. Pskov retained their tribute from some of the Letts, just as it had right from the start. And the great bishop [papal legate William of Modena] came from the Rome [in 1225] and we also confirmed a peace with him [in 1225].

Although a good peace had been concluded with the people of Riga, the Lithuanians started to conduct campaigns more often at the time, to pillage villages and imprison people. They came to Toropets and killed my brother Davyd [in 1225/1226] and wreaked havoc. Iaroslav will probably have to wage war with them a lot in the future, once he becomes the eldest in the family after me. I can't leave him much more than what I once inherited from my father. Toropets still does not have much wealth and power. Will the people of Pskov – fickle and looking out only for themselves – request him to be their prince? Will he be able to rebuff Vsevolod's sons'[13] desire for Novgorod and Pskov? Will the kinsmen of Tartu and Riga be a source of support or conflict? God bestows and decides.

* * *

Notes

1 *Crusading and Chronicle Writing on the Medieval Baltic Frontier: A Companion to the Chronicle of Henry of Livonia*, ed. Marek Tamm, Linda Kaljundi and Carsten Selch Jensen (Farnham: Ashgate, 2011).
2 *The Chronicle of Novgorod 1016–1471*, trans. by Robert Michell and Nevill Forbes (London: Offices of the Society, 1914), 51. The chronology of the chronicle is sometimes incorrect.
3 *The Chronicle of Novgorod*, p. 52.
4 *Crusade and Conversion on the Baltic Frontier 1150–1500*, ed. by Alan V. Murray (Aldershot: Ashgate, 2001).
5 Probably Mstislav Rostislavich the Brave (d. 1180), prince of Smolensk and Novgorod. As the patronymic of Vladimir and his brother Davyd is not mentioned in the contemporary sources, the hypothesis also exists that their father was Iaroslav Vladimirovich (d. after 1205), prince of Novgorod.
6 In Tālava region in Northeast Latvia.
7 The military order of the Brethren of the Sword (est. c. in 1202, in 1237 incorporated into the Teutonic Order).
8 In regions of Autine and, later on, Ydumea, on the road between Riga and Pskov.
9 Henry (d. after 1259), the probable author of the Livonian Chronicle (1220s), then priest in Ymera, next to Ydumea.
10 Vladimir probably resided in Valmiera castle, Latvia.
11 The Battle of Lipitsa.
12 Vsevolod the Big Nest in 1211 gave the throne of Vladimir to his son Iurii Vsevolodovich (1188–1238) against the priority right of the older brother Constantine.
13 Around 1230 four sons of Vsevolod the Big Nest were alive including Iurii, the Grand Prince of Vladimir in 1218–1238, and Iaroslav (1191–1246), prince of Novgorod in 1226–1229, 1231–1236.

Suggestions for further reading

Primary sources

The Chronicle of Novgorod 1016–1471. Translated by Robert Michell and Nevill Forbes. London: Royal Historical Society, 1914.
Henricus Lettus. *The Chronicle of Henry of Livonia*. Translated by James A. Brundage. 2nd ed. New York: Columbia University Press, 2003.

Secondary literature

Bysted, Ane L., Carsten Selch Jensen, Kurt Villads Jensen, and John H. Lind. *Jerusalem in the North: Denmark and the Baltic Crusades*. Turnhout: Brepols, 2012.

The Clash of Cultures on the Medieval Baltic Frontier, edited by Alan V. Murray. Farnham: Ashgate, 2009.

Fennell, John. *The Crisis of Medieval Russia, 1200–1304*, 5th ed. London: Longman, 1993.

Selart, Anti. *Livonia, Rus' and the Baltic Crusades in the Thirteenth Century*, Leiden: Brill, 2015.

4

MOTHER OF A TRIBAL HÄME WARRIOR – KUUTAMO HYVÄNEUVO

Mari Isoaho

We have no information about the individual Häme people before the fourteenth century. Even their names must be reconstructed from the later medieval sources, which reveal a variety of old Finnish pagan names in usage. The lack of information concerns especially women, as elsewhere in early written records. Together with archeological findings and the sparse literary references, there is still one source, however, which aids in reconstructing the daily life and hints at the pre-Christian worldview of the Häme people. This is the evidence of folklore, which was enthusiastically documented in the nineteenth century during the Finnish national movement, the results of which were collected by Elias Lönnrot into the book of epic poetry entitled the Kalevala. *The* Kalevala *preserved many of the pagan mythological motifs and beliefs long into the Christian era, such as mythical weddings of the bear, offerings to ancient gods and ancestors, and spells and charms, like the incantation to stop blood from bleeding, used also by the heroine of the vignette examined below, Kuutamo Hyväneuvo (Moonlight Good-Advice).*

She represents the silent group whose voice is totally missing from the medieval source material, a mother who misses her son who has disappeared in battle. She belongs to a Finnic tribe that in the Swedish and Latin sources is called Tavast, *and in the Novgorodian sources is called* Yem, *and finally in the Vladimirian and Kievan sources is referred to as* Yam. *In the Finnish language their land is called* Häme, *and their people are the* hämäläiset. *It was first mentioned around the same time on both the Swedish runestone of Söderby* (Tafeistaland) *and in the Russian chronicles* (Novgorod First Chronicle *and the* Primary Chronicle of Kiev – Povest vremennykh let') *in their annals of the year 6550 (1042), as a target of Viking-type plunder expeditions. During that time they already inhabited an area in south-western Finland, their core area being situated around Lake Vanajavesi.*

The Häme people are one of three Finnic tribes who are recorded as living in the area of present-day Finland in the late Iron Age and early Middle Ages, the other two being the so-called Proper-Finns (Sum *in the Russian chronicles), inhabiting the southwestern coastal area, and the Karelians, inhabiting the area north of Lake Ladoga. According to the linguistic evidence, all these groups trace their origins to a so-called proto-Finnic past. However, it is relatively complicated to unite the linguistic theories with archeological facts, which verify that the inland area of Finland has a long and continuous history of habitation from the Stone Age onward. It is an open question as to exactly what kind of relationship these Finnic tribes had to the nomadic hunter-gatherer population of Northern Fennoscandia referred to in the medieval sources as Lapps (or Saami population), which also share common linguistic roots.*

In the area of present-day Finland both archeological and linguistic evidence shows that there have always been people and cultural influences flowing from both East and West. Even today great genetic differences can be seen in the DNA of the present-day Finns between those living in the western and eastern parts of Finland. The people of Häme, although living in a sparsely populated woodland area, were thus by no means isolated, but had a wide net of contacts with their neighboring areas. It was a natural crossing point between East and West, and its archeological finds from the Iron Age point to influence coming from the East, from the Karelians, and from the West; that is, the Proper-Finns. In the north they were in contact with the Lapps and Norwegians; in the west and south and in the coastal area they were in contact not only with the Swedes, but also with the Danes and German merchants.

Little is known about the history and lifestyle of the old Finnic tribes. The people of Häme had large hunting and fishing areas, and they moved easily using the vast lake and river systems of Finland. One peculiarity of the inhabitants of both Häme and Karelia were the Iron Age hill forts, which were erected in the vicinity of their villages in order to guard their most important trade and hunting routes. Some of those hill forts were in use well into the medieval era, as is testified to by the description of the Novgorod attack on Häme in 1311.

As was the case with numerous European prehistoric tribes, the Häme people were illiterate until the establishment of Christianity, from around 1100 onward. This left the literary descriptions of the Häme people to others: to the neighboring Swedes and Novgorodians, as well as a few papal letters. Swedish sources are scarce, consisting only of the above-mentioned runic inscription and some opaque references in the later medieval sources. Papal letters, for their part, describe the concern of the Catholic Church over the newly Christianized area, which was believed to be in danger due to the close proximity of the enemies of the faith.[1] Moreover, the pope expressed opinions and worries similar to those connected with the Christianization of Livonia. Since papal letters are very formal and rhetorical, the reality of the spreading of the Christian faith is not easily reconstructed. We can conclude from the various sources that the Häme people were amazingly flexible with their dealings with the Swedes. In 1237 Pope Gregory IX invoked a Crusade against Häme – "Tauestia," against people "qui Tauesti dicuntur nacio" (who are called as the Tauesti) who had brutally cast aside their Christian belief because of the people living in the vicinity who were enemies of the Cross.[2] Because of the above-mentioned bull, and the reference in the much later fourteenth-century Swedish Erik's Chronicle, *Finnish historians have earlier talked about the Swedish Crusades as targeted against Finns and the people of Häme. However, it appears that the Christianization of both the Proper-Finns in the coastal area and the inland people of Häme was a relatively peaceful process, the result of sustained, peaceful contacts.*

By far the richest literary material on the Häme people is derived from the Chronicle of Novgorod, which gives an enigmatic picture of a remote country, to which Novgorodians made altogether nine recorded trips in the years between 1042 and 1311. The Chronicle also tells that the people of Häme raided the Lake Ladoga area in 1142, 1149, and 1228. Moving easily along the complicated water routes was essential for the livelihood of the Häme people; they used light boats and reached Lake Ladoga using the waterways such as the Vuoksi River, which led them straight into the heartlands of Karelia, to a fortified city that the Novgorod chronicle called Korela, later known in Finnish as Käkisalmi (Cockoo strait). During the thirteenth century, independent forays of Häme into the northern Novgorod districts ceased, so that in 1240 and 1256 they were already part of the Swedish fleet. They participated in military campaigns led by the Swedes in 1240, when they took part in the famous battle of the Neva in 1240, where Alexander Nevskii defeated the intruders, and in 1256 Alexander Nevskii again fought with the Swedish army and a Häme contingent in Narva, on the Estonian side of the Gulf of Finland. After these campaigns, there is no more information on independent Häme groups moving in the Novgorodian districts. From the beginning of the fourteenth century, the Novgorod chronicle treated the Swedish, Finnish, and Häme population under the common term nemtsy.

The story appearing below is placed somewhere in the heartlands of Häme, one year after the battle of the Neva, where the heroine, Kuutamo Hyväneuvo, waits for her only son, Kekro Kaukomieli (Will to fare way), to return home from a long journey. All the persons are fictive, since there are no sources indicating any individuals of the tribe; however, these persons are placed in the historical settings described above.

* * *

FIGURE 4.1 Akseli Gallen-Kallela *Lemminkäinen's Mother*, 1897, tempera on canvas, Antell collections, Finnish National Gallery/Ateneum Art Museum,

Photo: Finnish National Gallery/Jouko Könönen

Picture: The painting of *Lemminkäinen's Mother* (1897) by Akseli Gallen-Kallela, depicts a scene from the *Kalevala*, where the hero Lemminkäinen has been killed, his body hacked to pieces and thrown into the dark river that flows through the underworld, *Tuonela*. His mother, having both collected the parts from the river and sewn them back together, looks up to see a bee bringing back honey from the halls of the god Ukko, a wondrous ointment that would bring her son back to life. Lemminkäinen's mother wears a dress similar to that of the fictional heroine of this vignette, Kuutamo Hyväneuvo, who relies upon traditional knowledge of healing, and the secrets of life and death.

* * *

She had always been close to her ancestors, always. Every year the village elder, Kuutamo's uncle, Sampo Yletyinen, offered the ancestors the first fruits of the new crop of grain, serving them the first beer, speaking to their honored, long-gone kinsmen with respect and noble words, asking them to support the growth of next year's crop, as well as for luck in fishing and hunting. This had been a rite from times immemorial, and Kuutamo had witnessed this taking place every year. The big stone in the grove was full of small cups, carved in the stone, where the meals and drinks were served to those who had gone to the realm of death, or *Tuonela*. Dark, heavy, and cold stone was a gateway to the watery underworld, where the ancestors lived. In the sacred grove the ancestors were contacted not only through the offerings of a cup-stone but also through the sacred trees. Kuutamo had often talked with her grandmother while sitting by the big spruce by the sacred well. Conifers, with their long roots piercing through the limits of the spiritual worlds, were known as the trees for the spirits of the underworld, while the deciduous trees with their sighing, elegant leaves delivered messages to the upper world, to the world of gods and forest spirits.

Now Kuutamo was in need of a short consultation with her long-gone grandmother, Pihlava. She washed her face with sacred water, sat by the three-topped dark spruce, and closed her eyes, feeling the tree's comforting support. Such a tree had a strong power, and Kuutamo could feel the presence of her old granny, who had passed away years ago. Kuutamo was pale with fear and trembled when she asked a question, the answer of which she was afraid to hear. "Pihlava, my dearest granny, please tell me, have you seen my son there? Please tell me, has he arrived through the dark river to the realm of the dead? Pihlava, my sweet granny, is he there? I have a great fear for my Kekro, my only son, my sweet apple, who left to wage war in the faraway lands." She waited in silence, feeling the presence of her grandmother. She felt her grandmother's answer in her mind: Kekro was not there, among the dead. Good. Kuutamo was relieved, her heart lighter. But still, a year had gone and not a word from him.

Others had returned home many months ago, but Kekro had gone missing, not even his best friend and comrade in arms, Kölli Luupää (Bonehead), knew exactly what had happened. When Kölli and others had returned home, they had given Kekro's mother and his bride Kylli a description of a mighty war, of fierce combat that had taken place in the Land of the Karelians, near Lake Laatokka [Ladoga], by the swampy river, Neva. Kölli and others had joined the Swedes and their fleet had been bigger than ever. They had taken the Karelians by surprise, planning to build a fortress on the riverbank, but then the Novgorodians had come and given them a good fight, forcing them to leave. As Kölli testified, everything would have gone well but for the clumsy old chieftain of the Swedes, who was too slow and stiff in combat against the young and enthusiastic Novgorodian prince.

The Swedes had sailed home, but Kekro and the others decided to take the usual route through the Karelian land. They went raiding and plundering, now that the plans of the Swedes had dried up. Kekro, Kölli, and others of their tribe had tried to invade the Karelian fortress on the island, but the attempt was doomed from the beginning, since the Karelians were already alarmed and on their guard. They had then swiftly taken the route home before the Novgorodians could follow them, but there were too many Karelians on the alert along the way, and many of them were captured as soon as they had landed. Kekro's and Kölli's boat was ambushed, so they swam to shore, where the Karelians had then attacked them, shouting and swearing. Kölli had hidden himself in the woods and managed to reach the nearest Häme post after a long and tiresome march through the woods.[3] What became of Kekro no one seemed to know. Damn his excess pride! Why did he have to leave in the first place, his mother now thought. Always seeking after silver and the honors of war. This was something that he had learned from his father.

Kekro's father had been a victim of the great raiding expedition years ago,[4] when Kekro was only a boy. Karelians and Novgorodians had suddenly appeared on their home lake, sneaking through the southern rivers. Kuutamo's brother, Huru Arkapoika (Timid-boy), had spotted them first, but it was way too late to organize a proper resistance. While women escaped into the forests with the elderly, taking as much cattle with them as they could, the men of the village had retired to the high rocky hill fort, giving part of the Novgorodians a proper resistance. The hill fort kept only some of the enemy occupied, however, while others had hurried on in search of the escaping women and children. A messenger was hastily sent to neighboring villages, to spread word of the attacking enemies. In addition, a great warning fire was lit on top of the hill fort, to signal to others in nearby forts, who then lit their own fires, spreading the message of warning yet farther. Kuutamo remembered how it had taken too long for the others to come to their rescue. When the great host of Rapola[5] had finally arrived, nothing was to be done anymore, the battle was already over, the harm done.

The Novgorodians had come late in the autumn, when all the barns of the village had been full of grain, and the animals had already been taken into their shelters for the winter. It was an easy task for the intruders to burn down the crop and kill the cattle from the stables and cowsheds. They managed to capture many of the young girls and boys with them, taking them as their slaves.[6] Kuutamo could not remember which was worse, the misery of the mothers and others, who were left alive to weep for their stolen children, brothers, and sisters, or seeing the victims of a bloodbath, so many dead men. Kuutamo had done her best to heal the wounded.

Then the old spell for stopping the blood was still in use. Treating the wounds and bruises, she had sung the old song:

> *Hear me, Blood, and ease your flowing,*
> *O you bloodstream, rush no longer,*
> *Like a wall, O Blood, arrest yourself,*
> *Like a fence, O Bloodstream, stand still,*
> *As a sword in sea is standing,*
> *Like a reed in moss-grown country,*
> *Like the bank that bounds the cornfield,*
> *Like a rock in raging torrent.*
>
> *Therefore, Dear one, cease thy flowing,*
> *Crimson Blood, drip down no longer,*
> *Not impeded, but contended.*
>
> *Ukko, O thou great Creator,*
> *Jumala, aloft in heaven!*
> *Come here where you are needed,*
> *Come here where we implore you,*
> *Press your mighty hands upon the wound,*
> *Press your mighty thumbs upon it,*
> *And painful wound close firmly,*
> *And the door whence comes the evil,*
> *Spread the tender leaves upon it,*
> *Leaves of golden water-lily,*
> *Thus to close the path of bleeding,*
> *And to stem the rushing torrent.*[7]

It was after that devastating shock that the village agreed to allow the Finnish preacher to come to the village permanently, together with a properly armed Swedish escort. That escort lifted the spirits of the wounded and shamed village. But there were those who never forgot. There were some whose blood boiled with the idea of revenge. Most of the villagers had only contempt for the new, seemingly peaceful and orderly way of life. They continued their daily businesses, most of them burning down the woods to make way for the new crops. There were many who traveled to their trading posts to the North, to the Land of darkness and the *noita* (witches), the Lapps, and came with wondrous stories and odd silver jewelry and equipment. Some had met Norsemen on their trips. Many others went to the West, to the Finns, where they became increasingly acquainted with Swedes, trading their furs for the fine swords and spears. Others sailed south to their salmon rapids.

Kuutamo's husband, Silvo Väiräjälka Kovasydän (Crooked-Legged Stone-Heart), earned both of his nicknames after that horrific slaughter. His second name – Vääräjalka – came after being wounded in the combat with the intruders, and third name – Kovasydän – after becoming embittered by its consequences. Silvo thought he was stripped of all his manhood, first being wounded and crippled, and then yielding to the habits of the preacher man. Silvo's destiny was his burning blood, which drove him to revenge the next year. He never came back from that trip.[8]

Many of the villagers thought differently, and several, especially the brides taken both from Karelia and Suomi (Finns), were pleased to hear about Kiesus[9] and his holy mother, Marjatta, the graceful damsel.[10] Kuutamo had heard women singing a song about the wondrous birth of the new God, as his mother had conceived by a cranberry, when the maiden Marjatta was herding her father's cattle:

> *Marjatta, the graceful damsel,*
> *For a while lived on as herd-girl.*
> *Evil is the life of shepherd,*
> *Far too heavy for a maiden;*
> *In the grass a snake is creeping,*
> *In the grass the lizards wriggling.*[11]

Kuutamo was amused by the story of how the cranberry had lured Marjatta to swallow it. From that cunning cranberry, that modest virgin Marjatta came pregnant, and after her belly started to grow, she had been faced with the contempt of the others, having a fatherless child. Therefore, when the time of her labor was at hand, she wasn't even offered a *sauna*[12] but gave birth in the stall with only the warm breath of the horses and cows to relieve her pain. Children were indeed, Kuutamo thought, a gift from God, but also a constant reason for worry.

The sacred grove where the ancestors lay was given as a place for the new house of the preacher man's God.[13] None of this hindered people from talking with their ancestors in the grove, and having a connection to the underworld through its trees and the well. What the preacher man could not tolerate, however, was the respect showed toward the spirits of the woods and waters. Hunters and fishers as they were, they showed great respect to spirits who mastered the game and fish, since they knew that everything that they managed to hunt was given them by the grace of Tapio, lord of the woods, or Ahti, master of the waters. The preacher man had stripped even the skulls of the bear from the sacred pine tree deep in the woods.

Kuutamo remembered well that one feast for the hunted bear that the villagers had organized back then in her youth. She and Silvo had been selected as a bride and groom for the feast, and the spirit of a hunted bear had been invited as guest of honor. The service had been lavish; the whole village had prepared food and drink for three days of feasting and celebration. They were excessive in drinking, and wild in their mating – the whole village. The king of the woods, the bear, was with them, and looked approvingly on the abundance of it all. In that feast Kekro was conceived, as were many others of his future comrades. At the end of the long banquet, the skull of the bear was fixed to a tree, his eyes directed to the Northern Star, to the pillar of the sky. They all knew that the bear was the ultimate guardian of their lives, the king who carried the weight of heaven on his mighty shoulders. What would come of them, when the preacher man had insulted the king, the golden apple of the woods?[14] Silvo had died in the far-away lands and Kekro, their son, had gone missing. Would the world ever be the same, Kuutamo wondered.

She spotted a mighty old alder with a blood-red side. People had tied white ribbons to its branches and forks, as did Kuutamo also. "Please, dear tree here is white linen, which I offer to you, my dearest alder. You which are taller than others, whose leaves whisper to gods who linger in the Upper World. Whisper this and sing it to the god Ukko, who is the chief of all gods:

> *O you sun, whom God created,*
> *Have you seen my son pass by you,*
> *Have you seen my golden apple,*
> *Have you seen my staff of silver?*
> *From the murky rivers of the world,*
> *From its raging whirlpools,*
> *Best it is to journey homeward,*
> *To see the eyes of a loving mother."*[15]

Kuutamo sighed. Now this was all she could do. To wait. This was something that she was already used to doing with her Kekro. She was always waiting for Kekro, her only son, who was dearest from all the treasures of the world. Even when she was expecting him, she had waited and waited, until the boy had finally been born. The reddish and strong baby was swaddled in linen clothes. Kuutamo had prepared a little bag with the left eye of a magpie to be placed inside the swaddling clothes. This was to protect the boy from the evil eye of the envious and malicious people. The same careful preparations were done when the baby was grown up a bit, so that when he had been dressed for the first time in real clothes, they were clad inside out, and his face was blackened with soot so that malicious spirits would not recognize him. All these preparations were needed to avoid bad things from happening to her dearest one.

Kekro had been the apple of his mother's eye and also a great joy to his father, who had proudly taken him into his arms and claimed Kekro as his son. Not all the children were so warmly and joyfully welcomed into the Middle World, to the realm of living human beings. Many children were taken into the swamp, stuffed into watery turf, and hidden there to find their way into the murky river of *Tuonela*, to the realm of the master of the Underworld, Tuoni. These were the children who had no father to accept them, no kin to take care of them.

Her son had always had an easy path, and many said that he was a spoiled brat. But his mother remembered only a boy who, in his dreams, never ceased to reach out for the best treasures in this world. He wanted it all, the best furs, the best silver, and the best girl. Kuutamo remembered Kekro's trip to fetch himself a bride. He had left with his fairest boat, brought many gifts to Kylli's father, and finally returned home with an astonishing bride: beautiful, playful, and from a distinguished house.

They had been a good match; Kylli was a good-looking woman, with the sparkle of life in her eye and with a mind of her own. She came from a big house where she had been surrounded by admirers and band of joyous and giggling girls. Her playful nature was a bit of a problem for Kekro, who was a jealous man. Jealous, in spite of his own history with women. But Kylli was from a big house, and with her Kekro's own prestige had risen. Kekro had made Kylli swear that she would stop playing around with other girls of the village and stay home as a good wife should do. The laughter of the girls giggling in the corners and courtyard, singing and dancing, made Kekro feel uneasy. Who knew the kinds of stupid things they would do? Who knew whose attention they would catch with their flirtatious smile and joyous play? Kylli had promised to stay home, but only if Kekro would stay home too. She would not have come to Kekro's modest house only to sit there on her own, feeling miserable. She was a lively girl, singing and playing all the time, making jokes of everything and everyone.

Kuutamo had known in that instant back then that Kekro's promise to stay home would never be kept. They had always been on the move, the men of her kin. And so too was Kekro Kaukomieli. Even though Kekro at first tried to settle down, had gone fishing only to the nearby rapids, laid his nets in the village's waters, his mother knew in her heart that his mind was already on the bigger fishes, bigger prizes, and on a wider world. And so he went. She sighed and started walking from the grove. First to the house, where she would make a meal and bake breads with Kylli. Then she would take Leino, her grandson, and together they would go down to the harbor, to sit down on the shore and look to the lake, to watch if there were boats in the wide open lake, to see if one of them would finally come to the shore.

Notes

1 Diplomataricum Fennicum, Signum FMU 80.
2 Diplomataricum Fennicum, Signum FMU 82.
3 A similar path was mentioned in 1228 for the Häme expedition to Ladoga, when the men of Häme needed to retire from their campaign, which had started well, but had then become problematic on the return trip home, that is, in sneaking through the woods after losing their boats.
4 Prince Iaroslav's trip to Häme in 1227.
5 Rapola is a large hill fort in Sääksmäki, at the northern end of Lake Vanajavesi.
6 It was mentioned in the Laurentian chronicle that Prince Iaroslav's trip to Häme took place in winter. Also the trip of his son Alexander Nevskii took place just before the winter, in autumn 1256. Usually the chronicle accounts are very short in describing what the Novgorodians actually did when they reached their target. The exception is the Novgorodian raid of 1311, where it is told that the Russians wreaked havoc in the vicinity for three days, burning the crops, and killing the cattle. What was the purpose of these raids? Jukka-Pekka Taavitsainen has pointed out that these trips were not so much expeditions that we would call collecting taxes; rather, their purpose was to plunder and to make the population weak enough not to cause harm or claim land or wealth in the frontier zone.
7 Adapted from *Kalevala*, poem 9.
8 The Häme raiding trip to Karelia in 1228.
9 Jesus in its old Finnic form.

10 Mary had many Finnic forms, Marjatta being one of them.
11 Adapted from *Kalevala*, poem 50.
12 A hot bathhouse of the northern Finnic people, used also by the Novgorod Slavs.
13 In Pope Gregorius's letter to the Bishop of Finland in 1229, the pope confirms that the sacred groves, which the converted pagans had donated to the Church, now belonged to the Church by papal authority. See Diplomatarium Fennicum, Signum FMU 77.
14 Well into the present day, Finns have preserved their many old nicknames for the bear, which all show tender affection and respect.
15 Adapted from *Kalevala*, poem 15.

Suggestions for further reading

Sources

A.N. Nasonov (ed.), *Novgorodskaja letopis' starshego i mladshego izvodov*. Moscow: Akademija nauk SSSR, 1950. English translation in *The Chronicle of Novgorod. 1016–1471*. Translated from the Russian by Robert Michell and Nevil Forbes. London: Offices of the Society, 1914.

The Finnish national epos, *Kalevala*, contains very old elements from the pagan past. It is a composite work collected by Elias Lönnrot, and was first published in 1835. The version most commonly known today was first published in 1849 and consists of 22,795 verses, which are divided into fifty songs. It has been translated in English several times by several translators. The one used in this story is *Kalevala. The Land of the Heroes*. Translated by W. F. Kirby. J. M. Dent & Sons Ltd, London 1907.

Lavrent'evskaia letopis'. PSRL I. Izd. 2. Izdatel'stvo Akademii Nauk SSSR 1926–28. (Contains also the earliest Kievan Chronicle, *Povest' vremennykh let*).

Papal letters and other sources concerning medieval Finland and Häme are printed in Reinhold Hausen (ed.) *Finlands medeltidsurkunder* (FMU). 1. – 1400. Helsingfors Kejserliga senatens tryckeri, 1910; and Reinhold Hausen (ed.), *Registrum Ecclesiae Aboensis eller Åbo domkyrkas svartbok*. 1890. They are available online in Diplomatarium Fennicum, http://extranet.narc.fi/DF/index.htm.

Research literature is mainly in Finnish; here are some few examples in English:

J.-P. Taavitsainen, *Ancient Hillforts of Finland. Problems of Analysis, Chronology and Interpretation with Special Reference to the Hillfort of Kuhmoinen*. Helsinki: SMYA/FFT 94, 1990.

Jukka Korpela, *World of Ladoga: Society, Trade, Transformation and State Building in the Eastern Fennoscandian Boreal Forets Zone c. 1000–1555*. Lit Verlag: Nordische Geschichte, Band 7, 2008.

Jukka Korpela, "The Baltic Finnic People in the Medieval and Pre-Modern European Slave Trade." *Russian History* 41, no. 1 (2014): 85–117.

Jukka Korpela, "'. . . And They Took Countless Captives': Finnic Captives and the East European Slave Trade during the Middle Ages." In *Eurasian Slavery, Ransom and Abolition in World History, 1200–1860*, edited by Christoph Witzenrath. Farnhan, Surrey: Ashgate 2015: 171–190.

5

FROM BUTCHER TO SAINT

The improbable life and fate of Vaišvilkas/
Vojšelk/Lavryš/Elisej of Lithuania and
Black Rus' (?–1267)

David M. Goldfrank

The ancestors of today's Lithuanians were the last Europeans to convert to Christianity, and the subject of the sketch that lies ahead was the first or second prince from among these erstwhile pagans to convert to Orthodoxy. The early Lithuanians may have been pressured by the long-standing demographic, political, and military expansion of the neighboring Rus' and Poles; the aggressive, semi-crusading German colonization of the Eastern Baltic that started in the early 1200s; and an overall situation complicated by Mongol suzerainty over most Rus' principalities as of the 1240s and papal claims to supremacy over all Christians. Yet not only could these pagan warriors and forest-peasants hold their own against Christian neighbors, but also an expansive Lithuanian polity was taking shape by the 1260s, the time of our story.

The career of our Vojšelk [VOYshelk] – we shall call him at the start by his Rus' name, the earliest so recorded – fascinated some contemporary and later bookmen interested in regional history. And for good reason. Vojšelk bridged at least four divides: Lithuania-Rus', paganism-Christianity, warrior prince-monk, and, at least by legend, several Lithuanian rulers and ruling dynasties – here leading to what became the fabulously successful Gediminid-Jagellonians of the fourteenth through sixteenth centuries.

Our chief sources here are the work of archeologists with material remains and the oldest written records, a few comments by outside observers of pagan Lithuanian life, extant codices for monastic life, and then the chronicles – Polish, Baltic German, but especially Rus' from Halyč-Volynia, for the flow of politics and the outlines of Vojšelk's biography. The creative historian's task is to make sense of all of this fragmentary material – some not at all easy – and craft out of it a reasonably plausible human life. For as a genre, chronicles contain the equivalent of "headlines," sometimes alone, sometimes with an explanatory sentence or two, sometimes with barely plausible literary embellishments. In the case of Vojšelk, the leitmotif of his stormy career and tragic end, as found in the Halyč-Volynian Chronicle was revised imaginatively over the next 400 years and served as potent foundation myths for both an important Orthodox monastery and the dynasty that initiated the Polish-Lithuanian union in 1386 and reigned over it for 200 years.

*The sketch that lies ahead here thus represents the latest attempt at reworking the Vojšelk
story – a reworking which hopefully will make sense to the modern reader.*

* * *

It is Holy Week, late-April 1267 in Uhrov'sk [Ugrovesk, now Uhrusk in eastern
Poland], where the Uherka River flows northward from well-fortified Kholm [now
Polish Chełm] into the Bug. Uhrov'sk is protected by earthen and wooden stock-
ades and a recently constructed 9m x 12m rick tower typical of the Volynian-Polish
border region. Earlier the episcopal seat of the current Kholm eparchy, this little
fortress-town has several dozen well-armored professional soldiers and a variety of
other townsmen, and is supported by the surpluses from the surrounding villages
and local trade. Nearby (now the village Novouhuz'ke) stands the Daniliv Monastery, the only place within thirty-two kilometers where a liturgy is performed every
day, and where one can learn to read and write and start training for a career as a
churchman. Except for a massive stone and brick pillar, where ascetics sometimes
imitate the cloister's patron saint, Daniel the Stylite (409–493), this is a modest,
totally wooden establishment, home to its superior, to a dozen monks dwelling in
slightly sunken cabin-cells, to two more brothers inhabiting slightly larger frame
houses, as does the superior, and also a cookhouse-bakery and some sheds and cellar storerooms. One of these cellars serves as the cloister's small book repository for
protection of the precious items from fire. The wooden monastery church, appro-
priately dedicated to Daniel, is full of icons and also potent incense to neutralize the
persistent stench of the day. It holds only about fifty worshippers.

Daniliv's church and library contain in Church Slavic almost the minimum
any bishopric or major cloister needs in order to function: the all-important basic
Orthodox service books for regular liturgies, the holidays, and the commemorations of all the saints; the *Palaia*, that is, Genesis and Exodus in "haggadah" [story-
telling] form; an abbreviated and glossed collection from the Prophets, and also
Psalms, Proverbs, and Ecclesiasticus (Wisdom of Sirach) from the Old Testament;
from the New Testament, a Gospel and an *Apostol* (Acts and the Epistles) – each of
the combined *Apraxos* type – set in liturgical reading order for the calendar year,
not as separate books or items; collections of model sermons by some of the greatest of the Church Fathers, Gregory of Nazianzus (329–389) and John Chrysostom (c. 349–407), and others attributed to Ephrem the Syrian (fourth century);
the standard monastic corpora credited to Basil of Caesarea (330–379]), John
Climacus (579–649), and Theodore the Studite (759–829); some saints lives, some
of the *Sayings of the* (Desert) *Fathers*; and a penitential handbook. It was no trivial
achievement for a small-town monastery in thirteenth-century Rus' to have such
a collection. But missing from what went for a well-rounded clerical reading
curriculum for the period in the major Rus' towns and cloisters are more Scrip-
ture (the Orthodox Church at that time did not conceive of a complete "Bible"
as we do today), standard Byzantine and Rus' chronicles, and Ioann the Bulgarian Exarch's eleventh-century update of Basil's pseudo-scientific *Hexameron* [Six
Days of Creation] and condensations of the philosophical and theological treatises

of John of Damascus (c. 675–750). Also missing for professional ecclesiastical administration and for Church law are a *Pedalion* [*Kornmčaja kniga*] compilation. But in case of need, these can be found in Volodymyr-Volynsk or Kholm, either a two-day ride by horse.

Those two special Daniliv cells noted above represent no trivial matter. Each houses an illustrious resident: sixty-year-old Hryhoryj, the most prestigious ascetic master in all of Halyč-Volynia, who earlier served as his prince's envoy to the Pope, and the forty-five-year-old erstwhile Lithuanian warrior-prince Vojšelk. Vojšelk had been tonsured by Hryhoryj twelve years earlier under the monastic name of the second-century stonemason martyr and patron of horses Lavryš [Laurus], but also bears the name of the brutal and vengeful Old Testament wonderworker-prophet Elisej [Elisha]. Thanks to these two residents, Daniliv alternates as a cloistered sanctuary for pedagogy, prayer, reflection, and spiritual counsel under expert direction, and as a destination of visitors seeking serious discourse or interaction on this-worldly matters with battle-hardened royalty, self-represented as on permanent spiritual and penitent furlough from his princely duties. These contradictory functions combine and clash as our narrative commences with a knock on Lavryš's cell door.

At this very moment Lavryš has been contemplating for several hours as monks are wont to do. Hryhoryj, who was Lavryš's original mentor in Polonina in the Halyčan Eastern Carpathians and recently summoned by his princely disciple back to Daniliv, whence he had twenty years earlier served as a special envoy to the Pope in Rome, has provided sound guidance. Sincere tonsuring wipes away earlier sins. So Lavryš need only concentrate on his words, thoughts, and deeds since the time he became a monk and prepare for a future calling on earth and for the judgment that awaited afterward. But he is all too human, and his thoughts wander. Indeed, lacking either a Christian or a literate upbringing, not to say both, he is far from ideal material for the ascetic life. His thoughts migrate back to his childhood in central and eastern Lithuania as "Vaišvilkas" – literally, the friendly/generous wolf. He imagines the thick forests; the lakes, streams, and swamps; the huts and frame houses standing upon the earth, rather than half sunken as is often the case in Rus'; and the sturdy forester-peasants, who reap crops by rotating their planting among three fields – leaving two fallow – and also heed the call to arm and join their elite soldier countrymen in sly ambushes and counterattacks against invaders. Some of his happiest memories are of times spent with his beloved wet nurse. He recalls the time she explained to him the ever-present danger of fires and how low-hanging clay canopies allowed peasants safely to keep small fires inside their huts – they did not yet have clay ovens inside as did the Rus'. However, his thoughts of how much he enjoyed the festivities surrounding the periodic human sacrifices – chiefly of elite, captive Germans – are troubling. And he recalls the disgust that Christians, either visiting merchants or resident captives, expressed toward the venerated local priests who presided over these rituals, as well as over the custom of cremating the dead, and the numerous public pleas to the various gods and spirits responsible for favorable weather, harvests, hunts, health, and pregnancies.

Lavryš has also been focusing on his tortured relationship with his late father Mindaugas [Mindovg, ca. 1203–1263] – something that Hryhoryj definitely counseled against. Mindaugas, we ought note, was one of those gifted offspring of pre-modern royalty, whose brutal fighting prowess, personal charisma, and generous bonhomie toward loyal subordinates attracted followers. He had readily fought, feasted, and politicked his way to the position of leading Lithuanian *kunigas* [or *kunigaikštis* = (Rus') *knjaz'* = king, prince, duke], but not without making enemies. Among his weaknesses was a readiness to strip royal relatives of their wives and appropriate them for himself – not a sound recipe for natural death in those days. Vaišvilkas, as eldest surviving son, had been expected to follow in these footsteps and had trained hard with horses and weapons, speared boars and fed his companions by bonfire, but was less coordinated and gifted in combat. And a vicious groin injury had ruined his enjoyment of women. He assumed he would be bypassed for the ultimate succession in favor of a younger, fecund half-brother, yet had to do his father's bidding lest he end up prematurely dead, as had several royal cousins, who dared to oppose the redoubtable Mindaugas.

At this point in the flashback review of his previous life, Lavryš hears the knock, rises from his couch-bed, and opens the door. Accompanied by one of the monks, a messenger tells Lavryš that his trusted "uncle," Prince Vasyl'ko [Romanovič, 1203–1269, of Volodymyr-Volynsk] has arrived with a summons for a meeting à *trois* with the latter's nephew Lev [Danilovič, 1228–1301, of Halyč]. This is absolutely the last scenario that Lavryš wishes to consider, but to disobey Vasyl'ko, the senior family prince [in age, if not power], whom Lavryš vowed to treat as his "father"? Never! "In the name of God and His Most Pure Mother, please wait until I consult Father and Lord Hryhoryj, whom I have also vowed to obey," is the initial reply.

Lavryš's earlier calm now turns into a cold sweat. Just the thought of Lev drives away any trace of monastic calm, virtue, humility, and forgiveness and clouds Lavryš's mind with pernicious turbulence. For this man Lev is an able brute, just as his grandfather [Roman Mstislavič, 1150–1205] and father [Danilo Romanovič, 1201–1264], and also the all-too familiar Mindaugas had been. What they say of one, applies to all: "O evil Roman: you enslave in order to plow with the Lithuanian."

So now politics and war occupy Lavryš's mind. After the Mongols had made themselves indirect masters of Rus' [1238–1240], and their favorite, Aleksandr Iaroslavich ["Nevskii"] had driven back the Germans from Pskov [1242], the papacy mobilized Hungarian, Polish, and Baltic-German power to expand the reach of the Roman Church eastward into Orthodox Rus' and pagan Lithuania – the most resistant of all the Baltic lands to proselytization. In one year [1253], Rome scored a resounding success, with both Danilo and Mindaugas accepting royal crowns and the title *Rex* (= "King" as recognized in Latin Christendom: Danilo's title Slavic *kniaz'* was sufficient for Rus'). This forced some reorientation of policy for both new "kings," as they were expected to cooperate with each other and with neighboring Latins at the expense, for Danilo, of Orthodox loyalty to the Eastern Church's Greek hierarchy, and for Mindaugas, of native and neighboring paganism.

To complicate matters, slightly earlier Lithuanian power had extended eastward into Palatsk [Polotsk] under Tovtivl [Tautvilas], one of Mindaugas's kinsmen, and southward into the lands known as Black Rus' under himself, Vojšelk, who now held Volkovyjsk and Slonim in his own name, and Navahrudak [Novogrudok] as his father's town.

As he mulls over these events, the ex-Vojšelk Lavryš realizes how central his Rus' years became for who he is today. These towns had been established as outposts of Rus' power in the sparsely populated southern reaches of what had once been Lithuania. But with the in-migration of Slavic peasants this zone – its language, agro-techniques, and popular superstitions that did not challenge Orthodox authority – a new *Litva* was taking shape [the future Belarus]. It was in Navahrudak, Lavryš recalls to his dismay, that he performed his last human sacrifices to satisfy his elite Lithuanian armed retinue. Then as soon as his father converted to Latin Christianity [Roman Catholicism], "Vaišvilkas" converted to his Christian subjects' liturgically Slavic Orthodoxy. And then the senseless butchery ceased under the Christian "Vojšelk."

Sadly, thinks Lavryš, God did not intend for him a smooth reign over a transformed Black Rus'. Danilo and his clan had their own claims there, and the Mongols hoped to limit Lithuanian expansion. The pagan-at-heart Mindaugas, moreover, faced far more opposition to his trading even nominal conversion to Catholicism for the prestigious title *Rex* than Danilo ever did for his nominal and never effective subordination to Rome. The upshot was that in the face of Danilo's military demonstration, Mindaugas had to relinquish Black Rus'. Soon [1254], on the latter's orders, Vojšelk gave his own sister in marriage to Danilo's youngest son Švarno [ca. 1242–1269] and turned Navahrudak, Slonim, and Volkovyjsk over to Danilo's second living son Roman [ca. 1230–1258/60].

Continuing the review of past events, Lavryš now muses over what in retrospect was his great gamble.

> Mindaugas demanded that "Vaišvilkas" return home, but the latter was a genuine Christian now and had resolved that if he did so, it would be as bearer of Orthodoxy. But he first had to acquire some training. So off he went, with Danilo's and his clan's blessing, to Polonina and became Hryhoryj's disciple. Not so strangely, as the thought of Hryhoryj enters Lavryš's mind again, he remembers why he is pondering all of these matters, and feels he must consult the great elder immediately.
>
> Already alerted by Prince Vasyl'ko's messenger, Hryhoryj has been preparing for a visit from his unique disciple. At the age of thirty-three, when he took the tonsure, Lavryš was capable of repenting the big sins of his pagan days and of avoiding new ones, but was too beat up and spent to retrain as a hieromonk [monk-priest] much less as a missionary bishop. He could not even shake his drinking habits. Hard mead had been a staple from his Lithuanian youth through his days in Navahrudak, and this did not change in the cloister. Nor did anyone expect it to change. He could learn the [Cyrillic]

alphabet and sound out some words, but genuine, concentrated reading was beyond him, something that Hryhoryj quickly recognized.

So the master's plan for his disciple was to build on the warrior's ethic of stoic self-control and loyalty and apply it to emotions, so that this royal novice might stay out of trouble and serve as a model and advisor for laymen and mediate quarrels. This worked [sort of], and after two years of training, Hryhoryj found a suitably mature hieromonk and sent him with Lavryš back to Navahrudak. Not far from the town Lavryš established his own small cloister on the banks of the Nieman on the border of Roman's and Mindaugas's domains. Always happy to receive prestigious visitors, Lavryš helped to resolve disputes among Rus' and Lithuanians, even if Mindaugas displayed unconcealed contempt for his eldest son's new vocation. Hryhoryj was content with the periodic reports to him from Navahrudak, and indeed all would have been fine had the new peace between Danilo and Mindaugas prevailed. But the Mongols from the Rus' side and Lithuanian pagan magnates farther north broke up that alliance a few years later [1258]. Lavryš was haplessly caught in the middle.

Hryhoryj is rehearsing what he knows of this history, when Lavryš enters, clearly agitated, and in no mood to heed reasoned counsel to stay calm, keep absolute self-control, and so remain master of any situation, as a monk ought. "There's too much violence, killing, anger, and vengefulness in Lev's heart for your wisdom to prevail," protests Lavryš, as he recounts the highlights of past eight years.

"After that Mongol dog Burondaj forced Danilo to attack Lithuania, my father threatened Tovtivl and me, and we had to feign loyalty by kidnapping Roman, who died in captivity, but not at our hands. Danilo then sent my brother-in-law Švarno to Navahrudak. He and Vasyl'ko believed my innocence, but Danilo and Lev did not. Making matters worse, my father renounced Christianity altogether, and with my brothers and their allies launched continuous looting campaigns against other Rus' and into Poland. One group satanically surprised and massacred innocent Poles in Jazdów on the Feast of John the Baptist [June 1262].

"Finally my father's cousins tricked and murdered him and my brothers and then did the same to Tovtivl, who was maneuvering for the succession. As for the two villainous conspirators, my father's loyal grooms ambushed Trenjata when he exited his bath. The other, Dovmont [Daumantas], whose wife my lecherous father had appropriated, fled to Pskov, and now, as the local Christian prince there, pretends to be pious and attacks Lithuania. This was just three or four years ago [1263–64].

"I had fled for safety to Pinsk, but word came that my father's men wanted me to take his place. This, I thought, was my chance to serve God, but I sinned by not asking permission from you and my bishop. We defeated my father's enemies, and with so much vengefulness that my Christian Rus' warriors started to call me Elisej instead of Lavryš. But my pagan troops did not want to be Christians, only launch attacks and loot. And my former people remained true to their satanic gods. Švarno aided me, but he also relishes pillage too much, and he often acted more like a cursed pagan than a true Christian.

"Danilo had died [1264], and his son, our new 'King' Lev, was angry at Švarno and my Lithuanians for stirring up problems with the Poles and with me for everything. There could be no peace among us if Lev was unhappy. So Švarno and I met with our uncle Vasyl'ko last year and decided that Švarno, with my sister at his side and Vasyl'ko as shadow advisor, should take over as the chief prince of Lithuania, and I retreat to Daniliv, well away from Lithuania [ca. 150 miles] and not too far from Volodymyr [forty miles]. Lev thinks I killed his brother. Lev blames me for his inability to control Švarno. Even though I executed Prince Ostafij, the cursed villain of the Jazdów massacre, Lev blames me for his troubles with the Poles, and fears their designs on Halyč."

Hryhoryj has heard most of this before from Lavryš, but never such fright of Lev, and is speechless. A monastic mentor and even ecclesiastical statesman, but not a partisan domestic political advisor, what can Hryhoryj counsel except calm, patience, prudence, as well as obedience, repentance, and memory of death? Lavryš has heard all of this before too, and knows he must obey Vasyl'ko's summons to Volodymyr. Lavryš leaves on Good Friday [22 April] with a monastery servant and several soldiers sent by Vasyl'ko, spends two nights in villages along the way, and arrives in Volodymyr on Easter, in time for the end of the grand liturgy in the impressive, century-old masonry Dormition Cathedral, typical of the major Rus' regional capitals. Volodymyr had suffered terribly thirty-six years earlier at the hands of the Mongols during their initial invasion, but by now had largely recovered. After liturgy – attended by Vasyl'ko, but not Lev – Lavryš rests at the local Mikhajliv [St. Michael's] monastery. It is somewhat larger, but reminiscent of Daniliv. Lavryš is in for a surprise.

Late in the afternoon Vasyl'ko sends an escort to take Lavryš to the home of Markolt the German, a long-distant merchant and resident of Volodymyr with a plan to expand the commerce of Western Rus' with Central Europe. He brews good beer, keeps the best mead in town, and understands the Rus' love of drink. He will commence the post-Lent feasting with a jolly evening to induce the princes jointly to protect trade routes and bribe Mongol officials and border guards. His cousin, a long-time resident of Esztergom in northern Hungary, will grease the wheels from the other side. Already aware of this scheme, Lev and Vasyl'ko had summoned Lavryš to represent Švarno and put an end to Lithuanian raids. Widely ambitious to be a great as his father and grandfather, Lev is eager for more revenue to support elite troops, expand his network of fortresses, restore churches and monasteries, and, of course, pay off those insatiable Mongol visitors and ward off new invasions. Enticed by Markholt's vision of bags of gold and silver, Lev imagines himself as a great, magnanimous monarch. The evening goes well, as the four eat, drink, toast, chat, and plan. The old "Vojšelk" comes to life, and he and Lev are even treating each other as brothers. At last, having drunk too much, the sixty-four-year-old Vasyl'ko tires first, calls an end to the feast, and leaves for his small palace, where Lev is also staying as a guest.

Lavryš is a mite tipsy too, but remembers Hryhoryj's prudent counsel, thanks Markholt, takes leave of Lev, and returns to Mikhajliv. Lev is frustrated. On a bragging high, he sorely wants the party to continue, and is almost ready to trust his uncle Vasyl'ko that Vojšelk hadn't killed Roman. But then why did that hand-bloodied, battled-hardened part-time "monk" leave when Vasyl'ko did? Taking two scoops and a bucket of mead from Markholt's cellar, Lev goes to Mikhajliv, wakes the doorkeeper, and demands to see "Vojšelk." No one in his right mind would oppose the wishes of an angry medieval king, and soon "Vojšelk" appears, half-dressed, half-groggy. Lev gives "Vojšelk" a scoop and shouts, "Drink." They drink. Lev snatches "Vojšelk's" scoop, fills both again, hands one to "Vojšelk," and shouts, "Drink." They drink. Lev now looks "Vojšelk" straight in the eye: "Did you kill my brother Roman?" "Vojšelk" steps back. "Did you kill my brother Roman?" repeats Lev. "Vojšelk" steps back again. "You did!" shouts Lev, and grabs "Vojšelk" by the neck, slams his head against the hardwood floor, takes out a concealed dagger, runs it through his upper groin, and leaves him dying.

The next day Vasyl'ko accepts Lev's face-saving explanation – "Vojšelk" admitted to killing Roman. The Church prepares for Lavryš an honorable burial in Mikhajliv. But Markholt's fanciful commercial scheme dies with the murder.

* * *

In the aftermath of these events, Lev went on to have a glorious career as "King" of Rus' for a total of almost forty years. But Švarno soon died; both Lithuania and Black Rus' reverted to supreme pagan rule under Triadenis [Trojden, r. 1270–1282]; and Orthodox princes never again presided over the Lithuanian polity as it gradually absorbed more and more Rus' territory over the next 140 years. Both Vojšelk and Tovtivl prefigured the several dozen Lithuanian dynasts, who as Orthodox converts or their descendants reigned as subordinate princes in western Rus'. But the Lithuanian Grand Princes remained officially pagan until Jogaila [Jagailo, Władisław-Jagełło] converted to Catholicism in 1386, about 128 years after Mindaugas renounced it. As for Vojšelk's foundation Lavryšev, it became a key regional monastery. Reconstructed in the 1590s closer to Navahrudak, again with its church dedicated to the Prophet Elisha just before World War I, and for a third time in the course of 1993–2009, it now functions as "The Saint-Elisej Lavryšev Men's Monastery."

Suggestions for further reading

The Chronicle of Novgorod, 1016–1471. Translated by Robert Michell and Nevill Forbes. London: Royal Historical Society, 1914.

The Galician-Volynian Chronicle. Translated by George A. Perfecky. Munich: Wilhelm Fink, 1973.

Gimbutas, Marija. *The Balts.* New York: Praeger, 1963.

Goldfrank, David. "The Lithuanian Prince-Monk Vojšelk: A Study of Competing Legends." *Harvard Ukrainian Studies* 9, no. 1/2 (1987): 44–76.

———. "Some Observations Concerning the Galician-Volynian Chronicle and Its Lithuanian Entries for the 1260s." *Russian History/Histoire russe* 25, no. 1/2 (1998): 51–63.

Pashuto, V. T. *Obrazovanie Litovskogo gosudarstva.* Moscow: Akademiia nauk SSSR, 1959.

———. *Ocherki po istorii Galitsko-Volynskoi Rusi.* Moscow: Akademiia nauk SSSR, 1950.

PART 2
Eurasian steppe

6

THE RARE AND EXCELLENT HISTORY OF KONCHAK

A Polovtsian chieftain

Donald Ostrowski

FIGURE 6.1 Reconstruction of the head of a Polovtsian man by G. V. Lebedinskaia (1989) from a skull found in Kvashnikovo. 12th–13th Centuries. Maintained in the Saratov Oblast Museum of Local History, Saratov, Russia.

Our main source for Konchak is the Kievan Chronicle, *which mentions him a number of times in the entries from 1172 to 1187 as an adversary of the Rus'. The chronicler also employs invective in referring to him as an "evil leader," "despised by God," "accursed," and the "accursed, godless, and thrice-cursed Konchak."* The Tale of Igor's Campaign, *an epic poem reputedly from the late twelfth or early thirteenth century, also mentions him prominently and at one point calls him a "pagan slave." Yet, when one reads what Konchak was actually described as doing in these sources, his actions hardly seem to justify those epithets. He and Igor' Sviatoslavich, for example, at one point escape together in a boat when they are fighting Riurik Rostislavich together. Konchak's daughter subsequently marries Igor's son. And Konchak seems to treat Igor' well when Igor' becomes his prisoner after the battle on the Kaiala River in 1185. So, how "thrice-cursed" could he be?*

We have no accounts of Konchak from other than these biased Rus' sources, so, I wondered what if we were to tell Konchak's story from the Polovtsian side, also biased to be sure but leaning the other way. Perhaps it would help to balance the demeaning epithets of the Kievan Chronicle *and* The Tale of Igor's Campaign. *Although Konchak is a historical personage, I have created for my narrator an imagined character, a Rus' slave named Vaska, who is given by the* Kniaz' *of Suzdal' Iurii Dolgorukii (r. 1138–1157) to Konchak's father, Aterkek, and then passed on to Konchak after Aterkek's death. I have framed the story as though it were told to a certain Dusticello of Pisa after Vaska is captured in the steppe and sold back into slavery to a Black Sea merchant from Genoa. Readers familiar with the* Travels of Marco Polo *may recognize the slant allusion in naming. For the title of this piece, I pay homage to Bahā's* al-Nawādiral-Sulṭāniyya wa'l-Mahāsin al-Yūsufiyya *translated by D. S. Richards as* The Rare and Excellent History of Saladin.

Prologue: O, Emperors, kings, princes, dukes, and everyone who is curious concerning the different peoples of the world as well as regions to the east. Read this tale of the chieftain Konchak as it was told to me by the slave Vaska the Rus'ian who spent many years living as a Cuman in the camp of Konchak. Vaska calls them "Polovtsians" because that's what the Rus', of which he was one, called them, but they had different names elsewhere. They were called "Qipchaqs" by other Turks and by Mussulman [Islamic] historical and geographical writers, "Qumans" primarily by Byzantine authors, "Cumans" by us Latin authors, and "Quns" by the Hungarians. I even heard that they were called "Xartesk'ns" by the Armenians. I, Dusticello of Pisa, have written down the following tale exactly as Vaska told it to me.

* * *

My name is Vaska. My parents sold me into slavery because they were too poor to keep me. I was a slave of the Rus' *kniaz'* Iurii of Suzdal' but was given by him as a gift to Aterkek, chieftain of the Don Polovtsian camp. The Polovtsians west of the Iaik [Volga] River were divided into about a dozen different groups or camps each associated with the river or region where that particular camp was located. So, besides the Don camp, other river camps were the Iaik [Volga], the Donets, the West-of-the-Dnepr, the East-of-the-Dnepr, the Bug, and the Danube. Region camps were the Dnepr Meadow, the Azov, the Crimean, the Kiev-Korsun', and the Lukomor'e. All these camps were affiliated in one form or another with a loose confederation that stretched from the Carpathian Mountains in the west to Lake Balkhash in the east.

Aterkek, my new master, had formed an alliance with *Kniaz'* Iurii and his son Andrei. This alliance represented a change in policy from that of his father Sharukan, who had been in alliance with another family of Rus' *kniazi*. That family was the Ol'govichi who were the enemies of the Suzdal' *kniazi*. Without the Polovtsian alliance, the Ol'govichi went on to form an alliance with Geza, king of the Magyars. Whenever new alliances were made, the leaders would exchange gifts (including slaves) as a sign of their sincerity. Sometimes they would even wed their own sons and daughters to each other to really confirm the agreement.

Although I could have been sold on the Black Sea market for a substantial sum as a result of my fair hair and complexion, Aterkek kept me because he liked my cleverness and my usefulness as a translator when doing business with the Rus' *kniazi*. I had been able earlier to pick up some simple Tatar phrases during the negotiations between him and Iurii. In the Polovtsian camp, I quickly became fluent in the Tatar language. I adopted the Polovtsian way of life and ceased being a slave. Being kept close to Aterkek meant that early on I came into contact with his son Konchak. Upon our first meeting, Konchak and I realized an immediate affinity with each other. It was the beginning of a long-term friendship. He was much more skilled in riding, herding, and in handling weapons than I was, but he seemed to like my companionship, especially my telling of stories, which helped while away the many nights spent on the steppe by the campfire. We often visited other Polovtsian camps together. Once we even traveled as far west as the Danube River to visit a group of Polovtsians living there. It is a wide river, not unlike the Itil (Volga). At times we traveled to Rus' settlements to trade for products we couldn't make ourselves. Konchak spoke Rus'ian quite well but could not write it; there was no need for him to. So, whenever the reading or writing of Rus'ian was required, I came in handy.

It was during these trips that I fell in love with the steppe – its vastness, the many types of steppe grass, each distinctive in its own way, and in the spring the variety of vivid colors – blues, yellows, reds – from the flowers that bloomed. Animal life was abundant, especially birds, of which there were so many different kinds I couldn't even begin to keep track of the names the people of the steppe had for them. Marmots were widespread, as were deer and an antelope with a huge nose. My favorite animal, though, was the type of fox I saw there, which was different from the foxes of the forest where I grew up. This fox was slow and could easily be caught by a fast-running dog, so it relied more on cleverness than speed to elude its enemies (perhaps the reason I like it so).

As I came more and more wholeheartedly to adopt the steppe way of life, I gradually became a full-fledged member of the camp. I can't say exactly when I ceased being a slave and became a Polovtsian, but within a few years I was married to a Polovtsian woman named Valani whose husband had been killed fighting the Rus'. She did not seem to hold it against me that my background was Rus'ian as is evident by the three children she bore me. I learned a great deal from her about steppe ways, and I was an eager student to learn all that I could. Among other things, she taught me how to kill a sheep for eating without pain or suffering – just a quick incision in the chest large enough for me to reach my hand into the chest to grasp the heart and stop its beating. I am particularly grateful to her for that because I cannot stand to see an animal suffer, let alone be the cause of that suffering. She also instructed me to avoid contact with marmots that were acting in a sluggish way or that I found dead, and never to trap a marmot so that I could observe its behavior before I shot it. She said that great harm could come from violating these strictures. And I remember times when the entire camp moved when there was illness in a nearby marmot colony.

Around the year 6678, third of the indiction [1170], Aterkek died and Konchak became the chieftain of the Don Polovtsians. Konchak aimed to continue his father's policy in maintaining friendly relations with the chieftains of the other Polovtsian camps. Such relations were important mainly because of the moving of the herds from winter to summer grasslands and back. Each group moved their herds along different routes (although in some sections they could overlap) and to different grazing areas, and often at slightly different times. A chieftain in consultation with his council might decide to begin the move a week or two earlier or later than the chieftain of a proximate group. In that case, negotiation with the other group's chieftain was necessary, for having one's route or grazing areas encroached on was a cause for war. Nonetheless, disputes would break out. Sometimes the disputes were over serious issues such as the encroachment of one group on another group's grazing grounds. Other times the disputes had frivolous causes such as a misunderstanding or an imagined insult or unsanctioned raiding by juveniles seeking a good time.

Similarly conflicts with Rus' *kniazi* could have a range of causes. At first, Konchak believed that the Rus' were always the provokers of conflict. When a Polovtsian merchant or herder complained about some injustice by a Rus' merchant or farmer, Konchak at first typically took the side of the Polovtsian. But later, he would question more deeply the context of the "injustice" and realize that causes of resentments could often be complex. Such was especially the case when one had two different cultures living side by side. What might be considered insulting by a Rus'ian might not be by a Polovtsian and vice versa. Some of the stories I told Konchak had a moral that made exactly this point, and I hope that I was able to deepen his understanding that way. Sometimes, the power of a good story is greater than that of an entire regiment of mounted horsemen.

Shortly after becoming chieftain, Konchak heard of some Rus' raiders who robbed Polovtsian traders on the Zaloznyi trade route near Pereiaslavl'. He organized an expedition in alliance with Kobiak, the chieftain of the Lukomor'e camp. The combined Polovtsian forces rushed to Pereiaslavl' and demanded financial recompense from the people they thought were responsible. Learning about the Polovtsian forces in the area, the Novgorod-Severskii *kniaz'*, Igor' Sviatoslavich, caught up to and skirmished with the forces of Konchak and Kobiak. This encounter was the first meeting of Konchak and Igor', but by no means the last.

The animosities between the Pereiaslavian Rus' and the Lukomor'e Polovtsians continued. In retaliation against the Rus', Konchak lent his assistance again two years later in August of 6688, thirteenth of the indiction [1180]. It was at this time that he began to think that perhaps the Rus' were not always in the wrong and that they at times may have been justified in retaliating against the Polovtsians. He began to try to restore ties with the Ol'govichi. He managed to make peace with Sviatoslav Vsevolodovich and Igor' Sviatoslavich. He intervened in the fight between the Ol'govichi and Riurik Rostislavich for succession to becoming *kniaz'* of Kiev, the dominant city of Rus'. The intervention did not go well. Riurik routed the combined forces of Kobiak, Konchak, and Igor' at the Chertorye River. Konchak together with Igor' escaped and fled by way of Gorodets to Chernigov. Konchak told me later of their conversations. It was during this flight together that Konchak and Igor' discovered that both of them had children approaching marriageable age – Igor''s son Volodimir and Konchak's daughter Özgürluk. They agreed that if they succeeded in escaping Riurik's forces, they would form an official alliance. They thereby betrothed Volodimir and Özgürluk to each other. It was to be several years before that betrothal resulted in an actual marriage. I personally found Igor' Sviatoslavich to be quick to anger and impulsive. He rarely thought things through as Konchak did, and people tended to distrust him. Konchak, in contrast, was treated with respect by all sides, having earned it through honorable behavior.

Konchak made another trip to Rus' in the year 6691, first of the indiction [1183], in alliance with Gleb, son of Tirpeev, a wealthy Polovtsian merchant who had married a Rus'ian woman and who lived on the shores of the Black Sea. Konchak negotiated an agreement whereby the Rus' merchants would trade with Gleb. Later the same year in violation of this agreement, at Orel the Rus' *kniazi* captured Kobiak and later killed him. The following year Konchak undertook a large-scale campaign against the Rus' *kniazi* who perpetrated this outrage. Konchak employed siege weapons and negotiated a settlement whereby the Rus' *kniazi* paid compensation for the damages they wrought.

Although peace once again reigned between Rus' and Polovtsians, Sviatoslav seemed bent on provoking hostilities again. For what reason he did so, Konchak and the other Polovtsian leaders could not fathom. Sviatoslav sent the Black Hood people into the steppe, but they were so ineffective that they did no damage. Ignoring this violation of the agreement, Konchak brought herds of horses to Pereiaslavl' to trade. Sviatoslav and Riurik Rostislavich, like barking dogs, sent a message to Konchak to lift the siege, but there was no siege. Either Sviatoslav and Riurik were misinformed or they deliberately chose to misinterpret a peaceful action that Konchak and the other Polovtsians did almost every year. Nonetheless, not wishing to get involved in another conflict with Rus' *kniazi*, Konchak ordered his group to return to the steppe. He stopped just long enough on the way to help the people of Ream put out a devastating fire in their town.

Konchak's taking his Don Polovtsians back to the steppe seemed to satisfy Sviatoslav and Riurik that they had frightened him off. The hot-headed Igor' Sviatoslavich, on the other hand, thought he saw a chance for glory, false though it was, and decided to attack us on our way home. As we found out later, even Igor''s retinue advised against an attack, especially against the person whose son Igor' had betrothed his daughter to. Apparently only adverse weather conditions prevented his pursuit of us sooner.

After Igor' Sviatoslavich joined his forces with those of his brother Vsevolod Sviatoslavich and his nephew Sviatoslav Ol'govich at the Oskol River, a reconnaissance patrol of Polovtsians spotted them and sent warnings to camps that were close by. Those camps quickly martialed their forces to repulse the invaders. When Igor''s Rus' forces arrived at the Sal'nitsa River, his scouts informed him that they had spotted Polovtsian forces in battle formation. They advised him either to attack quickly before the Polovtsian band received reinforcements or to withdraw. Igor' and his relatives refused to return home because, as they argued, their peers would ridicule them for fearing to face death and heap shame upon them.

As Igor''s forces came to the Siuurlii River, the Polovtsian archers shot a volley of arrows at them and withdrew in order to entice the Rus' forces into an ambush.

Igor' and his brother Vsevolod did not fall for the trap, but his nephew Sviatoslav Ol'govich and his son Vladimir Igor'evich set off after them in pursuit. After all the contingents had reassembled, Igor' advised that they withdraw under the cover of darkness because they had seen how great a force the Polovtsians had already mustered. But Sviatoslav Ol'govich argued that he had pursued the Polovtsians too far to turn back and, besides, the horses were too exhausted to set off immediately. Igor', therefore, ordered his troops to rest for the night. The Donets Polovtsians sounded a general alarm. For three days their archers shot arrows at the Rus' invaders without engaging them in battle. The only hope of the *kniazi* lay in advancing toward the Donets River, but the Polovtsians surrounded Igor''s forces so that only fifteen of the Rus' men escaped. Igor' was captured by a Donets Polovtsian named Chilbuk.

When Konchak found that his future son-in-law's father was a prisoner, he assumed responsibility for him by saying that he was already his daughter's father-in-law. Igor' had been wounded in the battle, so Konchak made sure he received the best medical attention available – a doctor from Baghdad who happened to be traveling nearby was retained. Igor''s captivity in Konchak's camp was cushy. Although twenty Polovtsians were appointed to guard him, they actually did more to entertain him and to keep him from being bored than to prevent him from doing anything. Igor' was also given six servants to attend to him. He was free to ride wherever he chose and to hunt with hawks and falcons. He and Konchak would often go hunting together and enjoyed each other's company. Konchak even allowed Igor' to attend the morning open meetings that Konchak held. Anyone in the camp who had a petition or grievance could approach Konchak, whose tent flap was open until he had met with everyone who wanted to see him. Then he closed the tent flap until the next day. Igor' was dismissive of this practice, not understanding the reason Konchak would spend so much time listening to the complaints of those he considered to be Konchak's subjects. Igor' thought the people should just do what they were told and be like silent fish. But I could see that the Polovtsians did not have such a hierarchical ruling structure as the Rus' *kniazi* did. Konchak governed as chieftain as long as he had the respect of his warriors. This open tent-flap policy helped forge an unbreakable bond with those in his camp.

Another Polovtsian practice that Igor complained about was the freedom and independence of women in the camp. Polovtsian women could ride, shoot bows, and hunt as well as any man. When the men folk were off on campaign, the women tended the flocks and did everything the men did in addition to their own chores. I remember that women at the court of the *kniazi* had strict limitations on their activities and certainly were not allowed to hunt or perform tasks of men. That's what slaves like me were for. Among the Polovtsians, the only slaves were there to be transported to and sold at the slave markets. No Polovtsian was the slave of another Polovtsian, and no Polovtsian woman was a slave to a Polovtsian man. Igor' could not understand this, but to me who had lived the Polovtsian way of life for so long, it seemed most natural.

As soon as Igor' had recovered, Konchak offered to let Igor' return to Seversk anytime he wanted, but Igor' explained that for him to accept that offer of being released would be humiliating. It would be better if he could say that he had escaped. Igor' was always concerned about how his actions would appear to the other Rus' *kniazi*. He, for example, requested that a priest be sent from Kiev to minister to him, although Konchak already had a local priest of the Orthodox faith in the camp to administer to those Polovtsians who were Christian. Although Igor' complained that the Christian priest Konchak could provide was heretical (he said something about his being "Nestorian"), I think Igor' did it to show the Rus' *kniazi* at home that he hadn't given up the Christian faith. Konchak granted that request. Shortly after that, he had me help Igor' "escape." That way, Igor' could sound brave when he arrived home.

Trying to achieve a stable relationship with the Rus' *kniazi*, Konchak made sure that Igor' Sviatoslavich, while in captivity, reaffirmed the betrothal of his son Volodimir with Konchak's daughter Özgürluk. I was doubtful that Igor' would abide by that reaffirmation, but the marriage did take place two years later in the second year of the reign of Isaac Angelos, fifth of the indiction [in 1187]. Özgürluk was baptized in the Christian Church under the name Nastasia. Although Konchak and the other Polovtsians believe that living spirits occupied everything, they did not force their religious beliefs on anyone. I adopted their beliefs willingly, but I also kept some of the Christian teachings that I grew up with.

Shortly after this time, I was captured by the Azov Polovtsians, who were not in alliance with Konchak and the Don camp. This time the fox was not clever enough to avoid being caught. They sold me back into slavery to a merchant from Genoa who was plying the Black Sea trade. The merchant took me to Genoa to serve him and his family in his home. It is here in Genoa that I am telling my story to a friend of the family.

* * *

Epilogue: As the reader might imagine, after being captured and transported across the sea, Vaska lost track of Konchak and his doings. I just hope Konchak was able to forge that agreement among the Polovtsians and with the Rus' to bring peace and contentment to the steppe that Vaska told me about, and that Vaska's wife and children are safe.

– Dusticello of Pisa, St. Nicholas Day, 1195

For further reading

Dimnik, Martin. *The Dynasty of Chernigov 1146–1246*. Cambridge: Cambridge University Press, 2003.

Dimnik, Martin. "Igor's Defeat at the Kayala (1185): The Chronicle Evidence." *Mediaeval Studies* 63 (2001): 245–282.

Heinrich, Lisa Lynn. "The Kievan Chronicle: A Translation and Commentary." Ph.D. dissertation, Vanderbilt University, Nashville, TN, 1977.

"On Igor's Campaign." Translation with commentary by Jack V. Haney and Erik Dahl. 1992. http://faculty.washington.edu/dwaugh/rus/texts/igortxt2.htm.

Pritsak, Omeljan. "The Polovcians and Rus'." *Archivum Eurasiae medii aevi* 2 (1982): 321–380.

Vásáry, István. *Cumans and Tatars: Oriental Military in the Pro-Ottoman Balkans, 1185–1365*. Cambridge: Cambridge University Press, 2005.

7

SÜBEDEI BA'ATAR

Portrait of a Mongol general

Timothy May

In the thirteenth century, the Mongol Empire emerged from the steppes of Mongolia to become the largest contiguous empire in history. Although Chinggis Khan (1162–1227) founded the empire, it continued to expand long after his death. Much of the empire's success had to do with Chinggis Khan's latent ability for organization, emphasis on loyalty, military reforms, and his keen eye for talent. The most notable of all Mongol military commanders was Sübedei Ba'atar (1176–1248).

Sübedei was deeply involved in Chinggis Khan's unification of the Mongolian steppes. He entered Chinggis Khan's household as a slave and eventually became one of his most trusted commanders. He participated in the wars against the Jin Empire (1125–1234) and the rapid destruction of the Khwarazmian Empire that dominated much of Central Asia and Iran. He, along with the general Jebe, pursued the fleeing Sultan Muhammad Khwarazmshah II, who only escaped Sübedei by dying from dysentery on an island in the Caspian Sea. Sübedei and Jebe then continued westward, defeating a Georgian army (and possibly affecting the Fifth Crusade), before turning north and crossing the Caucasus Mountains. As they entered the Kuban steppe, they defeated an army of Alans and then a combined army of Kipchaks and southern Rus' at the Battle of the Kalka River (1223). Although the Mongols won an overwhelming victory, Jebe died during the battle.

Afterward, Sübedei withdrew across the Volga River, skirmishing with Kipchaks and the Volga Bulghars before completing a rendezvous with the armies of Jochi (d. 1225), Chinggis Khan's eldest son. This reconnaissance en force is a military feat that has never been duplicated and remains one of the most amazing actions in all of military history. Sübedei then led the initial forays into Xi Xia in 1225, which rose in rebellion while Chinggis Khan was in Central Asia. After Chinggis Khan's death, Sübedei remained active, probing the Mongols' western borders, which now reached the Yaik River (Ural River), before leading the final Mongol onslaught against the Jin Empire. Sübedei led a masterful campaign that culminated with the sack of Kaifeng, the remaining Jin capital, in 1233.

Sübedei then returned to Mongolia for a quriltai *or council in 1234. At this* quriltai *the second Mongol ruler, Ögödei (r. 1229–1241) (often referred to in the sources as Qa'an) ordered Sübedei to lead a Mongol army, estimated at 150,000 men to march west and bring all they encountered under the will of heaven (Tenggeri). It is for this campaign that Sübedei is best known. Although Batu (d. 1256), the son of Chinggis Khan's eldest (and possibly illegitimate) son, Jochi, was the nominal commander, Sübedei was the true commanding general. Under his direction, the Mongols subdued the Volga Bulghars, Kipchaks, Alans, the Rus' principalities, and the kingdom of Bulgaria as well as devastating Hungary and Poland. After this campaign ended in 1242, Sübedei returned and briefly retired to the steppes of Mongolia where he died in 1248.*

This brief sketch of his life demonstrates that we know a great deal about Sübedei's life. He has a biography in the Yuan Shi, *a Chinese history of the Mongol Empire, compiled from the court records during the Ming era (1368–1644). Sübedei is also mentioned frequently in other Chinese, Persian, Arabic, Rus', Latin, and Mongolian sources. All of these discuss his actions as a military commander.* The Secret History of the Mongols, *a Mongolian source that details the life and rise to power of Chinggis Khan, gives us but a glimpse into Sübedei's thoughts in a few brief passages. What we do not have, however, are any actual sources from Sübedei himself – and for good reason. It is almost certain he was illiterate and the Mongols did not have a tradition of memoir writing. Chinggis Khan, however, introduced literacy to the Mongols (although he remained illiterate) in 1204 and the Uyghur script is still used today.*[1]

The text below is a series of imagined letters from Sübedei, including one to his son Uriyangqadai (1199–1271),[2] *and grandson Aju (1234–1287),*[3] *both of whom served as notable generals. The letters are based on Mongolian, Persian, Russian, Latin, Arabic, and Chinese sources, and I have attempted to maintain a Mongolian idiom, similar to the anonymous author of* The Secret History of the Mongols. *The letters would have been written on parchment, birch bark, and perhaps paper. Due to the plethora of leather and sheepskin in nomadic societies, it is also likely that this would have been a common source of writing material. Due to the Mongols' conquest of China, Central Asia, and much of the Middle East, paper was accessible as well. Using the* yam *or the pony-express-like postal system of the Mongols, high-ranking Mongols such as Sübedei could send messages with little difficulty. These imagined letters are an attempt to view key events in Sübedei's operations in Eastern Europe through his eyes.*

* * *

Letter 1: Battle of the Kalka River
Year of the Ram (1223)
To my lord Chinggis Khan,

As I promised so long ago, I am your rat who will hoard goods for you, I shall be your black crow and gather all that is found outside your ger for you.[4] It has been several months since I sent my last message. I pray that *Köke Möngke Tenggeri* granted my rider good fortune to reach you in a timely manner. This was to report that Jebe and I were venturing across the mountains after defeating the Korguz. Not long after that we met a combined army of a people known as the Asud and Kibcha'ud. The Kibcha'ud are a people who are similar to the Ölberi, who harbored the rebel Merkit and the Qanglin that filled the armies of the thief Muhammad Khwarazmshah.[5] Though they live far to the west, they are People of the White Tents. We divided them through diplomacy, calling upon the Kibcha'ud to recognize our shared culture as People of the White Tents. Jebe and I sent bowls of *airagh* to them and they reciprocated.[6] I admit it was difficult as it was the last of our *airagh*. We were able to convince them that we simply wanted to return to our pastures far to the east and had no quarrel with them. We gave them many presents taken from the Sarts and Korguz.[7] The Kibcha'ud then abandoned the Asud to us. After we defeated them, we then attacked the Kibcha'ud and regained our possessions. Their leader, Koten Khan, fled with as many men as he could. We gained much from our daring – women, horses, booty, and more *airagh* which we would need later. From the plunder, we also gained some of what the Asud drink. It is not *airagh*. It is sweet, unlike our *airagh*, but potent. A prisoner told us that they make it from stuff that bees make and they call it *rong*.[8] It is a very strange place that we have entered – they drink the milk of bugs but not that of the five snouts! I saved a few flagons for my khan so that you do not think I'm telling tales! My messenger carries one for you.

We then pursued the Kibcha'ud. The Kibcha'ud leader's *quda* was among the Orusut and convinced them that we meant the Orusut harm despite our words that you ruled all of the People of the White Tents. The Orusut lived in cities, not white tents. Soon we encountered a joint army of Orusut and Kibcha'ud and sought to draw them into an ambush. Jebe led the vanguard to lure them into the ambush. It worked well, but his propensity to lead from the front also put him in harm's way. The Kibcha'ud recognized him and finally killed him with arrows. He died in the prelude to the battle by the Kalka River, but his men executed the *noqai kerel* with the skill one expected of Jebe.[9] Few Orusut or Kibcha'ud survived our onslaught. Still, it taught me that greatness still does not save one from arrows. We celebrated our victory in the remains of their camp. I also bring you tribute from the west. We return soon and will rest in the new pastures of Jochi before continuing to your ordo. We also sacked cities by a sea. Both the Orusut and these men, who spoke and dressed differently from the Orusut, had pale skins. The people by the sea are weak soldiers but have many boats.[10] Like the king of the Sarts, they fled to the water when we came. The Orusut people violate the earth and eat swine like those in Khitai.[11] From a distance we saw one city where their khan dwelt. It is not like Zhongdu or any of the Altan Khan's cities. We could see many domed building like those of the Sarts, but prisoners said they practiced a religion like some of the Kereit and Uighurs, not that of the Sarts. They also don't drink *airagh*. After our victory we tried the drink we found in their camp. One was not bad – it is made from wheat or other grains and golden in color. I have a few flagons for you. Another type was quite dark and made from bread.[12] Its taste is vile and better suited for extinguishing campfires than drinking, so I

FIGURE 7.1 Chinese woodcut of Sübedei Ba'atar (d. 1248). He fought in twenty campaigns, conquered thirty-two nations, and won sixty-five pitched battles. He is considered the greatest general of the Mongol Empire.

have not sent any. No wonder we defeated them so easily – they have nothing beneficial to drink.

Letter 2: On the dismissal of Güyük and Büri

Year of the Rat (1240)

To Qa'an

Before I hunted the Merkits in the year of the Serpent (1209), your father gave me instructions for my campaign on how to deal with those who did not obey orders or interfered with my mission. He instructed me: "Send to Us those who transgress Our order if it looks that they are *personally* known to Us."[13] The *qarachu* I always dealt with swiftly. Unfortunately, members of the *altan urug* have violated the *yosun* of Chinggis Khan. In accordance with *yasa*, your son Güyük, Büri, and Harqasun have been sent to you for judgment.[14] After our victory over the Orusut, Güyük and Büri insulted Prince Batu during our victory feast and threatened violence against him. Although Güyük and Büri have fought bravely on the campaign, their insolence toward Batu threatens division and to undermine your orders to carry out the will of Köke Möngke Tenggeri. Although Harqasun is not of the *altan urug*, I have sent him to you for his insult to another member of the *altan urug*.

As your servant, I swear the accusation is true. During our victory feast, Batu drank first, as fitting of his rank. Güyük and Büri drank too much *airagh* and their boasts soon equaled their thirst. They called Batu an old woman before the *noyad* and the other princes. Büri and Güyük became angry and departed, believing him not their equal. I am sure you understand my meaning. I know that Prince Batu sent a report as well. My testimony is sent by my own decision. I acknowledge that Batu, though wise in politics and at the *quriltai*, does not equal his father's skill in war. Still Qa'an placed Batu in command of all the princes who campaigned with me, thus elevating him above all others present. Just as I swore to destroy the enemies of your father, my *ejen* Chinggis Khan, I will do the same for you. If they turn into marmots and burrow in the ground with their claws, I will dig them out. If they turn into fish and plunge into the sea, I will cast a net and catch them. None shall escape me, but the dissension of the *altan urug* prevents me from carrying out Qa'an's wishes. Remind them for the good of the *Yeke Monggol Ulus*, what *minu ejen* Chinggis Khan told your brothers Jochi and Cha'adai when they quarreled:

> Do not let yourselves be scorned by people,
> Do not let yourselves be laughed at by men.[15]
> May the Qa'an end my life should I speak falsely.

Letter 3: After-action report for Hungary
Year of the Ox (1241)

My Qa'an, this message was written during lambing season. I imagine it will reach you in a few weeks. Your father, *minu ejen* Chinggis Khan once said, "The best things in life are to crush your enemies, drive them before you, to take their possessions, and listen to the lamentations of their women!" His wisdom still guides us and truly his *sülde* resides in our black *tuq* so that all of the *Irgen* tremble when they see it. We have once again demonstrated what it means to rebel against the will of *Köke Möngke Tenggeri*. The remaining Kibcha'ud and the Majarat (Hungarians) have all been chastened.

As the *yam* continues to expand with our conquests, you should now know that the Orusut city of Kiwa (Kiev) fell. I remember seeing this city from a distance when I first went west. For their offense of killing Adargidai and Chilger-bökö, two *minqan-u noyan* who served as our emissaries and their Kibcha'ud interpreter, we destroyed much of the city. They took refuge in their holy spaces. Considering they ignored the will of heaven, I don't know why they thought their *Tenggeris* would spare them from our wrath. We locked the buildings and burned them. We divided those who survived into tens and meted out justice. Those who travel to Kiwa will see their bones as they approach and will remember what it means to defy the power of the *Yeke Monggol Ulus*.

We learned that Koten, the Kibcha'ud khan, had fled to the land of the Majarat. You may recall his men killed Jebe Noyan. We sent *elchis* (envoys) to the Majarat khan, Bela demanding Koten's return to us and all of the Kibcha'ud. Additionally, we allowed a story to travel with refugees that Koten had secretly submitted to us and he was with the Majarat to cause mischief on our behalf.[16] We also demanded that Bela come to you and submit as was the will of heaven. We had no choice but to go and demonstrate your wishes and what happened to those who rebelled against the will of *Köke Möngke Tenggeri*.

The Majarat fortified the mountain passes. Can you believe they thought that wooden barricades in the mountain passes would halt us? Did they think we did not know of fire and axes? Was our destruction of Kiwa so complete that not a single survivor escaped when we burned it? We allowed a few to escape our wrath just so they would know and fear our coming. They also quickly learned that we were not Kibcha'ud raiders. Where their defenses were troublesome, we cut roads through forests to hasten our movements. I wonder what their reaction would have been if we had brought the exploding powder that we gained from the Jin. Useful stuff, but not reliable. Still, the noise alone would have them asking their god for help.[17]

Bela in the Majarat language must mean "fool," as he continued to prove a fool. Even when we carried out the will of Tenggeri among the Rus' and Kibcha'ud, Bela Khan ignored our actions and the portents that we were coming. Instead the Majarat dealt with their petty quarrels. By the time Bela awoke to the threat, it was too late. We invaded close to a religious celebration in the spring. I do not fully understand it, but it is when the Christians claim their savior returned from death. If he did, he helped them not. I know some of our people adopted this religion, but I don't understand it. When we left no one came from the dead, and we left plenty of corpses.

We bided our time, waiting for their khan, Bela, to commit his troops. As we waited for the main Majarat army, we attacked local forces and pillaged villages. In one instance, we placed puppets on our spare horses atop of a hill and in front of the sun, so that one approaching them could not see them clearly. Then we drew in the Majarat by retreating. When they saw our assembled army of puppets, they retreated in fear. We then turned and cut them down. Patience is a virtue, my Qa'an. We had to bide our time so that we could choose the battle-field and lure a larger force into a trap. Even with Bela Khan's incompetence, we had to be patient and wait. This not only ensured that it was not a ruse (could someone really be that stupid to think we were not coming?), but also so as not to be too eager for battle and make a mistake.

Bela finally accommodated us near the Sajo River, on a plain that the Hungarians call Mohi. Batu was slow to gain the bridge, eventually seizing it with siege engines. I wonder what he would have done if he had destroyed the bridge in the process. We are fortunate it was made from stone. He should have seized it before the Hungarians arrived. He eventually took it from them. My army marched far downriver seeking another spot to ford the river. In the end, we built a pontoon bridge and performed the *nerge* encircling Bela and his men. They huddled in their fort, made from wagons, like old women. This may have worked against the Kibcha'ud, but our men fought with iron discipline, shooting from a distance with an occasional probing attack.

We did this for a while, building the fear within their camp, and allowed them to see that we had surrounded them and that there was no escape. While during a true *nerge* hunt not even the smallest rabbit can escape, we did leave a slight gaps in our lines, obvious to the Hungarians. A few took the bait. They tested to see if it was a trap. Nothing happened. Soon from their fortified camp what started as a trickle became a flood.

The rest was easy. We allowed them to flee. Is it not easier to kill a wolf when it flees from you? Some say that war is like hunting. This is true, but never forget the lessons we all learned as children while tending to the flocks and herds. Controlling the enemy is much like tending to sheep. If they become scared, they are unpredictable and can be difficult to bring in, but if you can keep control of them, then you can direct the sheep or your enemies to where you want them. We allowed them to flee to their cities, but then we could cut them down. Also, those who escaped only brought back tales of woe and misery – terrifying those cattle within their walls. Once fear is rampant, then we become the wolves, destroying all that oppose us.

Letter 4: Letter to Uriyangqadai
Year of the Tiger (1242)
My son,

This letter comes to you from the lands of the Majarat. We have just learned of Qa'an's death and are preparing to return for the *quriltai*. I am feeling the years in my bones. This western land is not to my liking. After the land of the Majarat there is nothing but forests and small cities, not like those in Khitai.

As you know, we defeated the Orusut and the Kibcha'ud and then we prepared to invade the lands of the Majarat. This land in the west is known as Khun-gar-i to some. It was not until *chaqan sar* that we learned of Qa'an's death. It took several more weeks before all of our forces could begin to evacuate the Majarat lands. A sudden thaw also made it difficult, as we could no longer cross the rivers safely. We used to leave livestock across the river from where we though Majarat were hiding. Our spies would watch and if the Majarat retrieved the animals, we knew the ice was safe. We would then cross the river and kill the Majarat like the sheep we retrieved.

As you know, we were not going to stay here, but Qa'an's death has altered our schedule. Nonetheless, it was a masterful campaign if I say so myself. Perhaps Qa'an's *sülde* came and resided in our *tuq*.

One of the reasons we invaded was that some of our slaves among the Kibcha'ud had not submitted to the will of Tenggeri and fled there. These were from the Dnieper Kibcha'ud led by Koten – the same Kibcha'ud who killed Jebe so long ago. The rest had already submitted to us and were being assimilated into the army and their hair was cut in Mongol fashion. Prince Batu sent messengers to Bela, ruler of the Majarat, demanding that he send back Koten and the Kibcha'ud. Bela Khan of the Majarat refused to return them to him. I suspect Koten knew that we Mongols do not forget grudges. I had plans for Koten. As I understand it, this proved to be a poor decision for Bela, as their presence caused conflict within his kingdom. We never recovered them beyond a handful. Koten was killed by the Majarat, and so they fled southward – pillaging and plundering. We did not learn this until we had already invaded.

It is events like these that make me truly believe that Ögödei was right and that *Köke Möngke Tenggeri* had bequeathed the earth to Chinggis Khan and his heirs. How else does one explain the foolishness of the Majarat? The Hungarians were correct that we would attack them if they did not bend their knee and submit, but since they preferred to live in a state of rebellion against the will of *Tenggeri* and defy the Qa'an, why would they harm those who understood our ways of war? Koten was at the Kalka River – he witnessed our way of war. He was one of the few survivors – the Orosut learned nothing from the Kalka. The ease of extending Qa'an's golden rein over them was if they forgot we ever existed.

Remember, my son, always take advantage of your enemy's fear and stupidity. After we crushed their army, we found the *tamgha* of their khan.[18] Just as Chinggis Khan did against the Sarta'ul, we send letters written by a Majarat prisoner to every town and village for them to remain in place and that the rumors of Bela Khan's defeat was false. Like sheep they remained in one place instead of rallying to their khan. Then rather than fighting a second battle, all we had to do was take the villages one at a time, using the population in the frontlines against the next town or slaughtering like the sheep they are.

Much as I was a hound who hunted enemy leaders, I also assigned my own hounds. Prince Qadan led a special force to hunt down this King Bela. I'm sorry to say that Qadan was unsuccessful. Just as Khwarazmshah eluded Jebe and me, Bela fled into the sea. I hate boats.

As I said, pursuing the Kibcha'ud was only one of the reasons. By the will of *Köke Möngke Tenggeri*, we had the right to invade the Majarat. We did not plan to stay there – at that time. Since the time of Chinggis Khan we never occupy all of the lands we conquer. Instead, we destroy the territory beyond that which we keep. This does two things. It protects our pastures, as there is no longer an enemy who can attack or intrude in our affairs as the Altan Khan once did. Additionally, as we raze cities and depopulate areas, those territories become vacant, often turning to pasture, allowing us to move in when we are ready. I suspect we will return to the Majarat one day. Perhaps you or my grandson Aju will lead the army. If so, I have much more to tell you.

Glossary

Airagh – Mongolian for kumiss, or fermented mare's milk. Qimiz in Kipchak Turkic.

Altan Urug – The Golden Kin or members of Chinggis Khan's family. Gold (altan) was the imperial color.

As – Mongolian word for Alans or modern Ossetians. The Alans were nomads of Iranian origin. Plural is Asut or Asud. Some Alans were sent east and eventually became the Mongolian tribe known as the Asut.

Chaqan sar – The White Month (modern Tsagaan Sar) marks the Mongolian New Year and falls typically in February.

Ejen – Honorific title meaning "lord." Minu ejen means "my lord."

Elchi – An envoy. Mongols viewed envoys as sacrosanct and any harm done to them was a declaration of war.

Five snouts – Sheep, goats, cows/yaks, horses, and Bactrian camels. These five animals, in varying quantities, formed the basis of pastoral nomadic economy in Mongolia.

Irgen – A term referring to people, usually non-Mongols. It is most commonly associated with the Hoi-yin Irgen or Forest People (those groups that lived around Lake Baikal and were not pastoral nomads) or Khitat Irgen (Chinese people).

Jam – Also known as yam, this was a pony-express-style postal or messenger system the Mongols used throughout their empire.

Khitai – Northern China. In the thirteenth century it meant specifically the Jin Empire, but originally it referred to the time when northern China was ruled by the Khitans, a proto-Mongolian people, as the Liao Dynasty (960–1125). Khitai remains the Mongolian name for present-day China and from whence Marco Polo's Cathay is derived.

Kibcha'ud – Mongolian term of the Turkic Kipchaks who dominated the Pontic and Caspian steppes. They were known by various names such as Polovtsy by the Rus', Cumans in Latin sources, Koumanoui in the Greek, and Qifchaq in the Arabic. Kipchak, Qïpchaq, and Qipchak are the most frequent Turkic variants.

Korguz – Mongolian term for Georgians.

Majarat – Mongolian term for Magyar. The Hungarian language is still called Magyar after the Magyars, nomads who settled the region in the eighth century. Additionally, Onoghur nomads (Oghur Turks) joined the Magyar. This combination, along with those already present in what was known as Pannonia (historic Hungary), became the Hungarians.

Noqai kerel – Literally "dog fight," as when a dog suddenly turns around to bite. This was the Mongolian term for a feigned retreat, a common tactic in steppe warfare.

Noyan – Mongol Military commander.

Orusut – Mongolian for the Rus'. In Mongolian, a vowel is always pronounced before an "R."

Qa'an – The Middle Mongolian version of Qaghan or Khaghan (Emperor) and the title by which Ögödei (r. 1229–1241) was known.

Qarachu – The "black-boned" people, or those who are not of the royal lineage of Chinggis Khan. It could refer to both commoners or non-royal aristocrats.

Quda – In-law, usually one from a marriage alliance.

Rong – A form of mead and the preferred drink of the Alans.

Sart – Mongolian term for the sedentary Muslim population of Central Asia.

Sülde – The spiritual genius of an individual. It was thought that Chinggis Khan's Sülde remained and aided the Mongols.

Tamgha – A seal, brand, or mark of an individual.

Tenggeri – Heaven, the supreme sky god of the Mongols. In more general terms Tenggeri refers to a god. Köke Mongke Tenggeri refers the Blue Eternal Sky, the supreme deity of the Mongols.

Tuq – The standard of the Mongols. During times of war, it was made of black horse or yak tails. During periods of peace, it was white.

Yasa – Refers to the laws of the Mongol Empire.

Yeke Monggol Ulus – The Great Mongol State or Great Mongol Nation, and term the Mongols used when referring to their empire and themselves.

Yosun – Refers to the customs and practices of Chinggis Khan and the Mongolian culture.

Notes

1 After Chinggis Khan defeated the Naiman in 1204, as part of the spoils of war he acquired the Uighur, Tatar-Tong'a, who had worked in the court of the Naiman Khanate. With the destruction of the Naiman khanate, Tatar-Tong'a became the tutor for Chinggis Khan's children and taught them to read and write by adopting the Uighur script, it being based on Syriac, to Mongolian. From here, literacy became part of the education of the elite.

2 Uriyangqadai served during the Mongol conquest of the Song Empire. Uriyangqadai is best known for his conquest of the kingdom of Dali (modern Yunnan) in the 1250s. He served under the *il-khan* Qubilai, the future Qubilai Khan. While Qubilai held nominal command, Uriyangqadai held operational command. With the conquest of Dali, the Mongols now opened a second and southwestern front against the Song Empire.

3 Aju also served as a general under Qubilai Khan. He became quite adept at riverine warfare, something which had stymied Mongol operations in the past. He had also served with his father in Dali and assumed command when his father became ill. Aju, along with the Chinese general Liu Zheng (1213–1275), was responsible for the capture of Xiangyang. Aju also forcefully persuaded Qubilai in 1274 to commit to the final destruction of the Song Empire. While operational command was assigned to Bayan, Aju served as the primary field general. His skill at riverine warfare allowed the Mongols to resume of a war of mobility. Aju commanded the Mongol naval forces at Dingjia Island (March 19, 1275) and was instrumental in destroying other Song fleets. After the destruction of the Song, he was sent to deal with rebels in Mongolia and then west to Central Asia to fight the armies of Qaidu. He died in 1286 en route to Turfan in modern Xinjiang.

4 *Secret History of the Mongols*, trans. Igor de Rachewiltz (Leiden: Brill, 2004), §124. This is from an oath that Sübedei made to Chinggis Khan, proclaiming his loyalty and also his role as a *nökör* or servitor.

5 The Ölberi and Qangli are two other Turkic tribes that nomadized the region north of the Aral Sea. The Mongol invasion of the Khwarazmian Empire in 1219 was triggered by the massacre of a Mongol caravan at Otrar in 1218. Chinggis Khan attempted to resolve the matter diplomatically, with the stipulation that the caravans' goods be returned. This was not done and thus Chinggis Khan viewed the event as a theft of his property.

6 The sharing of *airagh or* kumiss was a typical method of showing amiable intent toward potentially hostile forces. This also was an attempt by the Mongols to demonstrate their shared culture.

7 The king of the Sarts was Muḥammad Khwārazmshāh. Sarta'ul is the plural but for the sake of simplicity it has been kept in the English plural form.

8 The Alans, many of whom were Christian of some form (Nestorian and Orthodox), viewed the imbibing of *kumiss* as unclean and a pagan act.

9 At Kalka, the Mongols retreated for nine days, luring the combined Rus' and Kipchak forces deeper in to the steppe and extending their lines so that the Rus' and Kipchaks were spread thin and no longer able to maintain formations.

10 Sübedei is referring to Venetian and Genoese merchants. The Mongols sacked some trading colonies in the Crimean peninsula including Sudaq.

11 By violating the earth, Sübedei is referring to farming. In Mongolian culture, disturbing the soil was often viewed as sacrilege.

12 Sübedei appears to be trying to make sense of *kvass*, a fermented drink made typically from rye or black bread. It has a very low alchoholic content of 1% or less.

13 *Secret History of the Mongols*, §199.

14 The *Altan Uruq* were considered white-boned, white referring to aristocracy. *Altan* or gold referred to imperial status. *Yosun* refers to the customs and practices of Chinggis Khan and the Mongolian culture. *Yasa* refers to the laws of the Mongol Empire. Güyük is the son of Ögödei Khan, the third son of Chinggis Khan.

15 *SHM*, §255. Jochi and Cha'adai or Chaghatay not only quarreled but broke out into fisticuffs during a meeting over Jochi's questionable parentage. Jochi was born after Börte, Chinggis Khan's wife, had been kidnapped by the Merkit. She remained with them for several months before being rescued.

16 It is not known if this truly occurred, but the idea was not inconceivable as the Mongols often preyed upon the fears of their enemies. Many Hungarians also arrived at the conclusion that the Kipchaks were agents of the Mongols, whom most did not see as different from the Kipchaks.

17 There is no evidence that the Mongols used gunpowder in this campaign, but it is clear that this is the powder that Sübedei mentions.

18 A *tamgha* is the seal, brand, or mark of an individual. In this instance it was the royal seal of King Bela.

Further reading

Buell, Paul D. "Sübötei Ba'atur (1176–1248)." In *In the Service of the Khan: Eminent Personalities of the Early Mongol-Yüan Period (1200–1300)*, ed. Igor de Rachewiltz, Hok-lam Chan, Hsiao Ch'i-ch'ing and Peter W. Geier, 13–26. Wisebaden: Harrassowitz Verlag, 1993.

Jackson, Peter. *The Mongols and the West, 1221–1240*. London: Pearson, 2005.

May, Timothy. *The Mongol Art of War*. Barnesly, UK: Pen & Sword, 2007.

Rachewiltz, Igor de., ed. and trans. *The Secret History of the Mongols*. Leiden: Brill, 2004.

Thomas of Split. *History of the Bishops of Salona and Split*. Trans. and ed. Damir Karbic, Mirjana Matijevic Sokol, and James Ross Sweeney. Budapest: Central European University Press, 2006.

PART 3

Byzantium and southeastern Europe

8

ANNA KOMNENE

Princess, historian, and conspirator?

Leonora Neville

Anna Komnene was a Byzantine princess and author of a history of the reign of her father,
Alexios I Komnenos (1081–1118). The International Encyclopedia of the Middle
Ages *summarized her life story as follows:*

> Anna Komnene (born Constantinople 2 Dec. 1083, died c.1153/4) was
> a Byzantine princess and historian, and the author of the laudatory his-
> torical biography *Alexiad* modeled on Virgil's *Aeneid* and Homer's *Iliad*.
> Eldest daughter of Alexios I Komnenos and Irene Doukaina, she received
> an excellent education from a young age (literature, historiography, philol-
> ogy, poetry,) and could easily be considered as one of the most educated
> women of the Middle Ages. While still an infant, Alexios I had betrothed
> her to Constantine Doukas, co-emperor and son of Michael VII Doukas
> (who had been overthrown by Nikephoros III Botaneiates in 1078). As a
> result, Anna always nurtured the hope that as the future wife of Constan-
> tine Doukas, she would succeed to the throne. However, the birth of her
> brother John (II) Komnenos in 1087 shattered her plans and she remained
> hostile to her brother throughout her entire life. After the premature death
> of her fiancé in 1095, Anna (now at the age of fourteen) married the
> young nobleman Nikephoros Bryennios (1097) who would subsequently
> become caesar and historian of the Komnenos family. When her father
> died in Aug. 1118 she and her mother plotted against her brother with the
> aim of securing the throne for her husband. The latter refused any involve-
> ment and retained loyalty to the family. When the conspiracy was brought
> to light, she was forced, following the death of her husband (1138), to retire
> to the monastery of Kecharitomene that had been founded by her mother.
> There she lived the remainder of her days and composed her historical

work (which she completed around 1148). She was tonsured a nun shortly before her death.[1]

In many modern histories Anna is characterized as ambitious and arrogant. The work of the great Alexandrian poet Constantine Cavafy reflects common perceptions of her character:

In the prologue to her *Alexiad*
Anna Komnina laments her widowhood.
Her soul is all vertigo.
"And I bathe my eyes," she tells us,
"in rivers of tears. . . . Alas for the waves" of her life,
"alas for the revolutions." Sorrow burns her
"to the bones and the marrow and the splitting" of her soul.

But the truth seems to be this power-hungry woman
knew only one sorrow that really mattered;
even if she doesn't admit it, this arrogant Greek woman
had only one consuming pain:
that with all her dexterity,
she never managed to gain the throne,
virtually snatched out of her hands by the impudent John.[2]

I believe that the perception of Anna as arrogant, embittered, and ambitious stems from a misreading of the rhetorical strategies she used in the Alexiad *in order to be perceived as humble and modest. Misunderstandings on the part of modern historians of how Anna's self-presentation interacted with twelfth-century conceptions of appropriate gender led them to see Anna as mannish, ambitious, and unnaturally interested in political power. Given this perception, their interpretations of the evidence for the events surrounding Alexios's death elevated Anna into the role of mastermind of an attempted coup. While we cannot know exactly what happened on the night Alexios died, when all of the available evidence is examined in light of current research on Anna's culture, there is little reason to think that Anna opposed her brother's accession. It certainly seems mistaken to see Anna's life as dominated by an attempt on imperial power. When we understand better what Anna was trying to accomplish through her self-presentation in the* Alexiad, *the reasons for thinking of her as a person who would want desperately to be empress fade away.[3]*

A standard part of secondary education in Anna's culture was practicing making speeches impersonating what a famous character from literature or history would have said at a particular moment such as, "what Achilles would have said upon seeing Patroclus body" or "what Niobe would have said upon seeing her dead children." This rhetorical exercise, called ethopoiia, taught students to imagine a situation from the perspective of another and to express that viewpoint convincingly. This chapter is an ethopoiia on what words Anna Komnene would say upon reading about herself in modern texts such as the International Encyclopedia of the Middle Ages *and Cavafy's poem.*

* * *

What strange people these future historians are! Have they not studied elementary logic? Have our efforts to preserve and elucidate all the works of Aristotle failed? The story does not even make sense. To be convincing, a historian must write at least what is plausible, or what would have been reasonable for a given situation. This historian claims that I conceived a desire in my heart for imperial rule when I was an infant, and that the birth of my brother dashed all my plans – when I was four. Do children in the future really establish life-long political plans as toddlers?

This historian also has me cast into a monastery as punishment in 1138 for revolt that supposedly took place 1118. What sort of emperor would leave his enemies at liberty for twenty years and only then imprison them? If this is a plausible political scenario, times have changed. I see that your historians of the eighteenth century established the tale that I had wanted to seize power from my brother without knowing of any of the court oratory that shows I was an honored member of court long after my father's death.[4] Apparently this historian was trying to reconcile that story with the more recently published evidence, and so shipped me off to prison twenty years after my supposed revolt. But his solution is absurd! Why didn't he ask whether his colleagues had gotten the plot line wrong so long ago? What about seeing me as a power-hungry woman was so appealing as to lead a scholar to distort all other evidence to fit?

What made you think that I disliked my brother? A number of your historians think that I showed my dislike when I described him as having a dark skin. I think this means *they* don't like dark-skinned people.[5] Why attribute their dislike to me? Historians are called upon to be truthful, and such a well-known characteristic of my brother's appearance was not something I could lie about. I also let you know that my father was short and stuttered. You say I criticize John's nose by saying it is between hooked and straight – but the mean between two extremes is ideal. I made a similar comment about the shape of my mother's face. You really must have lost Aristotle.

You think I hated John because I said it was stupid for Alexios's successors to overturn his policy of allying with Turks. In the middle of the twelfth century everyone had an opinion about whether the Empire ought to support the crusaders, because we were all Christians, or stick to the old ways of allying with whoever could help us best. Writing at a time when my nephew Emperor Manuel (1143–1180) needed to make vital decisions about these very issues, I used the *Alexiad* to make the best case I could that the Westerners could not be trusted and that abandoning Alexios's alliances with Muslims hurt the Empire. Recently your historians have realized how my work spoke to the politics of Manuel's day, and even that I portrayed my father as being more opposed to the Westerners than he really was. Why, then, do you insist that my criticism of Alexios's successors on this issue shows that I hated my brother? It is as if you think a woman could not have a reasoned opinion about politics. And sadly, did you notice I was right? The Crusaders conquered the Empire eighty-six years after my father died.

What evidence do you have that I plotted against John? The excellent jurist John Zonaras wrote a history closest to the time of my father's death, and he spread the rumor that my mother wished for my beloved husband, Nikephoros Bryennios, to succeed instead of John. But Zonaras nowhere says that I was involved. Zonaras also makes clear that my beloved mother Eirene and Nikephoros did nothing to dispute John's succession. On the contrary, he points out that the first group to proclaim John as emperor was the retinue of our future daughter-in-law, the Georgian princess, who that very day arrived in Constantinople. If Nikephoros was to rally anyone to his cause, it would be they. Yet he sat with my father as he died. Zonaras's history shows that the scandal of the hour was that John left his father's side to be proclaimed emperor before Alexios had breathed his last.

In my funeral oration, George Tornikes describes me as assisting my mother, Eirene, as Nikephoros assisted Alexios, with the work of ruling in the years before Alexios's death. He says that I was able to cancel debts and help those in need. In those days people certainly flattered us by saying that, if we were to rule, we would rule well. People will always flatter those in power, especially if they want a debt forgiven! If we had any power, it depended upon the will of the emperor Alexios, who needed help as his health declined. Did people say they would prefer Nikephoros to John as emperor? Perhaps. Some may even have meant it (though you never can tell). Nikephoros was as excellent a man as ever lived, skilled in war, beautifully educated, of matchless nobility and flawless character. He lived always knowing that had his grandfather captured and blinded Alexios, rather than the other way around, he would have inherited the throne, and John would have been a member of his court. It was not always easy for him. But were we deceived by the flatterers? No. What objections could be made to John? None. So we sat with my mother and sisters beside the dying Alexios and did not stir when John went off to be acclaimed and seize the Great Palace. Rumors may have flown far and wide,[6] but Nikephoros made no effort to dispute the claim of John.

While some doubtless whispered to John that Nikephoros had wanted the throne for himself, John saw through the chatter and knew that he could trust his brother-in-law. Nikephoros campaigned with John and served his government in the eastern provinces. John led our son's marriage procession. How does this behavior fit with your story that we had tried to murder him?

Do any of you wonder why, as my father's health failed, he did not give power to John – his son, heir, and co-emperor? Why did he rely on his wife, on me, and on Nikephoros, when he had a grown son already crowned? Alexios, it seems, learned distrust early, seeing a continuous stream of rebels trying to seize the throne throughout his youth. Once he had won the prize, he was careful with it. In the first years of his reign, he gave extraordinary powers to his mother who effectively ruled all matters of domestic administration while he was continuously on campaign against rival claimants for the throne and foreign enemies. Although many people criticized Alexios for relying on a woman, and depending on his mother like a child, she was someone he could trust to govern for him without ever becoming a potential rival. I think later he may have turned to Eirene, and perhaps to Nikephoros, because similarly they were never a plausible a threat to his power. He did not trust either Nikephoros or John with an army in his final years. Sometimes I wonder whether John was more nervous because of his father than his brother-in-law.

Nikephoros may have lamented the fortune that brought Alexios to the throne, but in the history he wrote, he demonstrates beyond doubt that the civil wars that preceded Alexios's rise had been devastatingly destructive for the empire. His history effectively calls on every loyal Roman to support the stability of the new dynasty. He did indulge, however, in tacitly arguing that it would have been better had his grandfather's revolt succeeded. Although I will always respect his memory, I was disappointed in how poorly he portrayed my father (John didn't seem to care). In Nikephoros's history, his grandfather, Nikephoros Bryennios, is a grand hero, and my father, Alexios Komnenos, appears craven, duplicitous, immature, and ruthless. In his description of the battle in which Alexios succeeded in capturing Nikephoros the Elder, my husband has Alexios win only because a band of Turkish mercenaries does everything for him while he stands by. Anyone reading his history would think that it was a tragedy that Nikephoros Bryennios the Elder had not become emperor. What a case he makes for the superiority of his own line! Yes, he knew that John was destined to rule and, by showing how destructive the civil wars were, his history argues that all loyal Romans ought to support the victorious Komnenoi. But Nikephoros worked effectively to convince its readers that he would have made a great emperor. Ultimately his book explained both why he would have ruled well, and why he chose to loyally serve his brother-in-law.[7]

As a good and loving wife, I deferred to my husband's views on these matters. Yet, years after his death, when I took my turn to write history, I refuted his case against Alexios, point by point. Every argument he made against the judgment and character of my father, I refuted.[8] My history resoundingly supports the house of Komnenos and rejects all the claims my husband made for his own line. And yet, you think that *he* failed to support *my* attempt on the throne?

It seems you must have been deceived by the slanderous account of Niketas Choniates. When, at the end of the twelfth century, that courtier tried to write history, he spat out base slander against everyone in my family, making the opening description of Alexios's death into a story of moral turpitude that sowed the seeds of destruction for the Roman Empire in his era. A grand ploy to mask the truth that *he* served the administration that led to the conquest of the Empire! Especially when he revised it in exile (after the Crusaders sacked Constantinople in 1204), his history dished out blame for everyone save himself. But even in its first version, he set my family up as the moral cause of all later ills. Like a twisted comedy, he had every member of my family play a role that was a direct inversion of the ideal behavior for their gender, age, and relationship: the wife does not defer to the husband; the son does not respect the mother; the husband cannot control his temper; the mother does not love her son! What more horrible calumny could anyone invent! He then talks about a conspiracy to replace John with Nikephoros – as a story of what *would have* happened, had something happened. Yet your historians take it as a story of what *did* happen. Then, as the crowning insult, he accuses me of declaring that I wished I had been a man and Nikephoros a woman – although in terms far too obscene for me to discuss. But rather than seeing this insult as a clear sign Choniates was writing an invective, rather than a history, your historians take it as something that I actually said! As revealing the truth about my character! How could Choniates, writing in the 1190s, *possibly* know what I had said in private about my husband in 1118? His story insists that *I* wanted power and that Nikephoros undermined my efforts to seize power on his behalf. How can this make sense in light of the politics of the histories we wrote? You have it clearly from our own pens – he put forth the case for the rule of the Bryennioi, and I refuted it to uphold the Komnenoi. If either of us wanted power, it was Nikephoros.

Choniates clearly wished to portray the house of Komnenos as the poison that eventually led to the Latins' conquest of the Roman Empire. Yet he also seems to have had an especial enmity toward me – to say that I wished to be a man. When I wrote my history, I knew well that it was not considered an appropriate task for a woman, and I strove vigorously to appease the possible objections of my readers. For many of my friends – or the men who said they were my friends – my methods worked, and they respected my writing as a great work of history, reassuring me that I succeeded at being both a good woman and a good historian. Yet it seems that it was not enough for Choniates. To him, by taking up the pen rather than the spindle and distaff, I became a mannish woman, a monster who wished to invert the natural order.

The slanders of Choniates are echoed in the insults of your poet Cavafy, who flatly calls me arrogant and power-hungry. Why do you call me arrogant when I tried so hard to appear humble and demure? I expected that my readers would think that a woman who wrote history must be conceited, and that is why I humbled myself repeatedly by drawing your attention to my piteous mourning. I know well that history is a matter for men to write, as it is a matter for men to discuss. History records the great deeds done by men in war and the great words they spoke in political deliberation. Women have no place discussing such public matters, let alone writing about them. I knew the matters of family and household were appropriate topics of concern for women. I often emphasized that I wrote about my father because my familial relationship with the subject of my history helped defend the morality of my choice to write. Since the palace was my home, and the emperor was my father, I did not transgress the boundaries of a woman's concerns, in a manner of speaking.

I knew that no one would expect a woman to have the education to write a history, and so I described my great learning in the opening lines of my history. Who would trust my history if it were written by a woman who could only read stories of saints and the scriptures? Yet even in the midst of that very sentence I explained that I wasn't boasting because it was necessary to clarify my credentials for writing. I wrote, not to show off, but because it was necessary to preserve the memories of Alexios's great deeds for the future. Listen to what I said:

> Having discerned [how time can destroy memory], I Anna, daughter of the emperors Alexios and Eirene, born and raised in the *porphyra* [palace], not

without some share of learning, but rather having studied Greek language in full and being not unpracticed in rhetoric and having read through well the Aristotelian treatises and the Platonic dialogs and having crowned my mind with the Pythagorean terms of mathematics – for it is necessary to betray these things, and this is not bragging, how much nature and the zeal for learning gave and God above granted and the opportunity supplied – I wish on account of this to tell in writing the deeds of my father not worthy to be passed over in silence nor carried away in the stream of time into the sea of forgetfulness. . . . In saying these things, I come not making some display of rhetorical exercise, but so that a matter so great may not be left without witness.[9]

Do I not immediately say that the situation compelled me to speak about my education, and that the point of writing was *not* to make a display of my skills? How then can you think that I boast of my own skills?

I anticipated that my audience would think that a woman could not have the emotional self-control to write a history. Historians must keep their own emotions in check so that they can fairly assess who had behaved well and who badly, without partiality or partisanship. Since women are naturally subject to emotion, they do not possess the dispassion necessary to write about history. But wise men know that nobility brings strength of character to both men and women. Noble women have a greater strength of character that allows them to control their emotions. I have a noble pedigree without rival, descending from two aristocratic lineages that had ruling emperors in their line, and having been born in the purple pavilion of the imperial palace, I can claim the title of *porphyrogennete*. One of your historians says my pride in my birth was "immeasurable,"[10] yet I only let my readers know of my nobility so that they would think I had the emotional control to write a history. Education and training in virtue can bring greater emotional self-control, and so I also emphasized my long study of philosophy.

But even though I wrote about my father, and even though I explained that I wasn't boasting about my education, and even though I insisted on my nobility to substantiate my emotional strength, I still knew that my readers would be affronted by a woman acting so boldly, so I immediately turned to tears and made myself piteous in my mourning for my husband. Your poet has no pity for my mourning. What sort of vile man would so disrespect a widow? Do not the psalms and the law enjoin all righteous men to pity the widow and orphan?[11] My tears call out your sympathy and condescension. Who could listen to a widow mourn and think her arrogant? I proclaimed my mourning in my history to gain my readers' pity. Listen again:

At these thoughts [of my husband] my soul becomes filled with vertigo and I wet my eyes with streams of tears. Oh! What a councilor is lost to the Romans. . . . Grace spread throughout his limbs and his appearance was not only worthy of royalty, as they say, but better and even divine. For my part, I have been conversant with terrible things since my birth in the purple as

they say, and I have been assailed by ill fortunes, if one could reckon it not
good and smiling fortune for me to be so born and a child of emperors and
produced in the purple room. The rest full of waves! Full of turmoil! Orpheus
moved stones and wood and even inanimate nature simply with his singing;
Timotheos the flutist once played the martial tune to Alexander and immediately moved the Macedonian to weapons and the sword. The narratives about
me are not the subject for movement to weapons and battle, but would stir the
hearer to tears, and not only a sensitive one, but would even force emotional
suffering from inanimate nature.[12]

Are you so heartless that you are unmoved by my cries? For hundreds of years writers have used mournful cries to mitigate the arrogance inherent in making people
sit and listen to them talk about themselves. Telling a tale of woe was a standard
way to humble oneself before an audience. I thought that by turning attention to
my piteousness I would overcome any annoyance at my stepping outside of the
boundaries of female decorum.

When I felt called to discuss my research and my sources for my history – which
entailed many clearly inappropriate conversations with strange men – I likewise
broke out in mourning for my parents and my husband and vigorously proclaimed
my isolation. I didn't put the discussion of my sources in my prologue, where you
would expect it to be, because I was already violating so many rules for proper
female behavior that I couldn't also mention all the time I spent talking about
politics and battles with old soldiers. But by the time I was writing book fourteen,
I realized that the quality of the research I had done was the main reason why readers should believe my history, and not think it base flattery of my father. So, even
though any proper aristocratic woman should only leave her home for religious
observances, I admitted that I had traveled with my father on campaign and had
seen many events first hand. I admitted that I had sought out accounts of events
written by old veterans, and that I had even had conversations with numerous men
about my father's deeds. Naturally I worked to mitigate these transgressions by
loudly proclaiming that I had lived an entirely isolated and cloistered life, by saying I was a victim of many woes, and by raising cries of mourning to the heavens.
Of course I knew that my claims that I lived entirely alone flatly contradicted the
statements that I had conducted research by conversing with witnesses. I trusted
you to see that the description of my research was the meat of the discussion and
the outbursts of grief were the sauce that made my behavior more palatable. But
your literal-minded historians have taken my wailing as evidence that I was incar-
cerated in a monastery! When I said I'd suffered blows of cruel fate blows even
before my eighth year, they date my fiancé's removal from imperial succession to
when I was eight! How does that even make sense? When I said "woe is me," it
never occurred to me that you'd search everywhere for an actual political event to
explain the cause of grief. I know in my culture women are expected to be subject
to emotion, but you people seem to think I was totally out of control, and that
I suddenly exploded into paroxysms of self-pity for no reason at all. At least you

don't seem to have asked why talking about my research methods made me break into a song of woe. If you had thought about why I expressed those emotions at that point in my writing, you might have seen how they work to mitigate my transgressions of female decorum.[13]

I thought I had proved my emotional control by telling you explicitly that I had recovered myself after I mourned for the deaths of my kinsmen in the course of the history. When the narrative of history called on me to describe the deaths of my brother and fiancé, naturally I allowed my audience to see me weeping, as is appropriate for a woman. How unnatural and monstrous I would be if I could mention the death of my brother without tears! Yet having mourned them, I told you that I put away my anguish, dried my eyes, and continued with the history. What better demonstration could I make than letting you all see how well I controlled my emotions?

In all these cases you take the vehemence of my emotion as real but disbelieve the reasons I gave for it. Your poet thinks that when I said I mourned my husband, I was really expressing anger and disappointment at not becoming empress. You do not believe that I was really mourning my husband and parents, so you try to find something else that would make me so upset, and fasten on the tension over John's accession to explain that I was really mad about. Well, as I have said, I am not such a hysterical and emotionally out-of-control woman that I let my real emotions flow all over my page like an untamed river. I am a careful writer, well-trained in rhetoric, and therefore I only display emotion in my writing when I am trying to provoke an emotion from my audience. In my day, my expressions of mourning would move an audience to pity the old widow and think me humble and lowly, and hence prevent them from being affronted at the boldness with which I took up the masculine task of historical writing.

Your historians have been entirely blind to my efforts to appear as a demure, modest, humble widow, and all my other attempts to be both a good woman and a good historian. Yet, like the twelfth-century audience I wrote for, they seem to harbor negative presumptions about a woman who would write a history. They seem to expect that a woman could not control her emotions; that any woman interested in writing about politics would be politically ambitious; that a female author would necessarily be vain; that a woman who wrote a history would have a masculine character and therefore want power. They see me *exactly* as I worked not to be seen: transgressive, arrogant, and disrespectful of natural masculine authority. Not only did my efforts to appear demure and deferential fail, they backfired. My piteous mourning does nothing to earn your sympathy but rather has become the fuel for seeing me as a hopelessly embittered power-hungry schemer.

And yet, when you want to know what happened in the twelfth-century Mediterranean, where do you turn, but to my history? Despite all of your calumnies, I have succeeded in preserving the memory of my father's great deeds for eight centuries. I could have written under a false name, but I wished to take my hand to the greater challenge of writing history as a woman. My history will likely last for centuries more, and perhaps in some future era people will begin to understand me.

Notes

1 Alexios Savvides, "Anna Komnene, Historian, 1083–1153/4," *International Encyclopaedia for the Middle Ages-Online. A Supplement to LexMA-Online* (Turnhout: Brepols Publishers, 2011), www.brepolis.net.
2 Constantine Cavafy, *Collected Poems*, ed. Geōrgios P. Savvidēs, trans. Edmund Keeley and Philip Sherrard, Rev. ed., Princeton Modern Greek Studies (Princeton: Princeton University Press, 1992).
3 Leonora Neville, *Anna Komnene: The Life and Work of a Medieval Historian* (Oxford: Oxford University Press, 2016).
4 Ibid., 154–171.
5 Ibid., 143.
6 Questions about the inevitability of John's succession may be found in a text known as the *Diegesis Merike:* Philipp Meyer, *Die Haupturkunden für die Geschichte der Athosklöster : Grösstentheils zum ersten Male* (Leipzig: Hinrich, 1894), 163–184.
7 Leonora Neville, *Heroes and Romans in Twelfth-Century Byzantium: The "Material for History" of Nikephoros Bryennios* (Cambridge: Cambridge University Press, 2012).
8 Ibid., 182–193.
9 Reinsch and Kambylis, *Alexiad*, Prolog 1.
10 Charles Diehl, *Byzantine Empresses*, trans. Harold Bell and Theresa de Kerpely (New York: Knopf, 1963), 180.
11 Psalms 12:5, 35:10, 41:1–3, 7:5, 65:5, 86:1, 109:22, 113:7, 140:12. Deuteronomy 10:18, Deut. 24:20–21, Deut. 27:19.
12 Reinsch and Kambylis, *Alexiad*, P4.1.
13 Ibid., 80–88.

Suggestions for further reading

Buckley, Penelope. *The Alexiad of Anna Komnene: Artistic Strategy in the Making of a Myth.* Cambridge: Cambridge University Press, 2014.
Kaldellis, Anthony. "The Corpus of Byzantine Historiography: An Interpretive Essay." In *The Byzantine World*, edited by Paul Stephenson, 211–222. London: Routledge, 2010.
Macrides, Ruth, ed. *History as Literature in Byzantium*. Farnham: Ashgate, 2010.
Magdalino, Paul. "Byzantine Historical Writing, 900–1400." In *The Oxford History of Historical Writing*, edited by Sarah Foot, Chase F. Robinson, and Daniel R. Woolf, 2: 218–237. Oxford: Oxford University Press, 2012.
Neville, Leonora. *Anna Komnene: The Life and Work of a Medieval Historian*. Oxford: Oxford University Press, 2016.
———. *Heroes and Romans in Twelfth-Century Byzantium: The "Material for History" of Nikephoros Bryennios*. Cambridge: Cambridge University Press, 2012.
Sewter, E.R.A., and Peter Frankopan, trans. *The Alexiad*. Revised. London: Penguin Classics, 2004.

9

ANGEL ON EARTH AND HEAVENLY MAN

St. Sava of Serbia

Florin Curta

With the exception of Sts. Cyril and Methodius, there is no churchman in the history of south-eastern Europe who had a greater influence on that region than St. Sava of Serbia. Dimitry Obolensky even believed that his reputation in Eastern Europe was second only to that of Alexander the Great. The beginnings of the Serbian Church (as an organized, independent institution) are linked to St. Sava. He is regarded as the founder of Serbian monasticism, both in his own country and at Mount Athos. The earliest pieces of original literature written in Serbia in Old Church Slavonic are associated with his name. Sava is also the first original author at Mount Athos to write in that language. He is the earliest known pilgrim from the Balkans to the Holy Land. He was a contemporary of the Holy Roman Emperor Frederick II, and like him, he met with the Ayyubid sultan al-Kamil. Sava played a key role in the regional politics of the Balkans during the troubled period that followed the sack of Constantinople by Western crusaders (1204). His dealings with the Empire of Nicaea and with Bulgaria are fundamental moments in the political history of the region. However, outside Serbia, he has rarely attracted the attention of historians. The biographical vignette that Obolensky dedicated to him almost thirty years ago remains unique. It was based on the attempts of the Yugoslav historiographical movement to shift the study of Sava from hagiography to biography. That, however, was done at the cost of neglecting the religious dimension of Sava's life, particularly the interesting combination of monastic qualities and features that one would associate primarily with the secular clergy. Occasionally, Sava's name appears in studies of Byzantine and Balkan history, but not in works dedicated, for example, to religious developments in Europe during the twelfth and thirteenth centuries. Some of Sava's writings and actions have been compared to those of St. Bernard of Clairvaux, but outside a small group of scholars dealing with the medieval history of the region, few English-speaking historians know who Sava was and what he did. The European dimension of Sava's personality has yet to be discovered.

The portrait that follows is therefore an attempt to depict Sava as a man of the Church. Much of what is known about him comes from the earliest of two biographies written by the Athonite monks Domentijan (in 1252 or 1253) and Theodosius (before 1336). Domentijan, a monk and a Serb, was Sava's disciple and had followed him everywhere during the last years of his life, most likely on his pilgrimages to the Holy Land and Egypt. A fellow churchman is best to draw a portrait of Sava as a man of the Church. I have therefore used Domentijan's biography to create an imaginary text, namely a letter from the Bulgarian Patriarch Joachim I to the Bulgarian emperor John Asen II. Joachim was appointed patriarch of Tărnovo (the capital of the Second Bulgarian Empire) in 1235, when, following his alliance with the Empire of Nicaea, John Asen II obtained the autocephaly (independence) of the Bulgarian Church. Joachim had been a monk at Mount Athos in his youth, and upon returning to Bulgaria in the 1220s, he established a cave monastery by the Danube. He became an adviser of Emperor John Asen II, who financed the enlargement of the monastery.[1] I have set the timeline of the imaginary letter during the second half of the previous year (1236), several months after Sava had died in Tărnovo during his short visit at John Asen II's court. During the months that followed Sava's death a number of envoys came to John Asen from Serbia, all requesting that the body of Sava (who had been buried in Tărnovo) be returned to their own country. The Serbian king Vladislav (John Asen's son-in-law) came in person to Tărnovo to beg the Bulgarian emperor to let him bring Sava's body to Serbia. According to Sava's biographers, Vladislav and his men eventually smuggled the coffin from the city, in what is one of the earliest instances in Eastern Europe of relic theft (furtum sacrum). Sava was re-buried in the exonarthex of the Monastery of Mileševa that Vladislav had built in 1224 in the valley of the Lim River (near the present-day border between Serbia and Montenegro). The imaginary letter of Patriarch Joachim would have reached John Asen before the relics were spirited away. The Bulgarian emperor, who had an enormous respect for Sava, could not understand why the Serbs were so bent on bringing the body of their former archbishop to their own country, and why they could not let it rest in its tomb in Tărnovo. This was an opportunity for Joachim to describe his fellow Athonite as a churchman of formidable spiritual and moral stature. I have inserted chronological markers between brackets in the text and added explanatory notes for person or place names.

* * *

The servant of God, Joachim, Patriarch of Tărnovo, to the Christ-loving, great emperor and autocrat of the Bulgarians, John Asen, the son of the old emperor Asen.[2]

Your imperial majesty asks for my advice on the matter of the repeated requests of the Serbs, especially of King Vladislav,[3] to have the body of Father Sava of blessed memory, who was buried in the Church of the Forty Martyrs in Tărnovo, moved to Serbia. I will try to explain to your imperial majesty their intentions and aspirations the best I can. This I will do on the basis of the conversations I had with Father Sava more than a year ago, when he arrived in Tărnovo, before his death on January 14 in the year 6744 from the creation of the world [AD 1236], as well on the information that I have obtained after that from his disciple Domentijan, who had always been with him over the last ten years or so. I have also relied on what I have learned about Father Sava from the good fathers and brothers at Mount Athos, where I have spent many years of my youth, before returning to Bulgaria more than fifteen years ago.[4]

Sava was born Rastko [in or around 1175] to the Grand Župan Stephen Nemanja of Raška. The Serbs believe now that when God chose Nemanja and his wife to

FIGURE 9.1 Portrait of St. Sava in the narthex of the monastery church at Mileševa, 1231/2. Courtesy of the Institute of Art History, Belgrade.

give birth to Sava, a new Chosen People appeared in the world. When still a boy, his father gave him a province to govern, namely Hum, the land by the sea [Adriatic Sea] that comprises Ragusa [Dubrovnik], the city to which your imperial majesty has granted a trade privilege some years ago. But one day, when he was at the court of his father in Ras, Rastko fled the country and went straight to Mount Athos. Domentijan says that he did so because of the great desire to serve God, but the Athonite monks told me that Rastko had betrayed his father when defecting to the Greeks [Byzantines], with whom Nemanja had been at war for some time. Be that as it may, Rastko was tonsured a monk at Vatopedi, one of the largest monasteries on Mount Athos, and took a new name – Sava. Some say that he first stayed with Rus' monks at St. Panteleimon. Meanwhile in Raška [in 1197] Nemanja abdicated and went to the monastery of Studenica that he had himself built [in 1183]. Soon after that, he left that monastery and came to Mount Athos to be with his son as a monk named Simeon. He brought lavish presents for the Athonites – horses, mules, buckets of gold and silver, and precious liturgical vessels. Father and son went around all the monasteries on the Holy Mount, in order to find a place for a Serbian monastery. They found a half-ruined house named Hilandar, a few miles away from

Vatopedi. The abbot at Vatopedi gave them permission to settle there, and Sava traveled to Constantinople [in 1198] to obtain the approval of Emperor Alexios.[5] The emperor first put Hilandar under the abbot of Vatopedi, then only under the authority of Simeon and Sava. That was now a self-governing, independent monastery, not unlike those of the Iberians [Georgians, the Monastery of Iviron] and Amalfitans [from the Italian city of Amalfi]. Simeon died soon after that [on February 13, 1199], and Sava went again to Constantinople to obtain full authority over the monastery. The emperor granted him Hilandar land and buildings, as well as permission to own a boat without paying any taxes. There were about ninety monks in the monastery, and Sava wrote its *typikon* [rule] by adapting that of the monastery of the Evergetis in Constantinople, where he had stayed during his visits in the great city. The rule gave great power to the abbot, but there are also many details about liturgy, confession, communion, fasting, clothes, and the election of officers. I have read the *typikon*, and recognized many Bulgarian and Rusian words. That is why I am convinced that the translator was not Sava, but a Bulgarian monk at St. Panteleimon.

To this day, Sava is known on Mount Athos as benefactor of many monasteries. He purchased a hermitage at Karyes, to which he often retired with one or two other monks to pray. He later built a church dedicated to his patron saint, Sabas [of Palestine]. A few monks, all Serbs, resided there, and Sava wrote the *typikon* for their community. The bishop of Hierissos [Nicholas, ca. 1196 until after 1213] ordained him deacon, then priest. [In late 1200 or early 1201] he traveled to Solun, where the metropolitan [Constantine Mesopotamites, ca. 1196/8–1222/8] ordained him archimandrite.[6] During that time, the Latins conquered Constantinople,[7] and then pillaged the monasteries on the Holy Mount as well. Sava's brothers, Stephen (the First-Crowned) and Vukan, asked him to bring back home their father's remains. So, in the middle of the winter [1206/1207], Sava returned to Serbia with Simeon's relics, which he re-buried at Studenica. On that occasion, Simeon was proclaimed a saint, and Sava wrote an order of service in his honor. He also wrote the *typikon* for Studenica, that was based, like that of Hilandar, on the *typikon* of Evergetis. The prologue is in fact a biography of Simeon, which I have once read at Hilandar. Sava compared himself with the Prodigal Son, and confessed that he had departed to a distant land, had fed with swine, and could not be sated with their fodder. I remember thinking that Sava's biography of Simeon is as much a glorification of his father as it is a form of repenting for the sins of his youth.

A second Cyril [of Alexandria], Sava took the seeds of God from the Holy Mount and planted them in his homeland. He became abbot of Studenica, but [in 1209] he began building a new monastery at Žiča, on the Western Morava River. He also fulfilled several diplomatic missions on behalf of his brother, King Stephen (the First-Crowned). For example, he went to Prosek, in Macedonia, to negotiate with the *sebastokrator* Strez [in 1212], your imperial majesty's cousin who had at that time allied himself with the usurper Boril against the Serbs and the Latins.[8] Strez was murdered shortly after Sava left Prosek, and Domentijan told me that it was a Bulgarian warrior acting on Sava's orders who stabbed the *sebastokrator*.

Domentijan also claims that upon his return to Studenica, Sava sent a bishop named Methodios to the pope in Rome with a request for a crown for Stephen. However, I believe that Stephen, whose second wife was Latin,[9] may have himself asked for the crown. At any rate, [in 1216 or 1217] Sava gave up being abbot at Studenica and returned to Mount Athos, where I had at that time already been residing for a few years. While at Hilandar, he maintained contacts with his brother, and must have had his approval and support when [in 1219] he departed for Nicaea, where he was very well received by Emperor Theodore.[10] On the feast of the Assumption [August 15, 1219], Patriarch Manuel of blessed memory consecrated Sava as archbishop,[11] a decision reinforced by a decree of the synod in Nicaea issued with the emperor's authority. The church in Serbia thus received autocephaly, much like ours did last year. The archbishops of Serbia were to be elected and consecrated without the consent of the patriarch of Constantinople, even though his name was to be mentioned first, before all others, in liturgical commemorations. Upon his return, Sava went to Solun to compile a body of canon law, which we now call the *Book of the Pilot*.[12] Back in Serbia [in 1220], Sava embarked on a new diplomatic mission to Hungary, in order to convince King Andrew[13] to make peace with Stephen the First-Crowned. In that same year, Sava established his archdiocese at the Žiča Monastery and began appointing bishops across Serbia, some of them based on monasteries. Three of them replaced Greek bishops under the jurisdiction of the archdiocese of Ohrid. This made Archbishop Demetrius furious.[14] But Sava also sent into the dioceses his "exarchs" to reinforce the sacrament of marriage laws and to root out the heretical beliefs. In a homily delivered at a council in Žiča [in 1221], he addressed both the Orthodox and the heretics. He asked the latter to return to the Church, and stressed the importance of venerating the cross and icons. He accomplished much more with this kind approach than his father had previously been able to accomplish with violence and cruelty.

When King Stephen the First-Crowned died [in 1228], he was succeeded by his son Radoslav, who had the support of his father-in-law, Emperor Theodore. After crowning Radoslav king in Žiča, Sava left Serbia for a pilgrimage to the Holy Land. Domentijan, who was with him, told me everything about the trip. They left from Brendič [in May 1229], and upon arriving in Jerusalem, they immediately went to the Church of the Resurrection.[15] Sava met with Athanasius, the most sanctified patriarch of Jerusalem, talked to him about Christ's passions and His Resurrection, and celebrated the liturgy with him by the Tomb of Christ.[16] He then went to Bethlehem, Mount Zion, and the Georgian monastery of the Holy Cross, which he liked very much.[17] In Bethany, he donated gold to the church keepers for a memorial service for his parents and brother Stephen. He set out for the river Jordan and washed his face with water from the river at the very spot where Christ was baptized. He went to the Great Lavra, where he venerated the tomb of St. Sabas.[18] He established a Serbian monastery in a dependency of the Great Lavra, the Church of St. John the Theologian on Mount Zion.[19] In July [of the year 1229], after visiting Nazareth and Mount Tabor, he returned home from Acre. On his way, he stopped in Nicaea to visit Emperor John Kaloyan, who gave him a warm welcome, as well as large amounts of gold and silver.[20] From there he went to Mount Athos, but spent the winter [1229–1230] in Solun, where he met with Emperor Theodore.[21] Upon his return to Serbia, he began introducing the church order of Jerusalem to Serbia, including the All-Night Vigil on the eves of Sundays and major feast days.

Emperor Theodore had been the ally of your imperial majesty [since 1225], when he suddenly decided to attack us only to be utterly defeated and taken prisoner at Klokotnica.[22] That was God's punishment for his arrogance, but Theodore's son-in-law in Serbia also paid for his insolence. The Serbian boyars [noblemen] deposed Radoslav and replaced him with his younger brother Vladislav, who is your imperial majesty's protégé and son-in-law.[23] By God's grace, I had just become Archbishop of Tărnovo and negotiations were under way for three years with Patriarch German [of Constantinople] in order to return our church to the Orthodox faith.[24] Vladislav therefore asked his uncle [Sava] to obtain the recognition of our church's auto-cephaly from all other patriarchs. So after crowning Vladislav king, at a council of churchmen and laymen summoned in Žiča, Sava announced his decision to resign his position of archbishop. A second Elias, he left Serbia on another pilgrimage to the Holy Land, which was also a delicate mission on our behalf. He embarked for Brendič [in 1234] and narrowly escaped being captured by pirates. From Brendič he sailed to Acre through a terrible storm. In Acre, he stayed at the monastery of St. George, which he had purchased from the Latins during his first pilgrimage. He stopped in Jerusalem to meet again with Patriarch Athanasios. From Jerusalem, he reached Egypt, where he met with Nicholas, the most sanctified patriarch of Alexandria and all Egypt.[25] The patriarch arranged for him to visit the monasteries of the Thebaid and of the Desert of Scetis.[26] Sava was received by the sultan al-Kamil, who gave him permission and an escort to visit Mount Sinai. In the spring [of the year 1235], he left the Holy Land to go to Antioch, where he met with the most sanctified patriarch of the city of God Antioch and of all Syria.[27] He then went to Constantinople, where he arrived shortly before your imperial majesty put that city under siege together with Emperor John Kaloyan. He was at the monastery of the Evergetis when the fleet of Emperor John Kaloyan was destroyed by the Venetians, whom John the Latin had called for help.[28] He responded to your invitation to visit Bulgaria, traveled to Mesembria,[29] and from there to Tărnovo on the horses and with the guides that your imperial majesty had sent to him. He arrived in our blessed city in December [of the year 1235] and your imperial majesty gave him the great palace in Tărnovo. On Epiphany [January 6, 1236], Sava celebrated the liturgy in the Church of the Forty Martyrs. A few days later, he became gravely ill and fell asleep in the Lord on January 14. Your imperial majesty has called upon me, the bishops, and all monks to bury his body in the Church of the Forty Martyrs. We have done so, and ever since miracles have taken place at his tomb. Learning about them, the Serbs have repeatedly asked us to give them the remains of their former archbishop. They rightly claim that he is the sail and lighthouse of their land. But he has also been a second apostle for our land as well. And should things go badly in the future, Sava will be our best shield against disasters. God has brought him to our blessed city – an angel on earth, and a heavenly man.

Notes

1 An English translation of the biography of Patriarch Joachim is available in Kiril Petkov, *The Voices of Medieval Bulgaria, Seventh – Fifteenth Century: The Records of a Bygone Culture* (Leiden/Boston: Brill, 2008), pp. 285–286.

2 John Asen II (1218–1241) was the son of Asen, one of the two leaders of the Vlach and Bulgarian rebellion of 1185 that led to the establishment of the Second Bulgarian Empire. He had to flee Bulgaria in 1207, when his uncle Johannitsa Kaloyan was murdered and power in Tărnovo reverted to Boril. John Asen returned in 1218 to claim the throne, overthrew the usurper, and became emperor.

3 Stephen Vladislav, king of Serbia (1234–1243), was married to John Asen II's daughter, Beloslava.

4 Little is known about the early life of Patriarch Joachim I of Tărnovo. However, he seems to have spent some time at Mount Athos as a young man, before returning to Bulgaria in the 1220s.

5 Alexios III Angelos (1195–1203), whose sister Eudokia had married Sava's brother Stephen (known as the First-Crowned, because he was the first crowned king of Serbia) in 1186.

6 Archimandrite is a superior abbot who is appointed by a bishop to supervise other abbots. Hierissos (now Ierissos) is the most important bishopric in the region of Mount Athos. Solun is the Bulgarian name for Thessaloniki.

7 During the Fourth Crusade, in April 1204.

8 Strez was a member of the Asenid family ruling in Bulgaria (thus, a relative of John Asen II). He was either the cousin or the brother of Boril (1207–1218), who became emperor after the assassination of Johannitsa Kaloyan that forced his nephew John Asen (future emperor) to flee the country. With the assistance of Stephen the First-Crowned, Strez seized Prosek, an important stronghold on the middle course of the Vardar River in Macedonia. In a few years, his power extended over the whole area between the Struma River to the east and Ohrid to the west. In 1209, he switched alliances, approaching Boril against their common enemies – Stephen the First-Crowned and the Latins. The title of *sebastokrator*, although of Byzantine origin, was used in the thirteenth century in Bulgaria as well. It is not clear under what conditions, and by whom it has been bestowed upon Strez.

9 Anna Dandolo, the granddaughter of the Venetian doge Enrico Dandolo (1192–1205), who had participated in the Fourth Crusade. Her wedding with Stephen took place in Venice. She is the mother of the Serbian king Stephen Uroš I (1243–1276).

10 Theodore I Laskaris (1205–1221), the son-in-law of Alexios III Angelos, proclaimed himself emperor at Nicaea shortly after the victory of Johannitsa Kaloyan over the crusader army at Adrianople (April 14, 1205). Three years later, Emperor Theodore re-established the Orthodox patriarch of Constantinople in Nicaea and appointed the former grand treasurer of the Church of Hagia Sophia in Constantinople as Patriarch Michael IV Autoreianos (1208–1214). Patriarch Michael then crowned Theodore as emperor.

11 Manuel I Sarantenos (1217–1222), Patriarch of Constantinople in Nicaea, had been deacon and the head of the university in Constantinople before the 1204 sack of the city by the crusaders. He opposed the marriage between Theodore's sister, Eudokia, and Robert of Courtenay, the Latin emperor of Constantinople, on grounds of consanguinity: Theodore was already married to Maria, Robert's sister.

12 The *Krmčija* (or *Kormchaia*) *kniga* is the most authoritative Slavonic body of canon law, which was adopted during the Middle Ages by both the Bulgarian and the Russian churches. It consists of a compilation of texts from several Byzantine collections in earlier Slavonic translations, to which Sava added Slavonic translations of commentaries by the twelfth-century canonists Alexios Aristenos and John Zonaras, as well as a complete translation of the Emperor Leo VI's lawcode known as the "Handbook" (*Procheiron*).

13 King Andrew II (1205–1235). Upon his return from the Fifth Crusade in January 1218, he agreed to the marriage between John Asen II and his daughter Anna Maria (at that time only thirteen years old).
14 Demetrius Chomatenos, Archbishop of Ohrid (1216–1236) had been in correspondence with Stephen the First-Crowned on matters of theology and doctrine. This reflected the rapprochement between Stephen and Theodore Comnenus Dukas, the ruler of Epirus (1215–1230), another Byzantine successor state created after the sack of Constantinople in 1204. Stephen's son and successor, Radoslav, married Theodore's daughter Anna in 1219 or 1220. In or soon after 1225, Demetrius Chomatenos crowned Theodore Emperor of Thessaloniki.
15 Brendič is the Slavic name of Brindisi, the main port on the Italian coast of the southern Adriatic Sea where most people going to the Holy Land would have embarked to cross the sea. Completely destroyed at the order of the Fatimid caliph al-Hakim (996–1021), the Church of the Resurrection in Jerusalem was restored with Byzantine funds in the mid-eleventh century and, a century later, by the crusaders.
16 Athanasius II, Greek Orthodox Patriarch of Jerusalem (ca. 1231–1244).
17 The Monastery of the Cross was established in the Valley of the Cross (now in Jerusalem) by King Bagrat IV of Georgia (1027–1072).
18 Great Lavra of St. Sabas (Mar Saba) was established in the late fifth century in the Judean desert. During the twelfth and thirteenth centuries, the lavra enjoyed enormous prestige and was richly endowed by both Melisende, Queen of Jerusalem (1131–1153) and the Byzantine emperor Manuel I Comnenus (1143–1180).
19 This was in fact the northern chapel of the crusader church on Mount Zion, which had been destroyed in 1219 or 1220.
20 John III Dukas Vatatzes (1221–1254), the son-in-law of Theodore I Laskaris and the second Byzantine emperor of Nicaea.
21 Theodore Comnenus Dukas, the ruler of Epirus.
22 The battle of Klotkotnica (March 9, 1230) put an end to the Epirote aspirations to dominate the Balkans and inaugurated a period of Bulgarian hegemony in the Peninsula, under the reign of John Asen II. In an inscription on a column in the Church of the Forty Martyrs in Tărnovo, John Asen celebrates the victory and proclaims himself "Christ God faithful tsar and autocrat of the Bulgarians," ruling over the entire land "from Adrianopolis to Drach [Dyrrachion], the Greek [part], as well as the Serbian and Albanian parts." After spending a while in relatively comfortable captivity at Tărnovo, Theodore was blinded at the order of John Asen II as a punishment for having attempted to spark a rebellion in Bulgaria.
23 Beloslava, Vladislav's wife, was the daughter of Anna, John Asen II's first wife, whom he had repudiated and sent to the monastery (where she became a nun named Anisia) in order to marry Anna Maria, the daughter of King Andrew II of Hungary.
24 Patriarch Germanos II (1222–1240) had been in negotiations with John Asen II since the latter's victory at Klokotnica. The issues at stake were the return of the Church of Bulgaria to Orthodoxy and the patriarch's recognition of its autocephaly. The Bulgarian-Nicaean rapprochement culminated in an alliance sealed by the marriage of John Asen II's daughter Helen (at that time only ten years old) with the son of John III Dukas Vatatzes, Theodore (future emperor Theodore II Laskaris, 1254–1258). The alliance was sealed in Gallipoli in 1234, and the wedding was celebrated one year later in Lampsakos.
25 Nicholas I, Greek-Orthodox Patriarch of Alexandria (1210–1243).
26 Thebaid is the region of Upper Egypt in which some of the earliest monasteries were organized in the fourth century by St. Pachomius. This is also the region in which St. Anthony lived a life of solitude that became the model for all subsequent hermits. Scetis (modern Wadi el Natrun) is a desert region in the northwestern part of the Nile Delta in which some of the most influential monasteries of Late Antiquity have been established between the fourth and seventh centuries.
27 Dorotheos, Patriarch of Antioch (1219–1245). From Jerusalem, Sava wrote a letter in Serbian vernacular to the archimandrite Spiridon, the abbot of Studenica, in which he

complained about not feeling well. Together with the letter, he sent to Spiridon a small cross, a belt (that he had placed on the Holy Sepulcher), a piece of cloth, and a small gemstone. The former were for Spiridon to wear in Sava's memory; the latter were Holy Land souvenirs for Studenica.

28 John of Brienne, King of Jerusalem (1210–1225) and Latin Emperor of Constantinople (1229–1237). Although he had only 160 knights, he valiantly defended Constantinople against the combined armies of John Asen II and John III Dukas Vatatzes. However, following the victory, some of his knights left for Bulgaria, for they had apparently not been paid.

29 Now Nesebăr, on the western Black Sea coast. Sava must have left Constantinople before the defeat of the Nicaean fleet by the Venetians.

Sources

Alpert, L. Annette. "The Life of Stefan Nemanja by St. Sava: A Literary Analysis." *Wiener slavistisches Jahrbuch* 22 (1976): 7–14.

Hero, Constantinidis, and John Philip Thomas (eds.). *Byzantine Monastic Foundation Documents: A Complete Translation of the Surviving Founders'* Typika *and Testaments.* Washington, DC: Dumbarton Oaks Research Library and Collection, 2000 (the typikon of the *kellion* at Karyes, pp. 1331–1337).

Kantor, Marvin. *Medieval Slavic Lives of Saints and Princes.* Ann Arbor: University of Michigan, Department of Slavic Languages and Literatures, 1983 (with an English translation of Sava's biography of Simeon, pp. 257–304).

Matejić, Mateja. *Biography of Saint Sava.* Columbus: Kosovo Publishing, 1976 (with an English translation of a fragment of Domentijan's biography of Sava, pp. 103–105).

Roach, Andrew P. "The Competition for Souls: Sava of Serbia and Consumer Choice in Religion in the Thirteenth Century Balkans." *Glasnik Skopskogo Nauchnog Drushtva* 50 (2006), 1: 1–30.

10

PAULUS DE BREBERIO BANUS CROATORUM DOMINUS ET BOSNE

Neven Budak

Pavao, Count of Bribir, Ban of Croatia, and Lord of Bosnia was the most outstanding figure of the Croatian High Middle Ages, one of the few whose actions and visions crossed the borders of medieval Croatia. In spite of that, there is no contemporary report about his life and deeds, and we have to draw our knowledge mostly from charters or other administrative sources. Only a few preserved artifacts add to the picture. Nevertheless, we can present a portrait of a lord skillful in both war and politics. What remains blurry is his private life.

Ever since the peace treaty of Aachen (812), which stopped the Carolingian-Byzantine war, the former Roman province of Dalmatia was separated in two. Coastal towns like Zadar, Split, Dubrovnik, and Trogir, together with most of the islands with the towns of Krk, Osor, and Rab, stayed under Byzantine authority. Although in the eleventh century they became politically integrated with their Croatian hinterland in what was to be known as the Kingdom of Croatia and Dalmatia, they remained to a large extent autonomous. Such a position was supported by the politics of Venice, which tried from the very end of the tenth century to dominate Dalmatia in order to control the sea route along the eastern Adriatic coast, which was of vital importance for its commercial activities. The other part of former Roman Dalmatia, which came under Carolingian domination after 812, developed into the duchy, and later kingdom, of Croatia. A major political goal of its rulers was to incorporate Dalmatia into their realm. Apart from that, they supported the development of new coastal towns, like Šibenik and Nin (which was actually a ruined Roman town), on their own territories. These towns, however, were soon subsumed into the rest of Dalmatia, taking over the social and political structures of the older centers.

The third party that got involved into the struggles over the coastal towns and islands were the kings of the Arpadian dynasty. Coloman, who was the first Hungarian king to be crowned as king of Croatia, conquered Dalmatia in 1105, but his heirs were less interested in the province or less successful in keeping it. Thus, Venice first gained control over the northern islands and later also over most of the others. Zadar resisted for a long time, raising four mutinies against the Venetians, and finally surrendered into the hands of King Bela III (1182). In

1190 the Zaratine navy won a decisive victory over their enemies, but the luck turned on the side of the Venetian Doge Henry Dandolo in 1202 when he used the knights of the Fourth Crusade to take the city. This put an end to any serious resistance for the next century. Three years later Dubrovnik, until then at least formally recognizing Byzantine sovereignty, was also forced to accept a Venetian count. In this way only Split and Trogir of Dalmatia proper, together with Nin and Šibenik, remained under royal control.

Two more centers on the coast followed their own destiny. One was Skradin, a developing town on the mouth of river Krka, since the thirteenth century a possession of the Bribirski family, and Omiš, on the mouth of river Cetina, a stronghold of the Kačići kindred and an old piratical naval base.

This was the political framework, within which the kindred of the counts of Bribir tried to build up its power, using the weakness of the kings, the ambivalent relationship of the Dalmatian towns toward Venice and the mutual conflicts of Slavic lords. Paul was the most efficient among his relatives, able to recognize the right moment for action and capable of using the heritage of his ancestors in the best way.

* * *

It is March 1311. Mladen II, Ban of Bosnia, rides through the gates of Zadar at the head of his troops. He is welcomed by the joyful citizens lined along the main street leading to the square with the communal loggia. On the way Mladen passes the church of St. Stephen and stops his horse in front of the church of St. Peter the New, opposite the loggia. The square is crowded with members of the aristocratic families, and *dominus* Corradus de Ancona, *defensor civitatis* (equal to rector or podestà), together with the Great Council, greet the Ban in the name of the commune. After getting off his horse, Mladen enters the loggia where Corradus hands over to him the keys of the city. John, the vicar of the monastery of St. Chrysogonus, approaches Mladen and expresses gratitude for his support in expelling Venetians from the city. The day before, namely, some citizens raised a successful mutiny against the Venetian count of Zadar and his entourage, bringing to an end a century-long domination of the doges over the Dalmatian capital. They knew, however, that without serious military help they would have little if any chance to maintain their newly acquired freedom.

Upon triumphantly entering Zadar, Mladen took the titles of Count of the city (*comes Jadre*) and Prince of Dalmatia (*princeps Dalmacie*), adding them to his previous title of Ban of Bosnia (*banus bosnensis*). It was to be expected that, after taking over the capital of Dalmatia, the mighty lord would decorate himself with a title second only to a king. It was a moment of Mladen's triumph. But even more so it was the lifetime achievement of his father, Ban Paul, the undisputed ruler of Croatia.

Paul, head of a kindred some time later known as Šubići, must have been between sixty or seventy when he sent his eldest son to take Zadar, for he had been mentioned for the first time in historical records in 1272 as podestà of Trogir. His kindred originated from the county of Bribir, situated in the most fertile part of medieval Croatia, in the hinterland of Zadar. The center of the county was a fortified settlement placed on a plateau on the top of a hill, overlooking a large area and also called Bribir (Roman *Varvaria*). The strategic position of the place was so good that it had been inhabited since pre-Roman times and throughout the Early Middle Ages. Together with the nearby castle of Ostrovica it was in control of the roads leading from the interior of Croatia, or even further, from Hungary, to Zadar and a number of other important places: Nin, Skradin, and Šibenik. Therefore, the lords of these strongholds were at the same time lords of a large part of the Kingdom of Croatia. Bribir was not just a castle; it was more like a fortified town with five churches, a friary, at least one palace, and many houses.

The beginnings of Paul's kindred can be traced into the eleventh century, in the time of King Zvonimir (1075–1089). During the reign of the Arpad dynasty over Croatia (from 1102) the counts of Bribir managed to turn their position of royal officials into a hereditary one, using the weakness of the Arpadian kings and their usually little interest in Croatian affairs. Although a member of the dynasty (usually the king's younger brother or son) was appointed as duke in charge of the area between the Drava River and the sea (*tota Sclavonia*), few of these acted with much engagement in the maritime region. Another representative of royal power in Croatia was the ban, something like a viceroy, appointed by the king among aristocrats not necessarily originating from Croatia.

Like other kindreds of free men, the Bribirians were a complex structure with several lineages. Through a large part of the thirteenth century at least two of these had been fighting each other in order to gain the leadership over the kindred. Finally, Paul's father Stephen (Stjepko) prevailed and secured further success to his three sons: Paul, Gregory, and Mladen.

After his father's death (before 1267) Paul inherited the title of Count of Bribir, holding in his hands the mighty castles of Bribir and Ostrovica, but also Skradin, a safe port for his ships. One year after being mentioned as podestà of Trogir, he became also Count of Split (and in addition to that, his younger brother George was Count of Šibenik).

Michael de Barbazanis, member of a distinguished Split family, described in his chronicle (written after 1330) Mladen II as a violent and unjust lord, ascribing to him the usual catalogue of vices. His officials raped women, robbed merchants, and plundered Dalmatian citizens, hanging hostages and decapitating noblemen. Mladen himself was arrogant, despising all the rulers of this world, ordaining bishops and abbots by his own will, listening to mischiefs instead of sober advisors. Though he used to read the Holy Script often, he did not obey to its words.

Obviously, this was a biased attitude toward a man who, like his father, ruled Croatia and all the Dalmatian towns, including Split. On the other hand, Michael's family fought for generations for more autonomy for their hometown, and any kind of pressure from the lords in the hinterland had to be seen as a threat and blamed for violence. Unless, of course, these lords came to rescue the town from the other enemy, coming from the sea, that is from Venice. Trying to keep the unstable balance of their autonomy, citizens had to try to play out one side against the other. Hence, as Mladen ruled Split, to Michael Venice seemed the lesser evil and he had to justify the attempt of the Republic to destroy the power of the Bribirians. However, although his account of Mladen was deliberately one-sided, we should not reject it as totally untrue. There is no doubt that the mighty lords were violent in trying to build up or keep their power. That was true of Mladen, and it had to be true of his father as well.

A trace of evidence for such a claim may be seen in the mutiny of the Trogirans against Paul in 1273. King Ladislaus IV, who took them under his protection, warned Paul in a letter written at his Buda castle, that he and his brothers should stop molesting the citizens of Trogir, they should return whatever they took from them, and they should also release the hostages they took. From the letter we also learn that Paul and George used citizens of Split and Šibenik to oppress Trogir, and those from Split who were not willing to support Paul were expelled.

Paul did not take this threat seriously. Ladislaus was still a boy, and it was his mother who ruled instead, backed by barons among whom was also Joachim Gút-keled, Ban of Slavonia, whom Paul supported in Joachim's clashes with competing barons. Showing no fear, Paul ordered the citizens of Split to attack the royal castle of Klis, close to both Trogir and Split, because its castellan supported the Trogirans. In spring of 1274 the resistance of Trogir was finally broken and Paul installed his cousin Stephen as count of the city. A temporary weakening of the Gútkeleds enabled the king to show his discontent with Paul and remove him from the office of ban, but already next year he was reinstalled as *Banus maritimus*.

Already in this early stage Paul developed the model of sharing power with his brothers and relatives. The position of count of a town meant incomes, military power, and access to the sea, but Paul was clever enough to leave much of that to his brother George who gradually became count of all maritime towns except for Zadar. Temporarily, like in the case of Trogir, important positions could be given to other members of the kindred. The third brother, Mladen I, was intended to take an important role in securing the spread of the Bribirians into Bosnia. At the beginning of the fourteenth century, Paul's sons governed a large border region between Croatia and Bosnia, the Three Fields. Taking care that everybody in the broader family was satisfied with his position, Paul was sure not to face any kind of resistance from his relatives. To the contrary, his relationship with both his brothers, and especially with George, seems to have been harmonious. To tell the truth, one of the reasons for this peaceful coexistence might have been the fact that neither of the brothers had sons of their own, so they had little interest to compete with Paul. Mladen II lacked his father's skills at least in this respect, so that one of the reasons for his fall in 1322 was the animosity of his brother Paul II.

Paul's ability in making friends or at least avoiding hostility came to the fore in the "games of thrones," which started after the murder of Ladislaus IV in 1290. One of the pretenders to the Hungarian throne was Charles Martell, son of Charles II, King of Naples, and Maria, a Hungarian princess. Relations between the court in Naples and Paul dated back to 1274, when Charles I started preparations for a crusade against Byzantium. For that he needed his fleet, and taking most of his ships with him to the Aegean would leave his Adriatic shores unprotected against the corsairs coming from Omiš. Therefore, he asked for help from the citizens of

Split and Šibenik, Paul's subjects, to support him in the war against Omiš. However, also Venice got soon involved wanting to put the corsairs' stronghold under control, but Paul did not like the idea of a Venetian base close to his territories. In a long-lasting war between the Bribirians and Venice Paul managed to take over Omiš and appoint George as its count (in 1282). In 1290 he finally decided to make piece, most probably because he wanted to concentrate on a more important goal: bringing Charles Martell to Hungary.

There were two reasons for Paul to take the side of the Angevins. On the one hand, Dalmatian towns, but sometimes also the Croatian hinterland, depended on the grain supply from the Kingdom of Two Sicilies (or Naples). On the other, in order to develop his power even further, Paul needed a benevolent king on the Hungarian throne, if not a weak one. Helping Charles to get the crown of St. Stephen secured many benefits, starting with a regular grain supply from the Italian Adriatic harbors. In November 1291 Paul's ships were allowed to export grain from Apulia in order to supply his castles and those of his brothers. These imports, sometimes freed from taxes, continued at least until 1303. Charles II wanted to be sure in Paul's fidelity because the Dalmatian towns and ports under Paul's rule were crucial for his support to Charles Martell. Therefore, in 1292 he confirmed the donation, previously made by his son, of all of Croatia (except the westernmost part, which was in the hands of the counts of Krk) "with all the barons, vassals, cities, castles, and villages, with adjacent islands and all the rights and appurtenances" to Paul and his brothers. Three years later, after the death of Charles Martell, when his son Charles Robert became the new pretender to the throne, Charles II confirmed to Paul the dignity of ban for life. Moreover, he made also gifts to the Bribirian brothers, like an expensive horse to George and a crossbow to Paul.

Both of them visited Naples, George more often than Paul, because he was obviously in charge of escorting Charles Robert over the sea to Croatia. In order to impress the Angevin king and display the power of the Bribirians, he was escorted by forty of his knights. We know nothing about Paul's escort, but we can be sure that it was by no means smaller.

But, clever as he was, Paul did not play only one card. He went on pretending his loyalty to Andrew III, the last of the Arpadian kings. Andrew III was aware of the importance of Paul's support, so in 1293 he confirmed to him and his brothers the hereditary dignity of ban of the maritime parts. However, he added a condition that for the Bribirians was probably not acceptable: they had to be subordinate to Andrew's mother, the duchess of all of Slavonia and the maritime regions, Tomassina Morosini. If until then Paul had some doubts as to whom to support, the idea of being subject to a woman and a Venetian must have made him come to the final conclusion to stand for the Angevin cause.

However, Paul also had reason to not be quite happy with Charles II either. In 1299 the king decided to confirm all the possessions of the three brothers anywhere in Croatia or Hungary, whether they had them already, or were going to obtain them in the future, but this time as a fief under the condition to serve him with "numerous troops" against his enemies. This was a kind of setback, compared to previous unconditioned donations, and it might have been the reason for Paul to distance himself from the court in Naples, leaving all the contacts to his brother George. So, when in August of 1300 the time came to bring Charles Robert to Hungary, it was George who went to Naples and who escorted the prince to Dalmatia. Though it seems that Paul was responsible for the rest of the voyage by land, later events show that he persisted in keeping his distance from the young ruler. Neither he nor any other member of his family attended Charles Robert's coronation in 1308 to which he sent only his emissaries.

While this was happening, Paul received an embassy from the counts of Görz (Gorizia, Gorica), coming with the mission to conclude a marriage contract with the Bribirians. The counts were an influential family with large estates in Istria and an important potential ally having no common borders with the Bribirians that might someday cause tensions between them. The charter was dated with "Actum Salone," which was strange because the Roman city of Salona, once the capital of Dalmatia, ceased to exist sometime in the seventh century. However, during the ninth through eleventh centuries Croatian rulers built a number of churches and at least two monasteries on the outskirts of the abandoned city. We know almost nothing about the condition of these buildings in Paul's time because with the extinguishing of the Croatian dynasty nobody had much interest in preserving holy places meant to keep alive the memory of mostly forgotten kings and queens. Paul must have chosen one of the better-preserved buildings to receive the distinguished embassy instead of taking them to nearby Split or Trogir, or at least his brother's castle of Klis. Was this a step toward identifying himself with the bygone kings of Croatia? It might have been so because the later history of the Šubići of Bribir would reveal such an attitude more clearly. Paul achieved another success in this respect when before 1310 Pope Clement V declared him patron and protector of the former Templar preceptory of St. Gregory in Vrana. Until 1075, when King Zvonimir donated it to Pope Gregory VII, Vrana was a possession of the Croatian kings, housing a part of the royal treasury. Thus, Paul extended his power over another important royal property, connected to King Zvonimir whose memory was for some reason cherished among the Bribirians. A fragment of a "chronicle," actually an invented story about the last days of Zvonimir, dated by some to 1308 and ascribed to the Bribirians, claims that Zvonimir was buried in the church of St. Mary in Bribir, which was the funerary church of Paul and his kindred.

In March 1304 the most important members of the family gathered in Split, in the Dominican monastery just outside the city walls. There were Paul and Mladen (George died some time before), together with Paul's sons Mladen II, George II, Paul II, and Gregory. They came to meet with Count Hrvatin, lord of the westernmost part of Bosnia called Lower Regions. Although Paul used on this occasion only his title of Ban of the Croats, the meeting was a display of his real power. His brother Mladen was Ban of Bosnia; Mladen II, Count of the Three Fields and all of Hum; George II, Count of Split. Paul did not bother to list all of his family's titles because even so it was clear that nobody between the River Sava and the Adriatic could compete with him. All Croatian noblemen, counts, and gentry were in his service, happy or not. Hrvatin enjoyed a better status because he was Paul's *cognatus* (kinsman) and *compater* (godfather), maybe a brother of Paul's wife Urša who had died a year ago. The Bribirians promised to love him and protect him and his possessions as long as he would preserve his loyalty. Paul wanted to bind Hrvatin with more than formal bonds, describing himself not only as his *maior et senior*, but also as father. Hrvatin's support was to Paul and Mladen of greatest importance in their attempt to rule Bosnia. This will become clear only three months later, when Mladen died from the hands of Bosnian rebels, described in the family necrology as heretics.

The rule over Bosnia was one of Paul's most important goals. Already in 1299 he called himself *dominus Bosne* (lord of Bosnia). It is not clear how he became lord over this land, which was changing its dependency from the Hungarian to the Serbian rulers. Most probably it was by force combined with Paul's ability to negotiate, at a time when Andrew III had little power to prevent Paul, and the two brothers on the Serbian throne, Milutin and Dragutin, were fighting each other. Resistance came from the Bosnian Ban Stephen I Kotromanić and war went on until the beginning of 1305 when the victorious Paul installed his son Mladen II as "Ban of all of Bosnia." However, he allowed Stephen to stay in the country and Mladen later even took his son Stephen II under protection against hostile Bosnian noblemen. In 1308, having no other choice, Charles Robert granted Paul the hereditary dignity of ban of Bosnia.

The war in Bosnia spilled over the borders of the province. Paul's ambitions made him in 1301 attack Kotor, then under Serbian dominion, using help from Venice, Dubrovnik, and Zadar. That was the farthest point of his outreach toward the southeast. He could not take the city, but he temporarily occupied Onogošt (today Nikšić in Montenegro) and the region of Travunija, keeping the newly conquered Hum (today Hercegovina).

So in 1305, Paul was the unchallenged ruler of Croatia, Dalmatia, Bosnia, and Hum. Only the counts of Krk in the westernmost part of Croatia remained independent of his authority, as did the Venetian towns of Zadar, Rab, Krk, and Osor. Paul needed to display his position also symbolically. We shall never know whether he ever really intended to renew an independent Croatian kingdom, but he surely acted as a king. With or without the consent of either Andrew III or Charles Robert, he started using the title of ban of the Croats rather than ban of the Maritime regions or ban of Croatia. In this way he was suggesting that his power came from his people, from the Croatian nobility, and not by will of some higher political authority. Using the title of *dominus* (lord) and allowing his son to call himself *princeps* (prince) had the same meaning. Maybe because of his relations to the Angevin court, Paul started imitating the habits of western chivalry and was the first Croatian nobleman to use a coat-of-arms (an eagle's wing on a shield), but we do not know from whom he received it (probably from Charles II). He was also the first in Croatia to mint his own money. The silver he needed must have come from Bosnia. In this way he even surpassed the Croatian kings who never produced their own coins because there were no silver mines in Croatia. Moreover, on his courts in Skradin and Bribir he kept not only a chancellery, but like his brother George in his castle of Klis he employed Italian physicians.

In order to ensure his position, Paul needed the support of the church. One big step in that direction was the establishment of the bishopric of Šibenik in 1298. Šibenik was part of the territory and diocese of Trogir, but since the town developed significantly and since it had much better relations to the Bribirians and was closer to their main stronghold, Paul and George were in favor of the new bishopric. At first Paul supported the bishop of Skradin, a certain Dominican named Galvanus, to perform episcopal duties on the territory of Šibenik. Neither Galvanus nor Paul was stopped when the Archbishop of Zadar excommunicated the Dominican for violating the Canon Law. Since Pope Boniface VIII supported the Angevins, it was easy for George to convince him, during a visit in Rome, to allow the establishment of the new diocese. That was not all: Paul succeeded in establishing two more bishoprics in his territory – one in Duvno, on the border to Bosnia (in the Three Fields), and another in Omiš. It seems that all the three new bishops were Franciscans. Paul was fond of the order and supported it. In 1299 he decided to build a church in Skradin, dedicated to St. John the Baptist, whom he chose to be protector of his kindred (the saint might have been chosen as a symbolic sign for Paul's intended invasion of "heretic" Bosnia[1]). Skradin became Paul's main residence and a generously subsidized friary would be another sign of his standing. He invited there the Franciscans, "*ad quem hordinem specialem deuocionem gerimus*" [to which order we cherish special devotion]. Next to the site of the new church stood already the nunnery of St. Elisabeth of the Clarisses, whose abbess was Paul's sister Stanislava. Paul brought Franciscans also to Bribir, where he established the friary of St. Mary, the mausoleum of his kindred. Of the undoubtedly rich donations he was giving to different churches almost nothing is preserved. In the treasury of the former cathedral of Nin there is still a golden reliquary that Paul donated on the occasion of George's death, and we know of at least one golden reliquary donated to the cathedral of Zadar.

At the peak of his power Paul had one more ambition. In order to complete his acquisition of Dalmatia, he had to take Zadar, the only Venetian possession on the Dalmatian coast. He had been preparing that undertaking for a long time, luring citizens of Zadar to his side in different ways. He gave them offices in his service, sending them as emissaries to Italy or appointing them to different duties in his counties, cities, and castles. He even made friends with the Venetian Count of Zadar, James Tiepolo, son of Doge Lawrence. Moreover, it seems that Tiepolo married one of Paul's sisters. Venice was at that time in a difficult situation because Clement V, who was at war with the Republic, laid an interdict on the city. Carefully observing the situation in Venice itself, Paul was waiting for the right moment, which came with the mutiny of Baiamonte Tiepolo and others against Doge Pietro Gradenigo in 1310. Baiamonte was Paul's nephew and the ban might have counted on an agreement with the new government on the status of Zadar. But, since the mutiny failed and Baiamonte had to escape to his uncle for safety, Paul decided that it was the right moment to make the move against Zadar, or better to say against the Venetian authorities in the city. Mladen's army stood before Zadar, prepared to act, and the Venetian count (who was not James Tiepolo at that moment) had no choice but to leave.

Venice tried to strike back, but both the pope and Charles Robert protested, asking the doge to stop the siege of the city. However, even without that support the citizens of Zadar defeated the Venetian navy and Mladen's army forced the Venetian troops to withdraw.

Paul, maybe too old to lead the army himself, must have received the news with a feeling of utter satisfaction. He was finally equal to the kings of the old days, not having to care about the real king in distant Hungary, victorious over Venice, lord over the Croatian and Bosnian nobles, over Dalmatian citizens and the pirates of Omiš, over cattle-breeding Vlachs, bishops, and abbots.

Venice accepted peace negotiations, which started in April 1312. Paul died on May 1.

The castles of Paul and his brothers and sons do not exist anymore. Bribir was annihilated in the wars of the sixteenth and seventeenth centuries and all that is preserved of it are two books from the friary's library. Family graves were devastated and only one nameless tombstone with an eagle's wing, lying among ruins, commemorates the mighty lords of the Croats.

* * *

Note

1 From the twelfth century till the end of the Bosnian Kingdom in 1463 Bosnians were constantly accused of being heretics, adherents of the so-called Bosnian Church, sometimes as Bogomils. The question on how far this church really was heretic is, due to the lack of sources, not definitely answered. However, all those who wanted to extend their power over Bosnia used this accusation as a justification for their actions. On the Church of Bosnia, see among others: John Fine, *The Bosnian Church: Its Place in State and Society from the Thirteenth to the Fifteenth Century: A New Interpretation* (London: SAQI, The Bosnian Institute, 2007).

Further reading

Unfortunately, most of the literature on Paul and his kindred is in Croatian. One important exception is the PhD thesis of Damir Karbić, *The Šubići of Bribir: A Case Study of a Croatian Medieval Kindred*, Budapest: Central European University, 2000. However, the thesis was not published and it is difficult to find. Still, as it is the most comprehensive study of both Paul and his kindred, it is also the basis of this portrait. Sources on Paul are mostly published, but in different publications. The majority are charters written in Latin and they can be found in Tadija Smičiklas (ed.), *Codex diplomaticus regni Croatiae, Dalmatiae et Slavoniae*, vol. 6–8, Zagreb: Jugoslavenska akademija znanosti i umjetnosti, 1908–1910.

11

KING MILUTIN AND HIS MANY MARRIAGES

(*1254, †November 21, 1321, r. 1282–1321)

Vlada Stanković

Barely two years after his death on November 21, 1321, Stephen Uroš II Milutin, king of Serbia, was proclaimed a saint. Unlike his ancestors who obtained sainthood, his great-grandfather and the founder of the Nemanjić dynasty Stephen Nemanja-St. Simeon, and his grandfather Stephen the First-Crowned, or his brother Dragutin, Milutin had not taken monastic vows and was married no less than four times during his sixty-six-year-long life, four decades of which he spent as the first king of Serbia. Yet his cult spread swiftly, well beyond the borders of medieval Serbia. Milutin's royal sanctity comprised two distinctive elements: a strictly speaking religious aspect and cult and its strongly pronounced political and ideological side, especially during the reign of his grandson, King, and from 1345 Tsar, Stephen Dušan (1331–55).

This portrait will look at these apparent contradictions in the life and legacy of the longest-ruling monarch of medieval Serbia, tracing the political rationale behind Milutin's four marriages, which may serve as a peculiar but accurate map for following and understanding the geopolitical changes in the volatile region of southeastern Europe in the second half of the thirteenth and the opening decades of the fourteenth century. Our main guides through Milutin's turbulent life will be his biographer and later Archbishop of Serbia, Danilo II (1327–34), and two Byzantine historians, George Pachymeres and Nicephore Gregoras, with many interesting contemporary details provided by the report of chief Byzantine negotiator in the years 1298–99, Theodore Metochites, numerous edicts of Byzantine emperors and Serbian king, as well as visual representations (fresco portraits) in the latter's many church foundations – all of which have been woven together to present the life and times of Milutin from his perspective.

* * *

In the cold winter days of early December 1282, Milutin, the thirty-eight-year-old king of Serbia, was awaiting with foreboding the latest among many unpredictable political moves of the mighty Byzantine Emperor Michael VIII Palaiologos (r. 1259–1282) – an out-of-season, punitive military expedition against his Balkan opponents that included Serbia too. The emperor, who had recaptured the capital Constantinople from the Latins in 1261, was famous for his quick and unexpected changes of tactics and plans, and feared for an amazing energy with which he reestablished Byzantine dominance over the rulers of southeastern Europe coupled with his embrace of unorthodox ways to achieve his goals. But a winter military campaign in the empire's deep Balkan hinterland was unusual even for Michael VIII. It would seem that the emperor's patience with his cousin, *sebastokrator* John I Angelos, the ruler of Thessaly (r. 1268–1289), was running thin. John I had assumed a role of the defender of Orthodoxy ever since Michael VIII signed the Union with the Roman Church and had accepted the primacy of the pope in all dogmatic matters in 1274 in Lyon. And in recent years, John I Angelos's actions had become more than a simple nuisance for Constantinople. Even though the grand coalition led by the king of Sicily, Charles of Anjou, with the Thessalian ruler as its key member among the Byzantines – whose primary goal was the reestablishment of the Latin Empire in Constantinople – was defeated by Michael VIII's sponsored coup against Charles in Sicily in March 1282, the Angelos's disruptive influence in the Balkans was a constant thorn in the emperor's side and a reminder that his dominance within the ramified ruling family is far from universally accepted. Freed from the hovering danger of an attack on Constantinople from the West, Michael VIII decided to put a swift end to the revolt of his cousin in Thessaly and to annex Angelos's domain to the core territory of the empire. Additionally, on the way to Thessaly, Michael VIII would have a chance to force the Serbian King Milutin back into obedience, since the latter was too welcoming toward a Byzantine aristocrat Kotanitzes Tornikios, the outcast and rebel against the Emperor. An offspring of the influential Macedonian aristocratic family and former close associate of Michael VIII's, Kotanitzes had led Serbian troops in plundering the Byzantine province of Eastern Macedonia in the previous years.

Excited about the prospect of finally finishing off his provocative cousin, Michael VIII did not want to waste time by waiting until the spring of the next year, 1283, and the usual beginning of campaigning season in the rough Balkan terrain. He wanted to begin the campaign as soon as possible on the wave of his great diplomatic success after thwarting Charles of Anjou's boisterous plans. Determined to reassert his authority over southeastern Europe, the Emperor had obtained the help of his son-in-law (through his illegitimate daughter), the Mongol Khan Nogai, leader of the Ulus of Jochi on the lower Danube, whose formidable troops had crossed the Danube in the fall of 1282 and were making their way to the south through Bulgaria without any significant resistance. Michael VIII himself exited Constantinople in November and planned to proceed toward Thessaly after meeting the allied Mongol troops. Unexpectedly, but somewhat ironically befitting his tumultuous career and life full of twists and turns, the emperor died in a village in Thrace called fittingly *Allage* (*Change*, for he had changed this earthly life for a spiritual one, as Byzantine authors of the time were quick to point out) on December 11, 1282, causing even with his death a political earthquake that heralded the beginning of a new era not only for the Byzantine

Empire but for the Constantinople-influenced world of southeastern Europe as well.

Emperor Michael VIII Palaiologos's sudden death reverberated throughout the entire region, which was already in turmoil after the swift sequence of changes that occurred in 1282. The year 1282 started with a highly anticipated eastern campaign of Charles of Anjou and his resolve to conquer Constantinople and oust the schismatic Emperor, and ended with a disappearance of both of them from the political scene, leaving many of their former clients scrambling for new alliances and in search of new patrons. At the beginning of the year, Bulgaria was firmly under control of the country's new Tsar George Terter (r. 1280–1292) and with Khan Nogai's influence contained on the northern shores of the Danube; but the year ended with Nogai directly dominating the land to the south of his territory by obtaining an absolute obeisance from the Bulgarian ruler. And last but not least, at the beginning of 1282 King Milutin was second in the hierarchy of a peculiar, three-headed ruling collegium in Serbia, deeply in the shadow of his older brother Dragutin and their mother, Queen Helen of Hungary. It ended with Milutin's leapfrogging his brother by becoming undisputed first king and rethinking his personal – and Serbia's, in general – absolute and multiple reliance on the Hungarian Kingdom. That reliance was evinced through his Hungarian mother, Queen Helen; Dragutin's Hungarian wife; and his own wife, Elizabeth, sister of his older brother's wife, Catherine.

* * *

If there was anything Milutin had become well aware of by that time, it must have been the consequential character of the significant political events, shakeups, and turnarounds – his entire life up to that point was in its essence a confirmation of the caustic nature of the politics in Serbia and southeastern Europe in the thirteenth century. He was born back in 1254, during the fifty-seven-year-long period of Latin rule over Constantinople and the former Byzantine territories that stretched from 1204 until 1261; he was born in the year the mighty emperor of the eastern Byzantine state of Nicaea, John III Vatatzes (r. 1222–1254), died, triggering a series of events that would lead to the rise of future Emperor Michael VIII Palaiologos with a direct influence on Milutin's life and the course the Serbian polity would take.

If the year 1254 turned out to be auspicious for the future of medieval Serbia, it certainly had not looked anything out of ordinary at the time, with Milutin as second son of the Serbian royal couple. His older brother Dragutin was designated early on as their father's heir and was married to the Hungarian princess Catherine soon after he reached maturity at the age of fifteen, strengthening the bond with the kingdom of Hungary. But an unlucky accident left Dragutin temporarily physically disabled soon after that marriage alliance. This accident coupled with growing political pressure from the ambitious Byzantine Emperor Michael VIII Palaiologos propelled young Milutin to the very center of the diplomatic power-play in the region just as he was coming of age, in the year 1269.[1] With all the attention suddenly turned on him, young Prince Milutin, portrayed together with his older brother

FIGURE 11.1 Prince-heir Dragutin and Prince Milutin, Sopoćani monastery, ca. 1265–66

just a couple of years earlier on the wall paintings of his father's foundation of the Sopoćani monastery with a typically "medieval" long hair and straight bangs, must have awaited the future events with some apprehension.

He grew up in a tight family circle with a dominant mother, Queen Helen of Hungary, whose family connections provided stability to his father's, King Uroš's, rule. These ties grew stronger just a couple of years earlier with Milutin's brother taking the same path as their father (a Hungarian dynastic marriage), the path that should have secured his inheritance of the royal crown of Serbia and continuous rule of their fatherland with an even stronger reliance on Serbia's northern Catholic neighbor. Instead, Milutin was now made to believe that his father's radical diplomatic turn toward the reestablished Byzantine Empire and its ambitious ruler would overturn the established order of things and make him – and not his brother Dragutin – the heir of the Serbian Kingdom, once he become the mighty emperor's son-in-law.

Milutin must have felt thunderstruck: marriage! At the age of fifteen! And with the daughter of the feared Michael VIII who spread his dominance in such a powerful manner that it seemed there could hardly be any limit to his rule over the vast region of southeastern Europe. After all, these were the lands that Constantinople traditionally dominated in the olden days before their empire fell to the Crusaders in 1204. But Anna, Milutin's future bride, was just a child, barely seven years old, and the actual wedding ceremony would therefore have to be postponed for five years, until the princess reached twelve, the legal marriage age for girls. But the deal was done, the alliance between the two rulers, corroborated by the betrothal of Prince Milutin – now his father's heir – and the princess Anna Palaiologina, and King Uroš's official recognition of the Emperor as in-law, friend, and ally repositioned Serbia as the empire's lesser but nevertheless worthy partner. Young Milutin looked at the world with new eyes. Now nothing was standing in his path to becoming king of Serbia with the all-important backing of the strongest ruler in the region, Emperor Michael VIII Palaiologos, a member of whose closest family circle he became even before formally marrying his daughter.

And then came the year 1274 and another – and as it would turn out not the last – political earthquake. Emperor Michael VIII signed the Union of Churches with Rome, accepting the primacy of the Pope and hoping to foil the attempts of the French Catholic prince Charles of Anjou to reestablish the Latin Empire. Emperor Michael VIII's coalitions crumbled, his relatives turned against him, and he scrambled to preserve his throne as well as his influence within the vast imperial family. That family included many foreign allies, especially in the region of southeastern Europe. He managed to impose personal dominance over the network of kinsmen through which the Byzantines controlled the empire's European hinterland by replacing the relatives of the Emperor John Vatatzes with his own kin. Similarly his own position as the leader of the ruling clan was now openly challenged by the lord of Thessaly, John I Angelos. The stage for the first act in the anti-Michael VIII movement was Serbia. The embattled emperor was no longer seen as the undisputed winner of the inner Byzantine struggle for prevalence within the ruling family. The Serbian King Uroš I was fast to accept John I Angelos's proposal for a close partnership between the two rulers, dissolving the engagement of Milutin and the Palaiologos's young daughter Anna, instead using his younger son to forge an alliance with a rising figure within Byzantium.

At twenty, Milutin was hurriedly married to John I Angelos's daughter (whose name is not known), playing the part of an unwitting political tool in his father's hands. Even if the provision for his inheritance of the royal crown of Serbia had remained intact in the new deal King Uroš struck with the Thessalian ruler in 1274, young Milutin learned a valuable, real-life lesson that would form the basic tenet of his political beliefs – the impact of the uncontrollable shifts in geopolitical balance on the larger scale could be best offset by allying oneself closely with the winning, most powerful party through a marriage union.

At twenty, Milutin had thus already been tagged as the emperor's – prospective – son-in-law, becoming soon thereafter the son-in-law of the emperor's cousin who seemed to be on the path of actually replacing Michael VIII on the imperial throne in Constantinople. But with John I Angelos's ambitious plans dispersing rapidly, and the reaction of Hungarian Catholic kings to Serbia's closeness to its new Byzantine ally growing stronger, King Uroš's days on the throne were numbered. In a synchronized coup by the brothers Dragutin and Milutin and their mother, Queen Helen of Hungary, in 1276, King Uroš was overthrown and sent into exile, with the new triumvirate taking the power in their hands. While both brothers claimed the royal title of king, the older Dragutin nominally became the first in the new hierarchy. Queen Helen received as her personal fief a significant portion of land in the hinterland of the predominantly Catholic southern Adriatic coast. With Queen Helen and Dragutin's wife, Queen Catherine, being of Hungarian descent, there was no space left for a political oddity that was Milutin's Thessalian wife, especially given the waning power and influence of her father on the course the political events in the region were taking.

At twenty-two, Milutin was consequently quickly divorced and even faster remarried: in a distinctly unimaginative move by the ruling triumvirate in Serbia, Milutin married Queen Catherine's sister Elizabeth, who had to be taken out of a nunnery and thrown back in the world of whirlwind diplomacy of thirteen-century southeastern Europe. The inauspicious circumstances of Milutin's fast-track wedding with Elizabeth left no consequences on their marriage – it would last much longer than his previous alliances, until 1284, and would give the Serbian prince his first offspring. In typically medieval fashion, in Byzantine sources these facts were translated to Milutin's passion for his Hungarian bride. That slanted view betrays the resentment of the Byzantine authors toward the close ties young King Milutin established with Hungary at the time. Later he would be included in the Byzantine world which involved his eventual absolute union with the Empire along with his fourth and fifth, and final, marriage.

* * *

In the months following the death of Emperor Michael VIII on December 11, 1282, faced with an intensive political reshuffling in the region, Milutin seized an opportunity to obtain, cautiously but unequivocally, political autonomy within the ruling trio of Serbia. This autonomy would help him eventually to prevail over his mother and his brother Dragutin, whose son was still officially considered the heir of the entire Serbian state. It took Milutin almost two decades and two more marriages to obtain his ultimate goal – the sole dominance over the kingdom of Serbia and a firm alliance with a Byzantine emperor. He showed his political prowess and almost Machiavellian vision by correctly recognizing that the only way to obtain his goals was by broadening his coalition beyond the borders of Serbia. The best way to secure new alliances was by marrying into the family of the currently most dominant political figure in the region. Milutin was not prepared to allow his political destiny to rest on the marriage alliances that he brokered for his children, although there were a few of those too. Instead, he insisted on personally being the protagonist of the major political marriages that he negotiated, painfully remembering the setback his ambitions took after the dissolution of the engagement with Emperor Michael VIII's daughter in 1274.

King Milutin jumped at the opportunity to benefit from the power vacuum in the region during 1283, establishing his newly acquired authority in the southern parts of Serbia with force, but it was the year 1284 that proved decisive for the king's future. In 1283 and the first half of 1284, Milutin and his older brother Dragutin were still working in unison. During that time they led military campaigns together, both in the south, penetrating deeply into Byzantine territory, and in the north, where they followed the Hungarian king in the punitive action against his two disloyal commanders of border fortresses on the Danube. However, the prevailing power of the Mongol Khan Nogai forced the brothers either to recognize his dominance by the summer of that year – as Milutin did – or to reinstate their vassalage to the king of Hungary. Dragutin's choice of the latter option thus strengthened his position in the Hungarian royal family and gave him the Belgrade fortress in lifelong personal possession in return. Milutin, on the other hand, was forced to cut his ties with the Hungarian king, expediently divorce his Hungarian bride, Elizabeth, and marry Anna, the daughter of Bulgarian Tsar George Terter, a client of Khan Nogai.

Anna Terter, the daughter of the new Bulgarian tsar who took the throne in 1280 but gained prominence in 1283 after accepting the supremacy of Khan Nogai in the wake of the death of their common patron Emperor Michael VIII, thus became King Milutin's third wife in the summer of 1284. She was the first one he had chosen autonomously, not in concert with his brother, the queen mother, or following decisions made for him by his late father, King Uroš. It was a significant and symbolic political action of the Serbian king. It also represented a step toward his total disassociation from the common family rule that he shared with his older brother Dragutin and their mother from 1276 and the toppling of King Uroš. It was also an announcement of the much bigger ambitions of the now thirty-year-old King Milutin, as well as a clear sign of his aspiration to spread his power and influence to the neighboring Bulgaria and the Byzantine lands that flanked his domains from the south.

Emperor Andronikos II Palaiologos (r. 1282–1328) had his hands tied with many challenges as he struggled to establish his personal authority within the empire. As a result, the Byzantine periphery was left fairly unprotected and Constantinople's influence in Bulgaria waned significantly. The path to the south was therefore open for Milutin. At the time, however, the king evidently judged that his main area of political interest lay to the east, in his wife's country. Nonetheless the lack of a clear border with Byzantium opened the way for plunder and the unobstructed spread of Serbian influence to the south. He went on to spend over a decade trying to build his influence in Bulgaria, creating a pro-Serbian faction around his father-in-law, George Terter. With the latter's death in 1293, King Milutin saw a chance to gain the upper hand in the neighboring land, backing first his brother-in-law, and later his son, as his proxies in the internal struggle for the prevalence within the Bulgarian ramified ruling family with the imperial crown of Bulgaria as the ultimate goal.

But Milutin overestimated his strength. He was no match for Nogai, once the Mongolian khan decided to force his will on Bulgaria, and by 1296 the Serbian king had to accept once again his supremacy by sending his son Stephen as a hostage to Nogai. It must have seemed at that time to the already forty-two-year-old Milutin that he was destined to spend his life being just another among the local rulers forced into submission to whomever the most powerful leader of the day was. He had to sacrifice the political future of his oldest son Stephen to appease the Mongol khan and send him to Nogai as a hostage. His other son, Constantine – born out of the marriage with Anna Terter, while Stephen was the son of Milutin's second wife, the Hungarian princess Elizabeth – could not have been more than ten years old at the time. Both of Milutin's sons were, however, facing uncertain futures, since the arrangement between their father and their uncle Dragutin unequivocally affirmed the latter's son Vladislav as the official heir of the entire united Serbian kingdom. All Milutin's attempts at overturning that specific provision of his agreement with his brother and their mother by positioning himself as capable to assert his power beyond the borders of his domain through alliances with a wider circle of powerful rulers seemed to have hit the wall. His power was far from comparable with the might of Khan Nogai, and the paths for spreading his influence seemed to be blocked on all sides, except toward the south, toward the farthest northwestern territories of the Byzantine Empire controlled by Constantinople. With nothing to offer to Emperor Andronikos II Palaiologos, Milutin also lacked the strength to dare to challenge openly Byzantine authority in this region, the empire's distant Balkan hinterland. As he was sending off his son Stephen to Khan Nogai in 1296, King Milutin must have realized that he was cornered and that the south was the only direction he could look toward for political survival. But even though – in hindsight – his turn to the south was a forced move, he still needed a near miracle to succeed in his by far most ambitious plan – that is, to become a relative of the Byzantine Emperor and to acquire the status promised to him back in 1270 when he was just fifteen years old.

The long hoped for reprieve, astonishingly, came before the end of that year. Kotanitzes Tornikios, the perennial Byzantine rebel, local magnate, and aristocrat, found sanctuary at Milutin's court yet again in 1296. His ambition and influence in Byzantine Macedonia forced in a way the Serbian king's military incursions in that region, after a dozen years of peace. It also finally gave solid political bases to Milutin's seemingly illusory plans for a close alliance with the Byzantine Empire and the coveted marriage alliance with the emperor in Constantinople.

After two seasons of inconsequential skirmishes, both Emperor Andronikos II Palaiologos – following the advice of his cousin and practically the semi-autonomous lord of Byzantine Macedonia, Michael Tarchaniotes Glabas – and King Milutin were ready to conclude a mutually beneficial alliance. That alliance would ensure stability in southeastern Europe by preserving overall Byzantine ideological dominance while strengthening the Serbian king's personal rule in what were traditionally his family's domains, controlled at the time by his brother and their mother. Both the emperor and the king had little to nothing to lose. Andronikos II could use the alliance with, and the nominal submission of, the Serbian king to restate his disputed leadership within the imperial family and position himself as the arbiter in all regional political disputes, more successful than even his late father, the mighty and feared Michael VIII. Milutin, on the other hand, with the emperor's support, could bolster his ambition for prevalence over his older brother and, consequentially, overturn the provision of their agreement according to which the heir of his dominion too, would be Dragutin's oldest son, Vladislav. Sacrificing Kotanitzes

Tornikios was an easy decision for the Serbian king. Emperor Andronikos II's sister Eudokia, a recent widow of the Trebizond Emperor John II "Grand" Komnenos, was designated as Milutin's future bride. The problematic fact that the planned marriage would be the Serbian king's fourth marriage, not allowed under any circumstance in Byzantine legal practice, was solved with a sophism that Milutin's first marriage with the Thessalian princess was never officially dissolved, and therefore his subsequent second and third marriages were practically non-existent. But then, in a surprising turn of events, the emperor's sister refused to marry the forty-five-year-old Serbian king, and Andronikos II was left with his five-year-old daughter Simonis as the only choice for Milutin's bride and the future Serbian queen.

Marrying the ruling emperor's underage daughter carried a much greater weight than taking his widowed sister as a bride, and there could have been no doubt among both sides that certain provisions of the deal needed to be renegotiated to mirror the new political reality of the alliance in the making. And while Emperor Andronikos II was faced with the strong resistance of the patriarch of Constantinople, John Kosmas, he was adamant to raise the stakes and to ask for a total submission of the Serbian king after the planned marriage. He also asked for the confirmation of the future alliance by Milutin's influential mother, Queen Helen, whose personal presence at the ceremony in late April in Thessaloniki the Serbian king managed to avoid. But that was the only compromise the Byzantine Emperor had to make. "For the sake of becoming the emperor's son-in-law, the Serbian king was ready to accept everything," stated, essentially correctly, the main Byzantine negotiator, the learned Theodore Methochites.

The alliance between Emperor Andronikos II Palaiologos and Serbian King Milutin in the spring of 1299 changed the course of the history of southeastern Europe, marking the beginning of a new and, it would turn out, latest phase in the tumultuous history of this region in the Middle Ages. The balance of power established at the end of the thirteenth century in the Balkans, with the ideological prevalence of Byzantine political Orthodoxy and the reality of the political rise of – toward the empire, the always friendly – Serbian state, replaced the long-lasting Byzantine-Bulgarian polarity and rivalry. That balance of power would be disturbed only with the fall of southeastern Europe under Ottoman rule, deep in the fifteenth century. The importance of the deal for both sides was evident from the determination of both the emperor and the king to overcome all the obstacles on the way to reaching alliance, from Milutin's acceptance to send his third wife, Anna Terter, and many Serbian noblemen together with Kotanitzes Tornikios to the emperor as "hostages" to Andronikos II's and the Byzantine church hierarchy's bowing to the king's insistence on marrying the five-year-old princess immediately, despite the transgression of the canon laws that prescript unequivocally twelve years as the earliest legal age for girls to enter into marriage. In this last instance, it is obvious that Milutin painfully remembered the missed opportunity from three decades earlier when his engagement to Michael VIII's underage daughter was easily canceled, ruining his hopes of becoming the emperor's son-in-law and the heir of the Serbian throne. The political trade, in which Milutin received the territory in northern Macedonia, including his future capital Skopje, as a dowry of Princess Simonis in exchange for accepting the absolute ideological supremacy of the Byzantine emperor, served just as an additional confirmation of the unusual but highly pragmatic political honesty of both sides. They embraced wholeheartedly the opportunity to strengthen each other within a new political union, into which – as Byzantine official documents point emphatically – the Serbian king willingly entered as the emperor's lesser partner.

* * *

The twenty-two years that elapsed between Milutin's marriage with Simonis and the king's death on November 21, 1321, could be best described as frantic, both regarding his building activities and his struggles to find a suitable heir to the now enlarged and, after some time, mostly unified kingdom of Serbia. Even though he had been on the throne as king of Serbia for almost two decades, ruling his own domain autonomously while wielding nominal authority over his brother Dragutin's lands to the north, it was only after he became the Byzantine emperor's son-in-law that Milutin started acting with the authority of an autonomous and complete ruler in his own right. One of the clearest signs of his changed status and self-perception but also his now much greater aspirations was Milutin's highly propagandized taking up of the role of New Solomon, the great church builder, that saw him found or rebuild dozens of churches and monasteries in the southern part of his polity in merely two decades. It was an amazing statement and a sharp contrast to his previous behavior and inactiveness in this regard. It was a statement of the political awareness and understanding of the unique importance of the status of the emperor's son-in-law by the experienced and crafty political actor who had patiently waited all his adult life for such an opportunity. By accepting the union with the emperor, Milutin had not only become a member of the imperial family, but was also given the right of participating in the unbroken imperial tradition – a circumstance he proudly underscored in many edicts that accompanied the restoration of churches across formally Byzantine Macedonia. The king's message that his new status marked the new beginning for the Serbian polity and the dynasty of the Nemanjić could not have been clearer. From the demolition and then complete renovation of the cathedral church of the Hilandar monastery on Mount Athos and the oversized but harmonious architectural masterpiece of the Church of Virgin Mary at Gračanica to his unfinished marble-covered mausoleum of St. Stephen in Banjska, all his foundations betrayed the splendor and immense riches of his new, exalted position.

But Milutin's frantic church building in the years 1299–1321 was overshadowed by the problem that was threatening to endanger all his political plans and endeavors – the lack of an adequate heir for his new kingdom. By entering the union with Byzantium, it was clear to all sides that Milutin's successor should be his and Simonis's son, but given her age it was also evident that the issue would not be resolved swiftly. While Milutin sent his oldest son, Stephen, to Constantinople as Emperor Andronikos II's "guest" after he rebelled in 1313/14 and kept his second son, Constantine, out of the political loop, by 1314 it became evident that the odd royal couple had a serious problem – Simonis could not become pregnant. The king even built a peculiar votive church in those years in the Studenica complex dedicated to Sts. Joachim and Ann, the Virgin Mary's parents, but to no avail. This last-ditch effort to cure Simonis's sterility only marked the beginning of the next, chaotic phase of Milutin's search for an heir, in which he was accompanied by his mother-in-law, Simonis's mother, Empress Irene-Yolanda of Montferrat. During the years 1314 through 1316, Simonis's older brothers, *despotes* Theodore and Demetrios, came to Serbia as potential heirs to their brother-in-law's throne. The sudden death of their mother, Empress Irene-Yolanda, in 1316, however, put an abrupt end to these plans that seemed to be gaining ground in Milutin's mind. Emperor Andronikos II Palaiologos had for his part no intention of pursuing the ideas of his estranged and stubborn wife who moved from Constantinople to Thessaloniki in 1308 in an unprecedented political act that highlighted her displeasure with Andronikos II's refusal to grant their sons personal dominions within the traditionally strongly unitary empire. By choosing Thessaloniki, the city, according to a half-legend, granted as a fief to the Montferrat counts by Emperor Manuel Komnenos in the late 1170s, Irene-Yolanda chose to be closer to Milutin, her main political ally in attempts to place one of her sons on a throne in southeastern Europe. These attempts additionally brought the Serbian king into the internal, highly personalized policies of the Byzantine Empire.

FIGURE 11.2 King Milutin and Queen Simonis, Church of Sts. Joachim and Ann, the Studenica monastery complex, 1314

Milutin – and medieval Serbia – stayed within the Byzantine orbit until the end of the Middle Ages, after his defining move toward political union with the Empire in the closing year of the thirteenth century. Obsessed with the problem of his heir and, related to it, of his entire legacy, Milutin seemed to have picked his son with Anna Terter, Constantine, as his successor during the last couple of years of his life. But in the end, his oldest son, Stephen, supported by Emperor Andronikos II, won the war for Milutin's legacy, quickly embraced and enhanced his father's policy of union with the Byzantine emperor by marrying Andronikos II's niece, and emphasized his own legitimacy by proclaiming Milutin a saint, a mere two years after the latter's death. As the famed *Holy King*, Milutin would be celebrated by his descendants, taken as a political role-model by his grandson King, and later Tsar, Stephen Dušan, and venerated far beyond the borders of medieval Serbia – and particularly in Bulgaria – until modern times.

Note

1 Both Milutin's biographer, Archbishop Danilo II, and Byzantine historian George Pachymeres report Dragutin's incident. However, while Danilo II presents it as the main reason behind Milutin's assuming the position of power within the ruling family in Serbia in 1282, Pachymeres stresses that Dragutin's injury forced him to lead a life of leisure in 1269, at the time when the emperor Michael VIII negotiated the engagement between his daughter Anna and young prince Milutin (Danilo II, p. 25–7; Pachymeres II, p. 453–7).

Further reading

Actes de Chilandar I. Des origins à 1319. Edited by Mirjana Živojinović, Vassiliki Kravari, and Christophe Giros. Paris: Editiones du CNRS: P. Lethielleux, 1998.

Daničić, Dj., ed. *Životi kraljeva i arhiepiskopa srpskih, napisao arhiepiskop Danilo i drugi.* Zagreb, 1866 (reprint with Introduction by Dj. Trifunović, London: Variorum reprints, 1972).

Georges Pachymérès Relations historiques I-IV (V Indices). Edited by A. Failler [CFHB 24/1–5]. Paris, vol. 1–2, 1984; vol. 3–4 1999; vol. 5, 2000.

Mavromatis, Leonidas. *La fondation de l'Empire serbe. Le kralj Milutin.* Thessalonica: Kentron Vyzanrinōn Ereunōn, 1978.

Nicephori Gregorae Byzantina historia I-III. Edited by Ludwig Schopen (vols. 1–2), and Immanuel Bekker (vol. 3). Bonn: Weber, 1829, 1830, 1855.

Stanković, Vlada. "The Character and Nature of Byzantine Influence in Serbia: Policy – Reality – Ideology (11th–End of the 13th Century)." In Mabi Angar and Claudia Sode, eds. *Serbia and Byzantium: Proceedings of the International Conference Held on 15 December 2008 at the University of Cologne.* Frankurt am Main: PL Academic Research, 2013, pp. 75–93.

Stanković, Vlada. "Rethinking the Position of Serbia within Byzantine *Oikoumene* in the Thirteenth Century." In Vlada Stanković, ed., *The Balkans and Byzantine World before and after the Captures of Constantinople, 1204 and 1453.* Latham-Boulder-New York-London: Lexington Books, 2016, pp. 91–102.

PART 4

Central Europe

12

HENRY ZDÍK, BISHOP OF OLOMOUC AND PREMONSTRATENSIAN

Lisa Wolverton

In the eleventh and twelfth centuries the Czech Lands (today's Czech Republic) consisted of two territories, Bohemia and Moravia, ruled by a single duke from a dynasty known as the Přemyslids. He governed Bohemia directly while delegating power in Moravia to three subordinate dukes, invariably his relatives, whose territories were centered on Olomouc in the north, Brno in the south, and Znojmo, further south, on the border with the Bavarian Ostmark (i.e., Austria). Bohemia and Moravia each comprised a Catholic diocese, centered at Prague and Olomouc respectively. The bishopric of Prague was founded circa 973, whereas the see of Olomouc was only established (or re-established, perhaps) a century later, circa 1065. Both bishops were subject to the Archbishop of Mainz in Germany, and ultimately answered to the Pope in Rome.

Bishop Zdík of Olomouc, who was also called Henry (in place of or together with Zdík), governed the church of Moravia from 1126 to his death in 1150. Nothing is known of his origins or of his life before becoming bishop, except that he accompanied other Czechs on a pilgrimage to the Holy Land in 1123. He appears to have spent the first half of his reign organizing the canons associated with the cathedral, consolidating the financial assets of his see, and generally attending to the institutional foundations of religious life in Moravia. The preeminent ecclesiastical figure in the Czech Lands during the last decade of his life, he also was well known to a succession of popes in Rome and was frequently in attendance at the court of King Conrad III of Germany. Bishop Zdík influenced the introduction of many religious reform ideals current in Western Europe to the Czechs. Although when and under what circumstances remains uncertain, Zdík is known to have joined the Premonstratensians, an order of secular canons that originated among the followers of the charismatic preacher, Norbert of Xanten.

The imagined letter below, from a young canon at Prague cathedral to his uncle, a canon in Olomouc, both unnamed, paints a portrait of the bishop at a turning point in his life and career, in the winter of 1140, a crucial time also of political transition, as the enthronement of Duke Vladislav I after the death of his uncle, Soběslav I, ushered in the reign of a new generation of Přemyslids. It strives to capture the ways Bishop Henry Zdík himself began to move within a wider world, stretching from Rome to the Baltic, from the Rhineland to Jerusalem, and the various reactions his activities might have elicited from a local observer. The imaginary letter-writer, as a canon of Prague, was well positioned to see and hear much about both political and religious life among the Czechs at the highest levels, without himself having influence upon these events or access to privy information.

The text below is based upon five different chronicles of Czech provenance, which record the deeds of Bishop Henry Zdík in varying levels of detail and from different perspectives, as well as the few authentic letters and charters that survive.

* * *

To N., servant of St. Václav in Olomouc, from N., fellow-servant of St. Václav in Prague, greetings and benediction.

I must apologize, uncle, for I received your letter some time ago, requesting news of your bishop, Henry, who is also called Zdík. You reported having seen little of him in recent years, since he set out with the others for Jerusalem and then went on pilgrimage to Rome. Moreover, he tarries so often and so long in Prague, and has spent so few days in his own diocese of Moravia that you and your brethren have despaired of his intentions and his fate. Yet I had hesitated to write when I knew nothing certain. I have decided finally to take up the pen and tell you plainly what people here say, so that you might weigh the significance yourself.

For of course, as you have surely heard, Duke Soběslav went the way of all flesh just two weeks ago, and his nephew Vladislav, the son of Duke Vladislav, Soběslav's predecessor, has been placed upon the stone throne in Prague. Anxiety prevailed here for several weeks when it became clear that the elderly duke was suffering the illness that would be his last. As he lingered in Prague castle, the leading men of the realm assembled across the river at Vyšehrad; while some preferred the safety of silence, others avidly debated the question of succession. Rumors flew, and at first it seemed there was little agreement, until finally everyone pledged to support whomever *Comes* Načerat favored. Thus Duke Vladislav assumed the throne on the third day after his uncle's death, and Soběslav's own son, also named Vladislav, was passed over. They say all the nobles present gave their consent. But some now fear the weight of Načerat's influence, and say that if he expects to hold sway over the new duke and finds himself thwarted, then resentment will fester and bring trouble all too soon. It may even come to war: then it would be "a war worse than civil" (as we read so often in old Cosmas's history).

Meanwhile Abbot Sylvester of Sázava, a close companion of your bishop (not least on his latest pilgrimage to the Holy Land) almost immediately renounced his election to succeed John, bishop of Prague, who migrated from this light last August. Since Sylvester was chosen by Duke Soběslav months ago and only declared himself unfit for the burdens of episcopal office after Vladislav was made duke, there are those who say he was ousted to make way for the new ruler's favorite. But I have heard from his own mouth the words of the Apostle: "No one serving in the army of God gets entangled in worldly affairs." As yet we are not certain who will lead our church, my brethren murmur and make plans, as if the election were in their hands. But the custom with us is the same as with you: it hangs on the duke.

But you asked not of public affairs or of our see, but instead about your own bishop – who, it must seem, has in recent years renounced the burdens of office while retaining fully its name and privileges.

I assume you have heard already that he returned from Jerusalem much changed. He went to pray and seek remission for his sins – but of course all pilgrims to the Holy Land say as much, though only the Lord on high knows their hearts. Those in his party who returned home described the journey as long and grueling, more so than usual. (As you well know, many have made this journey in recent years, including Henry Zdík himself on a previous occasion, before he was elected to the Moravian see.) Although they left early, right after Epiphany in the year of our lord 1137, they were delayed a long time at Constantinople, celebrating Easter in that great city. Then, on the voyage home, they endured terrible storms at sea. Thus, they were gone fully a year.

Ever since his return – so I am told by everyone – Bishop Zdik talks endlessly of the White Canons (as they are called from their dress) and the virtues of their life. It seems he encountered some of them while in the Holy Land, and heard how they strove to follow in the footsteps of the Apostles, not merely there, where they trod in ancient times, but here where we ourselves walk. And now the bishop speaks of a higher calling, of the contemplative life, of a move away from the worldliness required of bishops, and the importance of preaching to the people and teaching them by example. Many worry that he means to abandon the episcopacy altogether. All, it seems, have been pleading against this – even the dukes, both the old and the new. They lay before him Norbert's own example: for after many years of proclaiming the reform of the clergy and inspiring followers among the laity (including a great many women, which some consider a scandal) – eventually settled into monasteries and organized into the order people nowadays call "Premonstratensian" (after the first house at Premontré) – Norbert accepted appointment as archbishop of Magdeburg with all its responsibilities, spending much time at King Lothar's court and even involving himself in the dissension (fortunately resolved) around Pope Innocent.

For now, Bishop Henry's energies have been directed at the establishment of a house of these White Canons in Prague, atop Strahov hill. It will be named "Mt. Zion," the bishop has announced, as a symbol of the spiritual renewal it represents. Others say he chose that location, between the castle and Petřín hill (where executions customarily take place), to soften the impression of violence looming over the city below. The new duke, it seems, will support and endow the place, encouraged perhaps by Duchess Gertrude; they say she has experience of these zealous new canons and their good works back home in Swabia. The plans for this "Mt. Zion" are quite grand – even if, at the outset, there will only be simple buildings of wood. Bishop Zdík never lets go by an encounter with clergy – anyone, of any rank, from anywhere – without pressing them to join the community. They say he has also arranged for some Premonstratensian house in the Rhineland to send more monks and an abbot. All this, as I hear it, is set to occur very soon. And your bishop talks very freely of being buried there when his own time comes.

Moreover, he has enthusiastically suggested doing something similar at Olomouc, perhaps by installing White Canons at Hradiště and moving the Black Monks there who knows where else. They say Norbert did this too, at Magdeburg: with little hope that the cathedral chapter could be reformed in the radical manner he desired, the archbishop took over another church close by and installed his followers there. A priest from Magdeburg, who was our guest here several years ago, said the late archbishop pressed for all sorts of reforms that the clergy and people of Magdeburg found excessive. Your bishop too speaks this way, but so far his ideas have been moderated by others.

And meanwhile, what he talks most about is (and this seems frankly quite rash): preaching the Christian faith to the Prussians! I have not heard that Archbishop Norbert ever preached to the Slavic peoples beyond Magdeburg and the Elbe, or urged the White Canons to do so (though he boldly claimed their lands for his diocese!). So I think your bishop must be moved by the example of the blessed Otto, bishop of Bamberg, who migrated to the Lord only last year. Already many are saying that he has merited a heavenly reward, and has become a powerful intercessor to those in need of divine aid. Still, it must be said that the Prussians are a very different people from the Pomeranians, whom with God's help Otto brought under the gentle yoke of Christ. The Prussians are more obdurate in their paganism, more wary of outsiders and hostile to Christian clergy. Indeed they are not Slavs, as we are, so how will Bishop Henry communicate the Gospel's message? He speaks German surely, and knows a smattering of useful words in other tongues, but the Prussians speak a language neither Slavic, Germanic, nor akin to any other outside their own region (to the far north of the Poles, along the sea). Many grumble that it will come to nothing – that it is both a waste of effort and, furthermore, rife with danger. For as all know, Saint Adalbert himself met martyrdom in preaching to the Prussians 150 years ago. Few think them changed since then. All the more reason, the bishop claims, that further efforts should be made to bring them to Christ. He seems, against all arguments, determined to go.

Although certainly all this is commendable to God, it remains difficult to comprehend the bishop's zeal for endeavors that take him away from his diocese. You have written me of his extensive reform and reorganization of the Moravian church: how he built a new cathedral, dedicated to our patron, Saint Václav; how he established a collegiate church there and secured its endowment (even purchasing properties himself and granting them to the chapter); and how he diligently investigated all the see's estates, whether in the southern border regions (that is, Přerov, Břeclav, and Znojmo), attached to the new episcopal residence in Kroměříž, or set aside for his own or the canons' use. That was years ago now: I remember you wrote to me that Duke Soběslav, his wife, and many of our nobles were present at the dedication of the church of Saint Václav on June 30 in the year of our Lord's incarnation 1131, and that Bishop Henry subsequently issued charters in his own name listing the church's holdings and formally establishing the canons, twelve in number, as a community. Your brethren were moved from St. Peter's to St. Vaclav's, as you wrote me, with permission of Pope Innocent.

I still have your letter from that time, and others sent afterward. In them, you always extolled the virtues of your bishop – especially by comparison with that schemer Meinhard, who governed the church here in the early years of Duke Soběslav's rule. You praised Bishop Henry Zdík as an example of the kind of native clergy that might prevail here, for the good of both our land and Christ's faithful. And you reminded me that sometimes practical matters – of estates and endowments, of rights and laws – can go far in safeguarding the Lord's flock.

Seeing him in Prague recently and listening to his words: there is still no question he is a man of astonishing energy, all to the credit of God. But surely, by those same arguments, it is detrimental to the faithful in Moravia to be deprived of their bishop's protection and guidance. Not infidels but enemies nonetheless lurk around every corner there, as everywhere. A flock without its shepherd is vulnerable to injury.

Thus I must tell you: Bishop Henry has been diligently working here to arrange the return of young Otto from Rus', where he fled after his father's defeat at Chlumec. What a victory that was for Duke Soběslav and the Czechs, vanquishing King Lothar's army in the mountain snows of February! Oh, but exile from one's homeland is a bitter experience, as the young duke himself knows well – and Otto, the third of that name, has spent already fourteen years far away. Your bishop urges pity, and reminds everyone that the son ought not to be blamed for his father's misdeeds, especially now that Duke Soběslav no longer walks among us. But many argue against it, believing that Otto will join with his cousins, Vratislav and Conrad (who is said by many to be a man both aggrieved and implacable). Once Otto is invested with Olomouc in the north, if swayed to join with Vratislav and Conrad in the south, all of Moravia could be moved against Vladislav at the slightest instigation. The bishop insists that Otto seeks only to return home and live in peace. And he is determined himself to be a "minister of peace and concord," as was said of Archbishop Norbert (or as he said of himself). Bishop Henry openly alleges that Otto is quite tractable and thus will remain loyal with the right guidance, which he himself promises to provide. This view may yet win over the duke, but at present he postpones any action (I think, wisely).

I have real foreboding (and I am not alone in this): if Otto returns to give strength to Conrad's schemes, and Načerat turns against the ruler he chose, should the two ever combine forces in opposition to our new duke, the result would be a conflagration of the like unseen in decades. Duke Vladislav shows all signs of being most capable of rule; he is surrounded by many men of his own age, both loyal and ready to reap the rewards of loyalty; and his own brothers, Theobald and Henry, are expected to be steadfast. But precisely when two strong forces clash the din is loudest. Should it come to war – may God avert it! – this might provoke King Conrad to enter our land in aid of either party (most likely the duke's, since the duchess is his sister; but the German kings are said to be fickle and often swayed more by money or its promise than any other argument). Many on both sides would decry the loss of our native rule then.

Dearest uncle, I fear the times hang in the balance. Your bishop, burning with love of God, promises to work diligently in support of Duke Vladislav and of the general peace in our homeland. But how can he help us here when he is always abroad doing (so he asserts) Christ's work? Perhaps you can enlighten me, if your church has thrived in these years without him. Otherwise I regret to have dampened your spirits rather than raising them, as a devoted relative ought.

Sent in the year of our Lord's incarnation 1140, on the second day before the kalends of March. I beg you remember me in your prayers, and I shall you in mine. Amen.

Suggestions for further reading

Antry, Theodore and Carol Neel, eds., *Norbert and Early Norbertine Spirituality*. Mahwah, NJ: Paulist Press, 2007.

Christiansen, Eric. *The Northern Crusades*. London: Penguin, 1980.

Constable, Giles. *The Reformation of the Twelfth Century*. Cambridge: Cambridge University Press, 1996.

Wolverton, Lisa. *Hastening Toward Prague: Power and Society in the Medieval Czech Lands*. Philadelphia: University of Pennsylvania Press, 2001.

13

KING BÉLA IV OF HUNGARY

A monarch in a period of crisis and recovery

Balázs Nagy

It is difficult to draw a personal portrait of a medieval ruler because both the original sources and the later historiography typically focus on the events of public history. The details of private lives usually remain hidden. Modern historical research can sketch a profile of a medieval personality based on surviving sources, which usually reflect the political figure more than the whole complex personality.

In his youth Béla IV had strong ambitions and a distinct concept of how to govern the country that he had inherited from his ancestors, the Árpád dynasty. The course of history, however, confronted him with a very different challenge than he expected. He was the ruler who attempted to resist the onslaught of the Mongols in 1241–1242. This was almost a complete disaster; in one decisive battle he lost the main forces of his country, lost almost all the important members of his administration, and the allies he could rely on. He himself was forced to flee and find refuge in Dalmatia. After the retreat of the Mongols, when Béla returned to the country, he found it destroyed and desolate. Béla's real profile as an able monarch revealed itself in this situation. He was ready to change the main elements of his earlier policy and accommodate himself to the new situation. He made every possible provision to prevent a reported new Mongol campaign against Hungary and to prepare his country in the case of a new attack. In Hungarian historiography and historical memory Béla is usually referred to as the second founder of the country. It is not the task of this essay to decide if that claim is true or not, but Béla certainly was a true-born politician of exceptional abilities. He contributed significantly to the modernization of his country in the second half of the thirteenth century. The following portrait takes the form of an interview with a professor of history about King Béla IV and the significance of his reign.

* * *

What was Hungary like at the time of King Béla IV?

The territory of thirteenth-century Hungary in many respects was very different from its modern counterpart. It was approximately 310,000 km², roughly the same size as modern Poland, but only two-thirds of it was inhabited. It included modern Slovakia, Transylvania, some parts of modern Austria, Ukraine, Serbia, and modern Croatia (incorporating medieval Slavonia, Croatia, and Dalmatia).

Who were the Árpáds?

The Árpáds were the ruling dynasty of the Christianized country from as early as the turn of the tenth century; besides its canonized saintly rulers like kings St. Stephen and St. Ladislaus, the memory of the family went as far back as mythical non-Christian ancestry. Árpád-period Hungary was one of the largest centralized monarchies of Europe; its kings were significant rulers on the European level, with close contacts to both the Holy Roman Empire and Byzantium. The fall of Byzantium in 1204 and the rise of the Second Bulgarian Empire and the Latin Empire in the East contributed to the restructuring of southeast Europe's political map and strengthened the Western orientation of Hungarian politics. The Árpáds' power came down from the tenth century to the thirteenth century in the male line of succession; Béla IV's grandfather (Béla III) and father (Andrew II) were among the prominent rulers of Hungary in the late twelfth and early thirteenth century.

What was life like for the young Béla?

Béla IV was born in 1206 from the first marriage of his father. His mother, Gertrud, came from the dynasty of the Margraves of Andechs-Meran. Béla's childhood was marked by a fatal attack on his mother in 1213. His father, Andrew II, favored his wife's relatives, who formed a German lobby at the Hungarian royal court. When Andrew II left the country for a military campaign against Galicia, the anti-German party of the court murdered the queen in the Pilis Mountains. This assassination, which was supposedly conceived by Bán Bánk and co-conspirators, had a great impact not only on the life of Béla IV, but also on the Hungarian historical memory.[1]

Béla was crowned king of Hungary during the reign of his father in 1214, but that gesture really expressed only his position as heir to the throne. In 1217, Béla's father, Andrew II, decided to join a crusade and traveled to the Holy Land in a rather short and basically unsuccessful military campaign. Thirteenth-century Hungary, due to its large territory, was difficult to administer from the royal court. Some regions of the kingdom, for example, Slavonia and Transylvania, usually had local governments. These regional administrations provided excellent opportunities for their heads to build up alternative political centers. In 1220, Béla and his political party managed to press his father, King Andrew II, to acknowledge the power of the young duke over Slavonia, a huge territory incorporating the whole region from the Drava River to the Adriatic Sea. In this area, Duke Béla ruled basically as a sovereign ruler. In the same year Béla married Maria Laskarina, the daughter of the emperor of Nicaea, Theodore I Laskaris. The political tension between father and son intensified in the early 1220s, when Andrew tried to have the pope dissolve his son's new marriage, and finally forced his son to leave the country for a short while. When, after the mediation of the pope, the family conflict calmed down and Béla returned to the country, his father assigned him to govern Transylvania instead of Slavonia.

What was the cause of the political differences between Béla and his father, Andrew II?

The main political difference between Andrew II and Béla, father and son, in the 1220s and 1230s arose around the donation policy of Andrew II. Royal power in eleventh- and twelfth-century Hungary was based on extensive royal domains. Andrew initiated a new policy (*novae institutiones*, new dispositions) in this respect and donated extended estates to his followers. Making donations for royal service had been usual under earlier rulers, but Andrew continued this policy on a much greater scale. Béla opposed this process as heir to the throne and even later, after his succession.

How did Béla become king?

King Andrew II died in 1235 and Béla, his oldest son, succeeded him on the throne with no dispute. When Béla inherited the crown of the country he was twenty-nine years old, was already married, and had three daughters. He might have rightly expected to have a good chance to carry out his political agenda. This was basically the antithesis of his father's endeavors. He dismissed his father's court members from the royal service, even imprisoned some of them. His main concept was to strengthen the royal power and to regain the royal estates alienated during his father's reign. These steps, unsurprisingly, caused growing discontent among the groups of nobility who had been favored by Andrew II. As a reason for enmity between King Béla and the people, Master Roger noted that: "In order to repress the bold temerity of the barons, he commanded that if any of the barons – except his princes, archbishops and bishops – should dare to sit in his presence, he would be punished by due penalty. At the same time, he had the chairs of the barons burned, insofar as he could find them."[2] He also ordered that if someone applied to the royal court he should submit written petitions to the royal judge. All of his institutions aimed to return to a model of royal power that was already archaic at the time, and had been typical for the reign of his grandfather, Béla III.

What were relations like between Béla and his subjects?

There were additional issues that contributed to the tension between the ruler and his country. In 1223, the Mongols defeated the Rusians and Cumans at the Battle of the Kalka River, and thereafter the pagan Cumans moved west and soon arrived close to the eastern borders of Hungary. Two of their chiefs were ready to accept Christianity in 1227 and a special missionary bishopric was organized by the arch-bishop of Esztergom for the conversion of the Cumans. Prince Küten and the Cumans asked for admission and custody from the king of Hungary in 1239 and Béla hoped to increase his army by admitting Cumans who accepted Christianity. Moving the Cumans to Hungary, however, provoked the annoyance of Béla's own people. The Cumans, who resided in the Great Hungarian Plain, followed their own nomadic customs, disregarding the different rules of the native population.

Master Roger reported several cases of outrage between the Cumans and Hungarians. According to Roger, King Béla favored the Cumans over his own people when complaints arrived at the royal court.

How did Béla prepare for the Mongol invasion?

Besides the arrival of the Cumans, other news also confirmed that the Mongols were approaching Hungary. In 1235 and 1237, the Dominican Friar Julian traveled to the east to find the groups of Hungarians living there, but he returned with the news that the Mongols were advancing into Russian territories. In 1240, Kiev fell to the Mongols, which gave them an open route for an attack on Hungary.

In 1241 and 1242, Béla IV certainly confronted the most difficult task of his reign, the Mongol conquest of Hungary. The attack itself and the subsequent events were foreseeable. Orda and Baidar led the Mongol army, which seized Little Poland and Silesia and then defeated Henry of Lower Silesia at Legnica on April 9, 1241. The Mongols' main force crossed into Hungary at the Verecke Pass, the so-called *Porta Rusciae*, in mid-March of 1241. Not much later, another division of the Mongols also entered Hungary by crossing its Transylvanian frontiers. King Béla sent a military unit to the northeast border region of the country under the leadership of Count Palatine Denis against the invading Mongols, but these troops were easily split up by the enemy.

Why did Béla lose the battle against the Mongols?

In these weeks King Béla must have been confronted by two challenges. Prince Küten, the leader of the Cumans, had been massacred by a mob close to Pest, since he was believed to be an ally of the Mongols. Many people blamed the king for the pressing situation and were reluctant to help to defend the country. After crossing the border of Hungary, some detachments of the Mongols arrived in the central region of the country as early as March 1241. Béla finally set out from his camp against the Mongols at the end of March. The main battle between the army of King Béla and the Mongols followed a few weeks later. The Mongols, under the leadership of Chinggis Khan's grandson, Batu, and the warlord Sübetei, defeated and virtually destroyed the main forces of the Hungarian monarch at Muhi at the ford of the Sajó River on April 11, 1241.

What was the result of the defeat?

The victory of the Mongols was almost complete. Most of the Hungarian secular and ecclesiastic elites were lost in the battle, including Count Palatine Denis and Archbishop Matthias of Esztergom. Very few among the leaders of the Hungarians survived the battle, but King Béla and his younger brother, Prince Coloman, managed to escape. The mobilization of the Hungarian forces was not complete before the battle mainly because of the strong opposition against the political aims of King Béla, meaning that some of the Hungarian knights were not present at the devastating battle. This, and because the king and his brother managed to escape alive, gave the only chance for resistance. The eastern part of the country was completely occupied by the Mongols, but the king and his small retinue managed to cross the

Danube and reach the western border of the country some weeks later. Frederick, Duke of Austria, did not offer any help; on the contrary, he tried to use the situation for his own benefit. Frederick held Béla for ransom and in return Béla ceded three western counties to him.

Was Béla able to do anything to mitigate the impact of the Mongols on the country?

As monarch, Béla did everything that he could to get help for his own country. Despite the fact that the Mongols captured and looted the so-called *medium regni*, the central region of the country with most of the political and ecclesiastic centers, among them the towns of Esztergom and Székesfehérvár, Béla started an active diplomatic campaign in Europe. He conducted an intensive correspondence with Pope Gregory IX until the death of the latter in August 1241. Hungary did not receive any significant military or financial support for defense owing to the conflict of the pope and Emperor Frederick II; the death of the pope right at the time of the most serious devastation of Hungary; the very short pontificate of Celestine IV; and the longish vacancy on the papal throne thereafter. The idea of a possible crusade against the Mongols also failed.

King Béla had no other way out of the situation than to flee, from the western counties of Hungary to the south, first to Slavonia and then to Dalmatia. Béla found refuge first in Split and later in Trogir on the Adriatic coast. The Mongols only managed to cross the Danube in the early months of 1242 when they could cross the frozen river. General Kadan followed the route of King Béla with a squad of Mongols and tried to capture him. This action shows that it was an essential part of the Mongol military tactics to neutralize the ruler of their enemy.

How was Béla able to escape capture?

In March 1242, the Mongols left Hungary as fast as they arrived. The reason for the quick retreat is still a debated issue in the historical literature. After twelve months of basically continuous military activity they evacuated all of their troops from Hungary. The effects of the Mongol invasion were dreadful. The central territories of the country, which were under Mongol occupation for several months, were almost completely devastated. The eastern counties, where the rule of the Mongols was longer, were even more seriously affected than the western regions of the country. Given the lack of reliable sources, it is difficult to establish precise numbers of the population loss. The data vary from 15% to 75% depending on the individual regions. There was a clear military lesson in the events. Although the main forces of the Mongols were a nomadic-type light cavalry that was not prepared for proper sieges of fortified places, they still, with some exceptions, were able to seize all the settlements on their route. Béla realized that only well-fortified places could hold out in the case of another invasion by the Mongols. It was clear to many of his contemporaries that the 1241–1242 attack was only the first attempt to conquer the country and that a second, even more devastating, campaign might happen in the future.

Did Béla change his policies as a result of the loss to the Mongols?

Béla was ready to change the main elements of his earlier efforts and drop his intention to recover the royal domains alienated by his father. He realized that he could not return to his grandfather's model of government. Béla decided to adopt new military tactics in Hungary based on mounted armored cavalry and to build more stone fortifications. These castles, initially very simple structures, were typically built by noble families on their own estates using their own financial resources. The financial backing for these constructions was facilitated by extensive donations of landed property – something Béla had strongly opposed in his youth and in the first period of his reign.

The foundation of guest (*hospes*) communities was another important characteristic of Béla's new policy. Zagreb, the modern capital of Croatia, was burned down by the Mongols, who were chasing the king in 1242. In the same year, on his way back to the central territories of the country, Béla donated special privileges to Zagreb, elevating it to the rank of a free royal town. More than two dozen settlements received written privileges between the Mongol invasion and the end of Béla IV's reign.

The shock caused by the Mongol invasions influenced Béla's political actions in many respects. He made great efforts to ensure the support of the Catholic Church if there were a next wave of Mongol expansion; he also tried to improve his own position in communication with the papacy. In his letters to the pope he refers several times to Hungary as the frontier zone of Christianity, the "bulwark" or "shield" of Christian Europe. This concept was often used later in the period of defensive wars against the Ottomans. Béla IV also acted on his key role in defending Christianity against the Mongols when he tried to have the pope appoint his protégés to various ecclesiastical positions.

The foreign policy of Hungary after 1242 reflected Béla IV's active role in regional affairs. Béla's son-in-law, Rostislav Mikhailovich, Prince of Novgorod and Chernigov, led campaigns to conquer Galicia in 1244 and 1245, for which he received active military support from King Béla. This shows that despite the decisive defeat by the Mongols in 1241–1242 Hungary was again able to put a proper army in the field within a few years. In 1246, Béla decided to take part in a more ambitious military conflict against Frederick the Quarrelsome of Austria. Although the decisive clash at the Leitha River, in the border region of Hungary and Austria, ended with the victory of the Austrians, Duke Frederick was killed in the battle. He was the last member of the Babenberg dynasty in the male line, so the Babenbergs died out with his death. With the extinction of the Babenbergs, who had ruled the southeastern region of Germany for a long time, the rule of that area was contested. Béla IV and his successors, Stephen V and Ladislaus IV, and also Ottokar II Přemysl of Moravia and Bohemia, tried to gain the overlordship of the former Babenberg territories, which resulted a long and eventful military conflict. King Béla IV and Ottokar II's conflict ended at the battle of Kressenbrunn in 1260, when, after being defeated, Béla finally gave up his claim on the Austrian territories.

Did Béla ever have a male heir?

Béla IV was already thirty-three years old when, in 1239, after nineteen years of marriage, Queen Maria gave birth to a son; the baby was named István (Stephen) as homage to King St. Stephen. Béla faced the same conflicts with his son as his father had with him. Stephen was crowned junior king as early as 1246. From 1257 onward, father and son made various pacts about how to share the royal power. In 1264–1265 this disagreement even resulted in military conflict between them.

What was the result of that conflict with his son?

In hopes of settling the family conflict with his son, Béla convened a meeting of the royal servants (*servientes regis*) at Esztergom in 1267. The royal servants formed a special emerging social group who were dependent only on the royal power and not the local counts, even though their rights were traditionally not on the same level as that of the nobles. Their legal position was defined by the decisive legislative act of thirteenth-century Hungarian history, the so-called Golden Bull issued by Andrew II in 1222. This decree had been reissued in 1231 and later by Béla IV as a reaction to the demands the royal servants formulated at a meeting in 1267. Béla and his sons, who also ratified this decision, acknowledged that the legal status of the royal servants was the same as that of the nobles of the country. The 1267 decree confirmed several articles of the 1222 Golden Bull and modified others, basically defining and protecting the privileges of the royal servants.

What do you find particularly interesting about King Béla?

Béla IV's family history is especially interesting because of the large number of canonized saints among his relatives. Béla's younger sister, Elisabeth (1207–1231), was just one year younger than the king. She married Louis IV, landgrave of Thuringia, and lived with him at the court in Wartburg castle. She followed the ideals of the early Franciscans and was canonized in 1235 soon after her death. Elisabeth's aunt on the maternal line was St. Hedwig of Andechs (1174–1243), wife of Henry the Bearded of Silesia. Coloman, Béla IV's younger brother, married Salome (1211–1268), daughter of Leszek the White of Cracow. After she was widowed Salome joined the Poor Clares and when she died she was venerated as a saint. Béla's oldest daughter, Cunegond (Kinga) (1224–1292) lived in a chaste marriage with her husband, Bolesław V the Chaste of Poland. In January 1242, Béla's wife, Queen Maria, gave birth to a daughter in the castle of Kliš when they were in exile in Dalmatia. The newborn baby, later St. Margaret of Hungary, was offered to the Catholic Church as a nun to save the royal couple and Hungary from the Mongols. Margaret lived in a cloister from her fourth year onward and later joined the Dominican convent on the Rabbits' Island near Buda (now Margaret Island). The number of canonized saints among the close relatives of Béla IV shows the significance of saintly cults and also the influence of the mendicant orders in the period. For a long time Béla preferred the Dominicans; his confessors were usually from this order. Only later, around 1260, did the impact of the Franciscans become more intensive at the royal court. Béla even joined a secular community of Franciscans and stipulated that his body should be buried in the Franciscan church of Esztergom.

The younger son of King Béla IV, Prince Béla, died before his father, thus, in 1270, when Béla died, the inheritance of the royal power was uncontroversial and Stephen V was crowned as the ruler of the country. King Béla's death was followed some weeks later by the death of his wife and queen, Maria Laskarina. They lived together for fifty years, an unparalleled length of time in the history of the medieval royal couples of Hungary.

How would you sum up the reign of King Béla?

Béla IV was a prominent monarch in a period of vicissitudes of his country. He faced special challenges during his reign and he was brave enough to abandon his earlier concepts if these proved to be useless or outdated. After the Mongol invasion of Hungary in 1241–1242 he contributed to the modernization of his country by making substantial political and economic changes.

Notes

1 In the early nineteenth century, in the period of the national revival in Hungary, József Katona, a well-known poet and playwright authored a historical drama, entitled *Bánk Bán* (1821), on the assassination of Gertrud and one of the most important Hungarian national operas composed by Ferenc Erkel (1861) also features this event.
2 *Master Roger's Epistle to the Sorrowful Lament upon the Destruction of the Kingdom of Hungary by the Tatars*, trans. and annot. János M. Bak and Martyn Rady, in Martyn Rady, László Veszprémy, János M. Bak, *Anonymus and Master Roger* (Budapest: Central European University Press, 2010), Cap. 4. p. 143.

Selected sources in English translation

Archdeacon Thomas of Split: History of the Bishops of Salona and Split. Edited, Translated and Annotated by Damir Karbić, Mirjana Matijević Sokol, and James Ross Sweeney. Budapest: Central European University Press, 2006.
Master Roger's Epistle to the Sorrowful Lament upon the Destruction of the Kingdom of Hungary by the Tatars. Translated and Annotated by János M. Bak and Martyn Rady. In: Martyn Rady, László Veszprémy, and János M. Bak, eds. *Anonymus and Master Roger*. Budapest: Central European University Press, 2010.

Selected secondary literature

Berend, Nora. *At the Gate of Christendom: Jews, Muslims and "Pagans" in Medieval Hungary, c. 1000c. 1300*. Cambridge: Cambridge University Press, 2001.
Engel, Pál. *The Realm of St Stephen: A History of Medieval Hungary 895–1526*. New York: I. B. Tauris, 2001.
Jackson, Peter. *The Mongols and the West, 1221–1240*. London: Pearson, 2005.
Klaniczay, Gábor. *Holy Rulers and Blessed Princesses: Dynastic Cults in Medieval Central Europe*. Cambridge: Cambridge University Press, 2002.

14

ZALAVA, SLAVE IN THE KINGDOM OF HUNGARY

Cameron Sutt

The focus of this portrait is a slave on the estate of a lay landlord in the Kingdom of Hungary under the Árpád dynasty. The person, Zalava, was a real slave mentioned, along with his brother Zulav, in a series of charters from the 1270s. The central event of his life depicted in this portrait is also real and is the actual subject of these charters from which I have taken his name. Since the charters mentioning Zalava and all other servi *from the period were focused upon the transactions and activities of the elite in society, the* servi *who frequently appeared in them show up merely as items. Therefore many of the details of Zalava's life and the lives of other slaves mentioned in the portrait are in part the product of imagination and educated guesses. At the same time, all the events in this portrait are based upon actual incidents found in the charters. Of course they did not all happen around Zalava, but I have included them in his life story so as to give an impression of the lives of these voiceless men and women.*

The portrait of Zalava is representative of those slaves owned by lay landlords in the Kingdom of Hungary. The situation of subjects living on the estates of the great ecclesiastical institutions would have been different, and I have attempted to show that briefly. The organization and utilization of labor on royal estates had its own complexities, and I thought it best not to burden the portrait excessively with their complications.

Unfortunately, none of the charters used in this portrait have been translated, but they can be found scattered throughout the large collections of printed charters listed below. The Feast of the Ascension is one of the required celebrations mandated by the Synod of Szabolcs, found in the collection of the earliest laws of the Kingdom of Hungary. The description of Nicolas's castle-fort is taken from archaeological findings of the last couple of decades. Much of the discussion regarding these fortifications has likewise not been translated, but some summaries can be found in the volume edited by Zsolt Visy.

* * *

Zalava was born into the property of Nicolas, son of Arnold in the Kingdom of Hungary. Zalava did not know his exact birthdate of course, but he did know that he was born four years after the Tatars[1] had come to Hungary, so he was born around 1245. Nicolas was a man of great means in the western portion of the Kingdom of Hungary with significant holdings in Zala County. Zalava was born a slave because his father was a slave, and his sister was also a slave because his mother had been a slave. Zalava was not aware that the way birth status was determined in the Kingdom of Hungary was quite unusual. He just knew that a person's status was determined by the status of the parent whose gender he or she shared. Since Zalava's father was a slave, so was he, and since his mother was a slave, so was his sister. Of course, as Zalava grew up, he saw how status could become complicated. He remembered how the gossip mill ran in high gear when the owner of a small neighboring farmstead took up house with one of the slave girls belonging to Nicolas. If Zalava's memory served him well, the man's name was Gregory, and he even had four daughters by the girl. He evidently loved those girls deeply because he paid Nicolas a pretty penny to free them and their mother. Zalava also knew of an instance when another lord named Suge had seduced one of the slave girls that he had bought, and she had a son named Boxa. The boy should have been free, but he grew up as a slave in Suge's house. The boy's parentage was an open secret, but nobody would say anything as long as Suge lived. After he died, one of his daughters had him freed since he should have been free by right of his father. Besides, the boy was her kin and she felt an obligation to him. At least that was the story he got. In any case, such complications did not affect Zalava, but the juicy stories did make the time pass while they worked in the fields.

Zalava grew up with his brother Zulav and a sister on an estate belonging to Nicolas. When Zalava came of age, he married a woman who also belonged to Nicolas, and they continued their life together in the same farmstead where they had grown up. They had two sons and a daughter and all of them worked together on Nicolas's estate. They never saw Nicolas or any of the great men. There was no need because Lord Nicolas left the management of the estate to his reeve. The reeve would collect the harvest for the lord and make sure that the work was performed for him. Zalava's work was to plow the lands of his lord. Zalava did not own any oxen himself, but some of his neighbors did and with them, or with those that Nicolas's reeve provided, they plowed the fields of the estate. The whole family took part in the work. Zalava would take turns with men on the estate at directing the teams of eight oxen pulling the heavy, asymmetric plow. It usually took two men to keep the animals plowing straight while a third would walk behind sowing seed. One of the wives and some of the children would hold the seed bags for him. The work was hard, but not nearly as hard as the harvesting when all the men on the estate would work swinging the scythes and stacking the hay into sheaves. All of the land belonged to Nicolas or his kindred, and most of the harvest went to Lord Nicolas. The slaves were allowed to keep some of the harvest for themselves. The harvest was difficult, but far worse were the woodcarrying duties that Zalava some-times had to perform. Since Zalava was a slave, he had to perform whatever labor was demanded of him, and Nicolas and his kin needed firewood delivered to their house. Zalava did not have a cart, so he, along with the other slaves, had to carry the wood to the court on his back.

These arduous wood delivery trips were the only times that he would enter the court of one of the great men. The size of the court complex was impressive to Zalava though he could not have known that it was rather humble in comparison to other parts of the world. As he approached Nicolas's farm, he noticed the orchards and the fishponds on the outer edges, just inside the fields. The farm he was on was similar, but much smaller.

The court itself was a strong fortification surrounded by earthworks and a wooden palisade, and he could only enter through a gate. Many of the powerful had such "castles." The fortification, along with the handful of soldiers inside it, but as far as he knew, its purpose was primarily to intimidate other members of Nicolas's clan or maybe competing clans. Several years ago some of Nicolas's cousins became outraged over Nicolas's refusal to share the inheritance that his father, Arnold, had left behind. The cousins swooped down on one of the Nicolas's farms and burned everything to the ground. They carried off eight slaves along with their wives and children. It was a terrible thing, and Zalava felt bad for the poor slaves. At the same time, he was thankful that he and his family were spared. In any case, Lord Nicolas was unmoved because the cousins could not touch him in his castle, and he simply waited them out. They eventually came to terms and five of the slaves were returned. The remainder were divided among the cousins as a concession to their grievances.

Once inside the palisade, Zalava would stack the wood by one of the outbuildings. There were several such buildings inside the court-fortification. He did not dare approach the large house in the center of the courtyard. This was where Lord Nicolas lived with his brothers. Instead, Zalava would rest in the shade of the slave quarters, which was a separate building. There he liked to talk to the male and female slaves who worked in the great house. The cook and the laundress were quite jovial and loved to tell jokes, but the chambermaids had all the juicy gossip. The potential for gossip was ever present because Nicolas had a crew of young slave girls spinning and weaving for his court, and keeping the young noblemen away from them could be difficult, evidently. These girls lived in the slave quarters, but they worked in another building outside the fort.

After resting a bit, Zalava returned to his settlement with the other men. He particularly enjoyed talking with the other men on the trip back. Returning home always felt good, but Zalava had little time to rest – there was just too much work to be done. Zalava considered himself quite lucky because up to now he had lived in the same settlement undisturbed all his life. He knew it was not unusual for slaves to be moved. The great men often used their slaves as currency. Lord Nicolas was always acquiring property, and if he did not have any property that he was willing to trade for it, he would use his slaves as payment. A couple of years ago, several of Zalava's neighbors were removed from their homes and sent to live elsewhere when Nicolas's daughter married. Slaves were particularly susceptible to this sort of transfer because lords liked to make dower payments in non-moveables so as to keep their estates intact.

Well, never mind all that. The Feast of the Ascension was approaching, and Zalava would be able to rest a bit then. There was no church at Zalava's farmstead, but a nearby village had one, and there was usually a procession and celebration there that many from his farmstead would attend. That was one of the few times that Zalava and his family would set foot in a church. They were good Christians, mind you, but the trip to the village was arduous during the high holy days of winter. They did try to make the Feast of Ascension, however. First, they would hear the mass. The Mass was said by the priest whom the lord had employed for the village. He was not terribly educated, but as far as Zalava knew, he was just fine. He could say the Mass, or at least it seemed so to Zalava because he did not know Latin. In any case, the priest seemed like a fine fellow because he would join in on the drinking and dancing in the churchyard during the festival. The priest's wife and children were also there, and Zalava's children loved to go to the festival and play with the others. Zalava considered himself a good Christian, and he could not have known, but as early as the Synod of Szabolcs in 1090, the church in Hungary had declared that slaves had to be given a Christian burial in a churchyard.

Zalava was contemplating these things as he approached his home when his wife came running up to him with an extremely worried look on her face. She explained how the reeve had come while he was gone and told everyone that they were to be given to another owner. Almost eighty people were to be given to Ponik the bán of Croatia! Zalava knew that his life was about to be completely upended. They would have to go to another farm and work for another owner, a very powerful one at that. His wife explained that the reeve was unusually talkative and explained how they were all to serve as payment for an affair involving a couple of castles that Bán Ponik owned. Evidently, the bán had the castles for a while and had made numerous improvements on them during the war against the king of Bohemia. Well, one of Ponik's relatives now claimed the castles, and since Ponik had fallen from favor at the royal court, he was forced to hand over the castles to his relatives. As part of the settlement, Nicolas had to compensate Ponik for all the repairs to the castles, and the slaves were the compensation. Since male slaves cost around three marks, the total cost for the repairs was a sum that Zalava could hardly imagine. Zalava and his family were all very worried because they had no idea what conditions awaited them with their new lord, but Zalava was comforted somewhat by the fact that his brother, Zulav, along with his family would be joining them in the move.

On the appointed day, the bailiff arrived, Zalava and the other families, including his brother's, loaded their belongings, and they began the march to their new homes. Fortunately Zalava's children were old enough to take care of themselves. In fact, the worries of the parents could not dampen the children's excitement for the trip. They viewed the whole trip as the adventure of their lifetime since they had never been farther than the neighboring settlement. Neither Zalava nor his brother had an ox or a cart, so they only took what they could carry. Of course they did not have much to carry in any case, so they did not have to leave much behind. The first night the bailiff stopped everyone along a stream and something of a camp was set up. Zalava and his brother's family slept out under the stars since they had no other choice. Fortunately it did not rain, and Zalava slept well despite his worries for the future. When he awoke, Zalava could hear a commotion. The bailiff was shouting something quite agitatedly so Zalava ran over to find out what the matter was. "Where are they? How many are missing?" Ah, Zalava realized what had happened – several of the slaves had escaped in the night! This was rather exciting, and it distracted everyone from the worries of the move.

All of the escapees seemed to have been unmarried, and Zalava did not blame them at all. It was not terribly uncommon for slaves to run away in search of better conditions. It was common knowledge that if you could get connected with one of the agents organizing land clearances in the mountains of the Hungarian Highlands, he would give you a plot of land and you would only have to make annual payments to the lord. The rest of the time you could work for yourself. Zalava had heard that they had announced such opportunities in the market of Tolna. That is probably what the escapees intended to do, and they would have to be careful not to be caught. Zalava knew of several instances where slaves had run away. Several years ago a neighboring freeman, actually an officer in a nearby castle, promised some of the men on his farm that he would only demand some small annual payments if they would agree to clear some forest that was on his land. They moved to him under cover of darkness and even had their homes built and part of a field cleared when Nicolas's reeve found them and forced them to return. The officer was punished, but Zalava did not hear how severely.

Zalava had also heard rumors that many of the new German immigrants brought foreign customs like renting plots from lords instead of using slave labor. The slaves may have been trying to reach one of these communities though Zalava doubted it because he didn't see how they would fit in with a community of immigrant Germans. At the same time, so many slaves had been fleeing looking for better conditions that some Hungarian lords were changing their status and giving them their freedom rather than losing all their workforce. Maybe the slaves hoped to flee to one of those lords.

No matter, Zalava thought, he was not going to try to escape. How could he? He had a family to look after. It would not be so easy for him to travel all the way to one of the towns, try to find an agent, and to reestablish his life. No, he would just have to make the best of whatever conditions he found himself in the possession of his new master. Who knows, maybe his new owner would give him and his family to a great monastery or church. The subjects of the monasteries had easier times of it if they lived far from the monastery itself because the monks just demanded payments from them every year. They did not have to provide unlimited labor as they did on the estates of the lay lords. At any rate, Zalava felt fortunate that his family was not split up. Lords would on occasion divide up slave families if they needed to. Once when Augustine, one of Lord Nicolas's cousins died, Augustine left a slave named Paul from a nearby farmstead to the monastery of Saint Peter at Csatár while he gave Paul's wife and two daughters to one of his sisters.

Zalava was happy that at least nothing so catastrophic as that happened to him. He did not know what his future held with his new lord, but he hoped that it would be all right. He had his family and his brother, so that was something anyway.

Note

1 The Hungarian sources used the term "Tartars" to refer to the Mongol invaders.

Suggestions for further reading

Sources

Bak, János M., György Bónis, and James Ross Sweeney, eds., *The Laws of the Medieval Kingdom of Hungary, 1000–1301*, 2nd ed. Idyllwild: Charles Schlacks, Jr., 1999.

Secondary literature in English

Engel, Pál. *The Realm of St Stephen: A History of Medieval Hungary 895–1526*. New York: I. B. Tauris, 2001.

Sutt, Cameron. *Slavery in Árpád-era Hungary in a Comparative Context*. Leiden: Brill, 2015.

Sutt, Cameron. "*Parentela*, kindred, and the crown. Inheritance practices in Árpád-era Hungary," in *Inheritance, Law and Religions in the Ancient and Mediaeval Worlds*. Eds. Béatrice Caseau and Sabine R. Huebner. Paris: Centre d'Histoire et de Civilisation de Byzance, Monographies 45, 2014.

Szabó, István. "The Praedium: Studies on the Economic History and the History of Settlement of Early Hungary." *Agrártörténeti szemle* 5 Supplementum (1963): 1–24.

Visy, Zsolt (ed.). *Hungarian Archaeology at the Turn of the Millennium*. Budapest: Ministry of National Cultural Heritage, 2003.

15

JAN DŁUGOSZ ON KING WŁADYSŁAW JAGIEŁŁO'S MASTER CHEF AND THE INVENTION OF BIGOS

Paul Milliman

The following portrait blends fact with historical fiction to playfully explore why so many sites on the Internet claim that bigos, a hunter's stew and one of the national dishes of Poland, was invented by King Władysław Jagiełło, a Lithuanian pagan, who converted to Christianity, married Queen Jadwiga of Poland, and founded a dynasty that controlled much of Eastern Europe for almost two centuries.

Bigos is composed of a variety of different game meats, so the passage in Jan Długosz's Annales seu cronicae incliti regni Poloniae [Annals or Chronicles of the Illustrious Kingdom of Poland] *in which King Władysław Jagiełło returned to Kraków from a hunting expedition with diverse kinds of game meat in time to celebrate Carnival and his second marriage in 1401 seems like the perfect place to insert this bit of received wisdom into the historical record. Jan Długosz (1415–1480) is the main narrative source for medieval Polish history. His twelve-volume work,* Annales seu cronicae incliti regni Poloniae, *records the history of Poland from its founding in the tenth century until his own day. King Władysław Jagiełło's wedding to Anna, granddaughter of King Kazimierz the Great of Poland (1333–1370), is presented by Długosz as particularly important in the history of Poland because after the death of Queen Jadwiga in 1399, Władysław Jagiełło's claim to the throne could be challenged and the Polish-Lithuanian union was imperiled. Therefore, it was necessary to demonstrate to both domestic and foreign magnates that his reign was legitimate. What better way to do this than for the king to work with his master chef to invent a new national dish to be served at the wedding feast, where food could be used as propaganda to demonstrate the union of Poland and Lithuania under the rule of Władysław Jagiełło?*

There are many ways to prepare bigos, but its essential components are various meats, particularly game meats, which are first roasted then diced and cooked low and slow together with sauerkraut and vegetables and fruits for a long time. No recipe for bigos survives from the Middle Ages. The earliest recipes called "bigosek" appear in the first Polish cookbook, Stanisław Czerniecki's Compendium Ferculorum, *which was first published in 1682. But these recipes barely resemble traditional bigos. They are essentially just diced meat dishes,* composed of one or two kinds of meat, and many of the bigosek recipes are in fact for fish, so these dishes could be eaten on fast days. Medieval and early modern Europeans were concerned about mixing too many different kinds of meat in the same dish because different meats had different natures, which could upset the humoral balance of their consumers if those natures were not corrected by means of preparation or with sauces. People were also concerned about the order in which different foods were eaten. Digestion was looked upon as the final stage in the cooking process in which the stomach cooked the foods that were consumed. Consuming foods in an improper order could be the alimentary equivalent of throwing a frozen turkey into a deep fryer. Of course, just as today, not everyone heeded the advice of healthcare professionals, so some medieval dishes did combine a variety of meats, and it was common to offer a variety of meat dishes in the same course. Moreover, a thick, spiced, sweet and sour stew of meat subjected to multiple cooking techniques is something that would have appealed to medieval tastes.

We do not know a great deal about master chefs in the Polish royal court in the late fourteenth and early fifteenth centuries. We know the names of a few, identified in documents as regis magister coquine [master of the king's kitchen]. But we know very little about how the royal kitchens in medieval Wawel palace operated at the turn of the fifteenth century. Fortunately, the high cuisine at the time was very international, so it is likely that the royal kitchens in Wawel operated in ways similar to kitchens in the better understood courts of Western Europe. So, my Polish master chef is a pastiche, incorporating the characteristics of master chefs in courts throughout Europe in the fourteenth and fifteenth centuries. I also use as a model the author of the first Polish cookbook, Stanisław Czerniecki. Although many of the courts of Western Europe had rejected medieval cuisine by the late seventeenth century in favor of something closer to classical French cuisine, Polish courts continued to prefer medieval tastes, the heavily spiced flavors of which are closer to the cuisines of modern Middle Eastern and North African countries, but which had come to be thought of by some seventeenth-century Western Europeans as a uniquely "Polish" style which was not part of their collective culinary history and identity.

We do not know who the king's master chef was in 1401. But we do know something about Queen Jadwiga's master chef in the 1390s, Jakusz (or Janusz) of Boturzyn. It is possible that he may have occupied this position in her husband's court after Jadwiga's death in 1399. In any case, my master chef is intended to be someone like Jakusz, who Maria Dembińska has suggested "was quite capable of compiling his own recipe book since he spoke several languages, including Latin."[1] Dembińska also has this to say about the role of the master chef in medieval courts: "He supervised the nutrition of the court, discussed food products with the monarch he served, and oversaw the proper functioning of the royal kitchen. He also invented new dishes for state functions and sometimes compiled collections of handwritten recipes."[2] I hope the master chef I have inserted into Jan Długosz's Annals ably fulfills all these functions.

The title and first paragraph of what follows is a translation from Jan Długosz's Annales seu cronicae incliti regni Poloniae, Liber Decimus 1370–1405 (Warsaw: Państwowe Wydawnictwo Naukowe, 1985), 243–244. The rest is my own creation, an interpolation into the Annales in the voice of Jan Długosz to imagine what he might have written if he had written more about the wedding feast. It is intended to be as much a portrait of bigos as a portrait of the king's anonymous master chef.[3] It is also intended to prompt readers to consider *what cultural and culinary history can contribute to the study of nascent nationalism in the late Middle Ages.*

* * *

The Year of the Lord One Thousand Four Hundred and One
    Nuptials are celebrated between King Władysław and Anna, granddaughter of Kazimierz, formerly king.

Władysław, king of Poland, stayed in Lithuania for almost the whole season of winter and came to Kraków before the days of Carnisprivium [Lent], bringing with him into the kingdom of Poland the meat of wild beasts of various kinds, which he had taken while hunting in Lithuania. There the maiden Anna, daughter of the count of Celje and granddaughter of Kazimierz, king of Poland, betrothed by a solemn vow in a church in Kraków, also celebrated the solemnity of nuptials in the presence of the honorable persons, Alexander, the grand duke of Lithuania and his consort, Anna, and a multitude of princes and counts from various lands, who, having been invited, came together. Moreover the royal court proclaimed there would be for many days jousts and tournaments for the dukes, counts, and knights. After the solemnity of nuptials, Alexander, the grand duke of Lithuania, and his consort, Anna, as well as the other princes, counts, and guests were honored by Władysław, king of Poland, with magnificent gifts brought, presented, and returned by royal officials, and every necessity was bestowed in abundance.

But there was one more gift Władysław, king of Poland, gave his guests at the wedding feast. A novelty was created for this event, a dish that was truly a demonstration of the magnificence of the Polish royal court. King Władysław often returned from hunting in his native Lithuania with large quantities of game, which he customarily distributed to magnates throughout the kingdom of Poland. But he had a novel use of this meat in mind when he returned from Lithuania this time. Rather than simply making a gift of Lithuania's game to Poland's magnates as he had done in the past, he would instead transform that meat into a gift never before seen, a monument to his skills as both a hunter and a statesmen. Although King Władysław was for the most part better suited to hunting than to governing, in this novelty he demonstrated that his overenthusiastic passion for the chase could benefit the kingdom of Poland and raise the standing of the Polish royal court in the eyes of foreign dignitaries. For the wedding feast celebrating his marriage to the granddaughter of King Kazimierz, King Władysław ordered his master chef to create a novel dish, something never before seen, a dish that would symbolize the union of Poland and Lithuania and also demonstrate his skills as a hunter by using Polish cooking techniques to incorporate in the same dish all of the various game animals with which he had returned from Lithuania. Having created the idea of this new dish, King Władysław left the task of realizing his invention to his master chef.

The king's master chef was a formidable man, observing the workings of the royal kitchen from a seat perched high above the cooks and the rest of the kitchen staff. From here he would bark orders, and he would occasionally descend from this perch carrying a giant wooden spoon, which he would use both to taste the dishes being prepared and to punish those who were failing to meet his rigorous standards and high expectations.[4] In the days leading up to the wedding, the task with which he had been entrusted by the king was weighing heavily on him. He knew that the job of the king's master chef was not only to create dishes that dazzled the eyes and taste buds of the king and his guests but also to create food that was safe to consume, food that would keep the humors of the king and his guests in balance. Different animals have different natures, which affect the humors of those consuming them in different ways. How was he supposed to balance the different characteristics – hot or cold, dry or moist – of the various animals King Władysław presented to him, including elk, boar, auroch, deer, bison, hare, and wild fowl? The answer lay in different preparations for each game animal. Some would be roasted first, some boiled first; all would be given the proper treatment to correct their characteristics so they could be served harmoniously in the same dish. After preparing each animal according to its nature, all would be carved into bite-sized pieces and cooked together for a very long time with cabbage, sauerkraut, and other vegetables. So that the addition of these common ingredients and the final treatment of cooking food fit for a king in a manner fit for a peasant did not undermine the greatness of the dish, the king's master chef planned to give his dish three more treatments. First, he would use an abundance of spices – cinnamon, sugar, ginger, pepper, cloves, and nutmeg – in order both to balance the natures of the various ingredients in the dish and to elevate the dish by demonstrating the wealth of his lord, King Władysław. Second, he would add a variety of the most delectable fruits; the value of this food, which is suitable by its nature only for the high born, would increase immeasurably by its service at the height of winter, again demonstrating the opulence of the Polish royal court. As a finishing touch he planned to put the dish in an enormous serving platter and cover the whole dish with a pie crust emblazoned with golden decorations illustrating all of the various game animals contained therein. He also coordinated with other members of the king's court, particularly the royal huntsmen and falconers, to create an environment in which such a work of art and science could be truly appreciated.[5] I have heard that the French call such show-pieces *entremets* because they come between the courses. They are intended to delight the participants at the feast with their inventiveness.

With this vision in mind, the king's master chef started to realize his ambitious plan. Preparations for the feast began more than a week in advance. The king's master chef had to ensure that he would have a sufficient amount of fuel, particularly for his novel dish, which would need to cook for a long time. Also, the game animals had been salted and packed in barrels to preserve and transport them. The first task was to remove the salt from the meat. This was accomplished by soaking the meat for long periods of time and changing the water frequently. It was extremely important that the water used both for preparing and cooking be clean spring water, which had to be acquired. Then the game had to be marinated in vinegar and spices. Next the various animals had to be prepared in different ways in order to correct their natures and render them harmless to the king and his guests.

Finally, this large quantity of various kinds of meat each had to be properly carved and then diced so that the king and his guests could remove them from the dish while observing the proper rules of etiquette.

When the dish was presented to King Władysław and Queen Anna, they and their guests marveled at such a novelty, which delighted all the senses. First the sounding of horns and the barking of dogs delighted the ears, as it reminded King Władysław and his guests of the thrill of the chase. Next heralds announced the arrival of the dish and explained what was contained within the enormous crust, which was being wheeled around the great hall by a procession of chefs, including the king's master chef, who was beaming with delight. Even before the ears and eyes were delighted, however, the wonderful aroma of the dish astonished not only those in the great hall but everyone throughout Wawel castle and even those below in the city of Kraków. The brilliant display and aroma of the dish were enough to sate the appetites of those whose place at the feast was too distant from the king and queen to feel the dish with their fingers and taste it with their tongues. The wedding guests congratulated King Władysław on his invention, and the king in turn thanked his master chef for realizing his ambitious plan.

King Władysław had one final request concerning the creation of this novel dish. He asked his master chef to preserve the memory of this event for his lord, King Władysław, by committing to writing all of the recipes from the dishes served at this feast, especially the new dish which the king had instructed him to create. The king's master chef could write good Latin, but he had never before seen the need to write down recipes. He knew all the recipes of the dishes for this feast by heart, even the newest one. However, he happily honored his lord's request. This book is preserved not in the kitchen, for the king's current master chef also has no need for instructions on how to cook, but in the royal library. The instructions for the dishes are quite terse, both because the king's master chef took many things for granted that someone outside of his profession would not have and because he did not wish to give away all the tricks of his trade. He called several of his dishes, including the novelty created for the wedding feast, his "secret recipes."[6] The king's master chef wanted to give the reader a taste of what they could expect. But he knew that he alone would know all of the unwritten steps involved in preparing the dishes. Many of the king's master chefs since this time have attempted to replicate the recipe of the novelty created for this wedding feast. But it is said that none of these versions can compare to the novel dish that was served to King Władysław, his bride Anna, and their honorable guests by King Władysław's master chef.

Notes

1 Maria Dembińska, *Food and Drink in Medieval Poland: Rediscovering a Cuisine of the Past.* Revised and adapted by William Woys Weaver. Translated by Magdalena Thomas (Philadelphia: University of Pennsylvania Press, 1999), 134.
2 Dembińska, *Food and Drink in Medieval Poland*, 54–55.
3 If you would like to try to create your own version of medieval bigos, see William Woys Weaver's recipe in Dembińska, *Food and Drink in Medieval Poland*, 169–170.

4 This idea comes from Olivier de la Marche's depiction of the master chef at the court of his lord, Charles the Bold, Duke of Burgundy. Terance Scully, *The Art of Cookery in the Middle Ages* (Woodbridge, UK and Rochester, NY: Boydell Press, 1995), 243–244.
5 Maître Chiquart, the early fifteenth-century master chef for the duke of Savoy, calls cooking an art and a science (Scully, *Art of Cookery*, 40–41).
6 I took this idea from Stanisław Czerniecki, who includes three "Secret[s] of the Master Cook" in his recipe collection.

Suggestions for further reading

Czerniecki, Stanisław. *Compendium Ferculorum or Collection of Dishes*. Edited by Jarosław Dumanowski in collaboration with Magdalena Spychaj. Translated by Agnieszka Czuchra and Maciej Czuchra. Warszawa: Museum of King Jan III's Palace at Wilanów, 2014.
Dembińska, Maria. *Food and Drink in Medieval Poland: Rediscovering a Cuisine of the Past*. Revised and adapted by William Woys Weaver. Translated by Magdalena Thomas. Philadelphia: University of Pennsylvania Press, 1999.
Klemettilä, Hannele. *The Medieval Kitchen: A Social History with Recipes*. London: Reaktion Books, 2012.
Montanari, Massimo. *Medieval Tastes: Food, Cooking, and the Table*. Translated by Beth Archer Brombert. New York: Columbia University Press, 2012.
Scully, Terance. *The Art of Cookery in the Middle Ages*. Woodbridge, UK and Rochester, NY: Boydell Press, 1995.

PART 5

Travelers to strange lands

16

THE TRAVELS OF GORM IN EASTERN EUROPE

Heidi Sherman-Lelis and Arnold Lelis[x]

The Vikings were not just the raiders of monasteries and pillagers of towns in Western Europe; they also raided, explored, traded and settled along the river systems of Eastern Europe. The Viking travelers/traders/explorers in Eastern Europe are largely known from later sources in the Christian world, but archeology, runic and Islamic sources can provide us with contemporary records for what life was like among these Scandinavians in a foreign land. The archaeological record provides us with evidence for the trade undertaken by these Scandinavians; in this portrait particularly we have plentiful evidence of the glass trade undertaken by Gorm. Runic inscriptions in Scandinavia provide terse but fascinating evidence of Scandinavians who did not make it home from their travels in the east or Serkland as the Islamic territories were known. Finally, Islamic sources themselves, most famously that of Ibn Fadlan, describe the local Slavic population as well as the Scandinavians and their customs, including wearing their wealth, descriptions of their weapons and their burial customs. This portrait attempts to weave together this disparate source base to present a small slice of one man's life in medieval Eastern Europe bridging cultures, language groups and regions.

A brief definition of terms is required here. I mentioned above that Serkland *(possibly from* serkr *[gown] +* land*) was the Old Norse name in the Runic inscriptions for the territories to the east ruled by Muslims. Other Old Norse terms used throughout this portrait should also be noted. The term* Gardariki *(Realm of towns [or fortified settlements]) is the Old Norse name for the land that would later be called* Rus'. *The term* Miklagard *(from* mikill *[big] +* gard *[town]) is the Old Norse name for Constantinople. The term* Ostweg *(East way) refers to the route eastward through Gardariki via rivers and portages to Sarkland and Miklagard. The term* Holmgard *(holm [island] +* gard *[town]) is the Old Norse name for Novgorod (because of the island in the middle of the river on which part of it is located).*

* * *

Gorm's travels to Gardariki in the 920s

Gorm is from Birka, the largest town in the kingdom of the Svear in the tenth century. His father is a master glass bead maker whose silver and gold-foiled beads are sought after across the Norse world. Gorm studies bead craft under his father at their market stall, where he also talks with merchants who have traveled the Oster-weg to Gardariki and even Miklagard.

Gorm begins to dream of adventures in the Great East! At the age of sixteen, he has a vision of Odin prophesying a future of winning great fame and gold armrings in the East. Gorm haunts Birka's shipyard, and talks himself aboard a vessel preparing to head out East with the spring weather. Though hired as one of the rowers, he brings his war gear along and hopes to become a sought-after sell-sword. His pack sags with his *Ulfbehrt* sword, a chainmail shirt, and a bag of fine glass beads, given him as a parting gift by his father.

Setting off in May, the voyage from Birka across the sea to Aldeigejuborg takes five days, at the end of which the travelers spot the large burial mounds of their Viking ancestors at the bend of the Volkhov River's left bank. They have arrived at the Viking town of Aledigejuborg: gateway to Gardariki! Gorm's enthusiasm wilts, however, when he experiences the disappointment of the famous Viking destination, which is considerably smaller than his hometown with about twenty small wooden houses linked by wooden walkways, strung in two long rows along the river bank. "Good thing we're just passing through," he snarks to his skipper, Snorri, who replies, "Hold on, lad. We'll be at this foul cesspit of a town until we've found riverboats. This sea snake will get stuck in the shallows of Gardariki's rivers." Snorri's words depress Gorm, but he copes by learning some of the local languages from the children of the merchants. The company spends two to three weeks at Aldeigjuborg, regrouping and preparing for the next stage of their adventure. They find a party that is returning out of Gardariki with silver and other valuables that they have acquired during their own successful adventure. They exchange their seaworthy ship for a portion of the departing party's silver and goods, as well as two smaller boats suitable for travel on the inland riverways and hire local pilots to take them through the two dangerous sets of rapids on the Volkhov for their first inland stage to Holmgardand Lake Ilmen.

Gorm is disappointed with Holmgard as well. It is a fairly new town that is just catching on with Scandinavian merchants, so there isn't much for a young guy to do except take orders from his skipper as the crew makes further preparations for their long trek farther inland. When he does have time, Gorm and his mates steal away to the local mead hall. There they meet, boast, and occasionally fight with other boat crews as well as locals. Over several meetings, Gorm's crew arranges with another boat crew to travel together for safety and support along the way. One day while Gorm is larking about the busy marketplace he notices a somewhat older man, with armrings and tattoos, who is haggling with a silversmith over some brooches. The stranger notices Gorm as well, and the two start talking. The other man, Ingjeld, turns out to be a member of the company of warriors (*druzhina*) resident at the fort called Gorodishche a couple of miles away. [Ultimately, these are Jarl Igor's men, but while Igor resides at Kiev, the Gorodishche garrison is commanded by one of Igor's vassal commanders.] Ingjeld invites Gorm to come out to a feast that night. He goes as Ingjeld's guest, drinks large quantities of ale and eats much roasted meat, listens to songs and to tales of adventure, witnesses some brawls (no blood shed, this time) and meets a few more of the warriors. In the morning, after sleeping it off under a bench, he finds his way back to Holmgard on a ferry boat. His skipper, Snorri, yells at him, and says the expedition is setting onward at the break of dawn tomorrow and he'd better be ready or they'll leave him behind in Holmgard.

It's around the middle of June when Gorm's party heads into Lake Ilmen, finds the mouth of the Msta and proceeds to row upstream, with their goal – to cross over the watershed into the upper Volga basin and thence proceed eastward. Occasionally they meet boats in ones and twos coming downstream heading westward, exchanging brief greetings and news about what's happening around Holmgard and along the Volga.

One day they have a fright. Sweeping around a bend in the river, coming down fast, are three unusually large boats (for such a smallish river), all hung with shields, and with ten to twelve grim-looking men on board each of them. Standing at the prow of the lead boat is clearly a war leader, decked in helmet, shining mail, high leather boots and multiple gold armrings on both arms. Quickly assessing the situation, Gorm's skipper guesses that these might be Danes trying their luck in Gardariki (Snorri has been several times from Birka to Hedeby, and knows something of the conditions in southern Scandinavia – and speaks a bit of the Danish dialect of Norse); he tells everybody else to keep their mouths shut and let him do the talking.

"Hail, prince of Denmark!" Snorri calls out, climbing up on the forward thwart of his own boat when the two parties are about fifty yards apart. "We are honored to meet such rare and distinguished travelers here, in distant Gardariki. Has Odin led you hither to fortune and renown?"

The warlord turns and gives a signal, and his boats pull up into the slower-moving water nearer to their side of the river, while the oarsmen of Gorm's party do the same and tread water slowly with their oars. The conversation continues.

"Fortune and renown?" the warlord sneers, mockingly. "And who might you be, to know of such things?"

"I am Snorri, lord, from Gotland, where I have a farm and a wife and sons. I have been in all the trading places, large and small, from Birka to Haithabu, and even once up to Kaupang in Skiringsal, on the Skaggerak. I have traveled the great eastern way more than once, down to Bulghar [on the Volga], where the Serkland men [Islamic traders from the Abbasid Caliphate] will pay much silver for the goods we bring. But never have I seen before a war party of Danes on these rivers. Last I heard, you were busy plundering the Saxons and the Franks."

The warlord pulls his face into a sour grimace.

"Things in the West are no longer as they once were. In England, the cursed Æthelings keep building up their damned burhs. And no one wants to fight the

Franks any more – their kings will give bags of silver and free land to anyone who shows up out of the sea, just for the asking, so why fight? There's no work any longer in the West for an honest raider."

He spits and looks accusingly at Snorri. "I, too, have been in the trading places, from the Limnfjord to Haithabu, and more and more I kept hearing in these places men, such like yourself, crowing about the riches to be had for anyone bold enough to go east. At last, having few other options, I decided to see for myself. I outfitted a fine longship, gathered a party of good, tried warriors, and set out upon the Eastern Sea to seek this fabled Gardariki." He spits again.

"Have you ever sailed upon the Western Sea, Snorri of Gotland? There, with a longship and a sunstone, you can come out of the night or the sea mists and descend on any point along those endless shorelines wheresoever you will, plunder a monastery or a town and be gone again into the sea before the locals can gather any force to challenge you. What did we find here? Already at Aldeigjuborg we were shocked and dismayed that our beautiful longship with its proud beast-head could not enter the rivers, and we had to abandon it in trade for these miserable scows. And how do you raid where there is no sea to swoop in from and to return to? Not that there is anything in this wilderness worth raiding anyway. No monasteries. A few traders' towns, yes, and a few forts where the local jarls keep a few armed men, but these are a hundred miles or more apart along torturous riverways. When you try to come ashore at some native encampment [probably local Finnic tribes] everybody scatters into the thick woods, and all that's left to take is a few worthless cooking pots and half-dressed furs, if that. We ventured to raid one or two of the palisaded, riverside towns where we knew some good Norse people live, with some jewelry and hoards of silver to take, perhaps, but each time it nearly did us in. These people fight back! And if you manage to grab a few things of value and get back to the boats, your only hope is to get downstream as fast as you can – but then these people that you have roused cross the necks of the oxbows on foot faster than you can row the loops, and ambush you with spears and arrows as you have to run past them. We rowed all the way down the great east river to within sight of Bulghar, thinking that here, surely, would be a prize worth taking if half the tales of the traders be true. You may as well attempt to attack Paris with thirty men! High stone walls! Dozens of soldiers in strange helmets and black faces, as you said, atop them. We turned back. We had not the force to rob this city, nor had we gathered anything that we might trade. I led these fine men here. I promised them golden armrings. Where am I to find gold in this desert!" The warlord looks belligerently across at Snorri.

"I have heard, lord, that the king in Miklagard [Constantinople] will pay gold to warriors such as yourselves if you will join his royal guard. I have not been there, but they say that Miklagard is great and splendid beyond imagination. If you continue back down this river to Holmgard, men there can show you the way south, to Jarl Igor in Kiev, on the Dnieper. Thence lies the way onward to Miklagard."

The warlord looks thoughtful. "Yes, I have heard of this Miklagard. Perhaps I will venture there, after all. As for you, Snorri of Gotland, may Odin lead you to better fortune than I have had in Gardariki – or may Hel take you, I care not." He turns and signals again, and his boats put back out into the current and soon are out of sight downstream. Snorri, Gorm and everyone else heave a long sigh of relief and continue their laborious rowing upstream.

When Gorm's boat reaches the upper parts of the Msta, where it soon would become too shallow to navigate, they portage over to the Tvertsa, which shortly flows into the Upper Volga. The hardest segment of their journey to the rich markets on the Middle Volga is now behind them!

As they navigate the upper Volga to the east, they make occasional stops at riverside settlements. Snorri and several of the other men are experienced long-distance traders, and they know how to deal with the locals. In the Finnic villages, Snorri typically gives small gifts (beads, some silver coins, maybe a comb or a knife) to the local chiefs or elders, which secures their welcome in the settlement. Further business is all on the basis of exchanges voluntarily arrived at between the Norse merchant-adventurers and the locals of all ranks. Above all, the travelers are seeking high-quality northern furs (squirrel, sable, marten) and young, attractive slave girls, for these are the items that will bring the greatest profits down in Bulghar; but they also load some buckets of honey and rolls of wax. Such are the "products" of the northern forests, which have a market down to the east and south.[1] Gorm finds that he lacks the experience and the goods to do much trading, but he manages to obtain a few forties of furs anyway in exchange for some of his stock of beads.

The major stop that Gorm's party of merchant-adventurers makes along the way between the outflow of the Tvertsa and Bulghar is at Timerëvo [near later Iaroslavl], which impresses Gorm much more than Holmgard or Aldeigjuborg. Scandinavian people from the Lake Malaren area [Middle Sweden] have been resident here since at least the early ninth century; it is a permanent and growing settlement, a fort with a garrison of warriors and a local chief, nominally subordinate to Jarl Igor in Kiev, and of course an important staging post for the trade on the Upper Volga. Here the travelers make the final major adjustments and exchanges to their cargoes. Snorri and the senior members of the ship's company know what special items are most desired by the Scandinavian men and women: fine brooches, combs, swords and other gear. For the local smiths in Timerëvo, Snorri has brought some bars of zinc-alloy metal, obtained in the West [originating in Britain], which superficially looks much like silver and is used to make cheap copies of more expensive jewelry for trade with the indigenous peoples.

After several days of complicated haggling and feasting, in which Gorm does not play much of a part (except he manages to get a fair share of ale and meat), Gorm's party sets out on their final leg of the journey to Bulghar. Their boats are quite crowded now with bales of furs and other goods, and blond northern girls situated amid the clutter here and there. Altogether, the journey from Holmgard to Bulghar up the Msta and then down the Upper Volga, including the stops, has taken some five to six weeks. July is mostly over by the time they arrive at this major international trading site, where under the auspices of the Bulghar *khan* and his Middle-Volga city-state, Muslim merchants from Central Asia and the Caliphate trade millions of Islamic silver *dirhams* (and other high-value items) for the goods brought from the northern pagan lands by Gorm's group, and similar traders.

A Viking funeral

When they arrive at Bulghar Gorm is surprised that there are Norse pagan shrines with carved wooden idols where the men go to give thanks for their safe arrival. They also ask the gods to grant them easy profits in the trading that they are about to engage in. There are crude huts outside the city walls where Rus' [Scandinavians who have taken up living in Eastern Europe] traders usually stay; Gorm's party finds a couple of these that are presently unoccupied, quickly erect some new ones for the senior crew members and start to plan their trading strategies. The marketplace inside Bulghar is large, crowded and loud, and Gorm follows in the wake of the older and more experienced men. Typically, the greatest profits (usually taken in the form of Islamic silver *dirhams*) are negotiated for the best-quality furs and for the girls; the men who own these choice items acquire considerable quantities of silver. Snorri, however, also has brought some rarer goods: he has some "Frankish" swords, both genuine items made on the continent and imitations forged in Scandinavia, both of which are highly prized in the Middle East, and these he sells to specialist dealers. Snorri also has brought some Baltic amber and some walrus ivory from the far North. Gorm also manages to offload the few forties of furs that he has acquired along the way for some silver *dirhams*, so he is fairly content. As a bead maker's son, he is attracted to stalls that deal in exotic stones (carnelian, quartz) and some interesting bead types as well as some raw glass (in rods) at a reasonable price, so he trades in some of his *dirhams* for these items. The entire process of scouting out the best buyers, negotiating the exchanges and completing the separate transactions takes about a week.

However, when they are all about ready to leave Bulghar behind and start the return journey up the Volga, unexpected news runs through the Rus' community: an important chief among the Rus' has fallen ill and is not expected to live, and his relatives and companions are going to put on an elaborate funeral to mark his passing. So Snorri and the other leaders of Gorm's party decide that it might be worth staying to witness this. The chief dies in about a week, and preparations for the spectacular funeral take another week. The ceremony is performed at riverside, in the midst of the makeshift Rus' settlement, and it involves the sacrifice of a slave girl and the burning of the deceased chief's body in an unusually large boat. Gorm is entertained by the spectacle. He has never seen anything quite like this back home in Birka, and he wonders if his countrymen living here in the East are getting a bit weird.

Gorm's return voyage

Gorm's party sets out on the return trip the day after the funeral, but the season has grown dangerously late. It is now mid-August, and the way back, upstream against the strong current of the Upper Volga, is much more laborious and time consuming.

Altogether, they do not complete their multi-stage return journey to Aldeigjuborg until late October. And they find that the last seaworthy ship that might take them back across the Baltic to Birka has departed. They are stuck in Aldeigjuborg until spring breaks the ice and ships from the West start arriving again.

Gorm has had enough adventure; he wants to be home, spending a snug winter with his family and working with his father in the bead workshop. "O Odin!" he cries out, "why did you lure me here to Gardariki with promises of wealth and glory, only to dump me in this stinking hole for a long, miserable winter and nothing to do?"

The party finds what accommodations they can, and settles in. Gorm makes friends with a local Finnic man's daughter, especially once he gives her some of his beads. Eventually, Gorm moves into the girl's hut and they spend the winter sleeping together. They cannot understand each other's language very much, and Gorm finds much about her to be mysterious. He lets her rummage through his pouch of beads and small bronze jewelry items, but the girl keeps talking and gesturing and trying to show him something that he doesn't understand. Like all of the local people, she has very strange taste in jewelry and clothes. For instance, when he tries to give her a pair of bronze turtle-brooches, which any Swedish bride or wife would be proud to have as a gift, the girl in turn is greatly puzzled and has no idea how to wear them.

In May of the following year, the first ships start coming in from points west via the Gulf of Finland and the Neva. Eventually, another complicated swap-and-trade deal involving river boats for a seagoing ship is negotiated with an arriving party similar to the one that Gorm's group made when they arrived a year earlier. By mid-June, Gorm is back in Birka, having left his Finnic winter bride with her father.

Gorm spends a year, more or less, back at home. He makes some smart trades with the modest profits he has brought back from the East and works diligently to improve his skills in bead making. When he goes east again, in May of the third year of our story, he is much better prepared and eventually returns to Birka with much greater profits than he did on his first voyage. He also reconnects with his Finnic bride and his father-in-law in Ladoga and finds that she has born a child while he was away. Gorm begins to plan on spending winters in Ladoga. After a couple more cycles, each of which takes a couple of years, he decides to relocate to Ladoga permanently. This time, he leaves Birka with a set of bead maker's tools and sets up as a practitioner of this highly specialized and prestigious craft right in Ladoga. He still goes on trading expeditions east to Bulghar in the summers, but the rest of the year he is at Ladoga, making beads, trading them both to long-distance merchants and to people in the local Ladoga region, building up stock for his next trading journey to the East, and thriving in the bosom of his growing Scando-Finnic family. His children grow up bilingual and able to negotiate the divide between the Scandinavian and Finnic cultural worlds with aplomb.

When Gorm is about thirty years old, his Finnish wife dies in childbirth. Soon after, Gorm decides to leave Ladoga and relocates up the Volkhov to Holmgard on Lake Ilmen. Thus begins a new phase in Gorm's life.

Note

★ Arnold Lelis died of cancer shortly after this biography was completed. The runic symbol Gebo (x), used after his name, symbolizes Arnold and Heidi's love and partnership.
1 For furs and wax and honey the travelers trade directly with individual Finnic producers, who are expert in extracting these resources from the *taiga* and welcome traveling traders. The local Finnic people produce more of these items than they need for themselves in order to be able to engage in this trade and be able to obtain things such as glass beads, silver coins, or small pieces of jewelry – the availability of which is slowly transforming the material and cultural lifestyle in these parts of European Russia. The traders, in turn, depend on the cooperation of the local people to get the wares that they need to make these long, difficult and dangerous river voyages worthwhile. The provenance of the slave girls is more problematic because slave trading tends to be highly disruptive for source societies. If slave girls are obtained from local Finnic villagers at all, it is likely that only village leaders have the authority to hand over these teenage girls to the strangers, and that the prices paid for them (in silver, fine jewelry and other exceptional items) are much higher even than for the choicest furs.

Further reading

Ibn Fadlan, *Ibn Fadlan and the Land of Darkness: Arab Travellers in the Far North*, transls. Paul Lunde and Caroline Stone (New York: Penguin, 2012).
Simon Franklin and Jonathan Shepard, *The Emergence of Rus, 900–1200* (New York: Longman, 1996).
The Russian Primary Chronicle, transl. and ed. Samuel Hazzard Cross and Olgerd P. Sherbowitz-Wetzor (Cambridge, MA: Mediaeval Academy of America, 1953).
Thomas S. Noonan, *The Islamic World, Russia and the Vikings* (New York: Variorum, 1998).

17

ANNA PORPHYROGENITA, BYZANTINE PRINCESS AND QUEEN OF THE RUS'

Susana Torres Prieto

Introduction

Anna Porphyrogenita is, despite her relevance for the history of Kievan Rus', someone we know very little about, and even the order of the few facts we know about her life is still contested among historians. We know she was the sister of Basil II, the Byzantine emperor and so-called "Bulgar-slayer." We know she married prince Vladimir Sviatoslavich – but historians disagree when or where – that she probably had no children (but the agreement is not unanimous on this point either) and that she died in Kiev, though the date is also disputed. Her paramount role in the history of Kievan Rus' derives from the fact that her marriage to prince Vladimir symbolized the entry of the newly created polity within the orbit of Byzantium (politically, culturally, religiously) and, therefore, the entry of Kievan Rus' in Christian history.

The present sketch is therefore based on the few historical facts that we know, without entering into the academic polemics but necessarily adopting one position against others, and, mostly, on what we know about material culture, about the cultural and social shock that for someone coming from Constantinople must have been to live among the Rus'. I have tried to underline the prominent role that she apparently kept, particularly in religious issues, despite not having apparently produced any surviving child.

I have adopted the form of a purported diary, a recollection of memories in the first person of someone who maybe, and only maybe, against her will, would contribute decisively to the change of the history of Kievan Rus' for what she represented. This is, therefore, a highly novelized sketch, and it is, as such, highly personal and potentially contested. In order to avoid misleading any reader, I have clearly identified in notes those facts in the life of Anna that are attested in the sources. All details of realia are taken from secondary sources identified in the Suggestions for further reading. The rest of the tale is my own.

* * *

Epiphany, year 6496[1]

These people stink. From the moment I arrived here I carry with me a handkerchief and a little bottle of rosewater that Ioannis readily provided. People look at me as if I was crazy when I spill the rosewater in the handkerchief and bring it to my nose. They laugh and look at each other and make a gesture as if whatever is in the bottle should be drunk, and not spilled. To be perfectly honest, they look at me, at all of us, as if I were a character out of the *Alexandriada* or we were a troupe of the circus, rather than an imperial delegation. Everything in them stinks: their mouths, their hair, their armpits, their feet, their clothes, everything. I should never, ever forgive my brother for doing this to me. Ever.

There is this woman who comes after me everywhere I go. She looks a little bit like an imbecile, smiling all the time and bowing constantly. Of course, she does not speak any language I know, so I cannot really enquire why she does it either. She was given to me in Cherson, just when I arrived, I guess she is a slave, because that man from my husband's personal guard could only manage to say in broken Greek, "She. With you," and then this poor thing has never left my side, so I guess she is mine now. She tries to be kind, but she leaves behind her this stale odor coming out of her clothes, of her head – you can always tell when she is around. Her face is all round, she is quite plump, and her skin is always greasy, shiny, but she is always trying to help and trying to smile, regardless. I wish she smiled less, her teeth are just a horrible sight. I really don't know what her name is, I call her Maria, I am sure our Theotokos will not get offended. She seems to have learnt the name and now responds to it.

The trip over here was a nightmare, the whole thing has been a nightmare. My stupid brother, who had no qualms in handing me over to this barbarian, didn't even have the guts to come with me and do things properly. I said to him: "Well, brother, are you afraid you could be kidnapped or something by your new, wonderful ally!" He looked at me, full of contempt, and muttered: "Perhaps." I exploded: "And what about me, then? Aren't you afraid I could be kidnapped?" He looked up from the papers he was reading: "I have already given you to him. I don't expect he would ask for ransom." And with that, he turned towards one of those horrible generals and ended the conversation. I guess my words didn't help.

Things had not been going well with Basilii lately. We have never been favorite brother and sister, him being the oldest and me the little one, and the girl. And he was never really very normal, particularly after Mother's demise from the court.[2] He became even more taciturn, more into himself. The relations with Uncle John were never easy, always complex, and Mother's leave must have been hard on him. I was only seven, I don't remember much, but he must. I don't remember how many times I prayed to our Theotokos to allow me to leave that horrible palace, where everybody suspected everybody and you could not trust anyone, lest they fall in disgrace tomorrow and you were also caught. It was horrible! Thankfully, Ioannis was always taking care of me. But God knows I certainly didn't want to leave the Court for this. I have often wondered what Basilii had against me. I have come to the conclusion he just hates all women. End of story. I guess he never forgave Mother for leaving him behind in the hands of Uncle John, surrounded by enemies: she, who was supposed to be his guardian and his regent. I wonder now if I am not paying for her sins. Only God knows how many they could be.

I tried to postpone coming as much as I could, I told Basilii he had to make sure this barbarian was already a Christian, and I said I needed more time to finish my lining and my ceremonial clothes. He said he didn't think I was going to need any of that where I was going. I tried to convince him that there were many other candidates to whom a marriage with his only sister could be advantageous. He said there was no time for that then, that the decision was final, and that was it.

The man is a brute. For the first couple of days after we arrived in Cherson he just looked at me and spoke broken Greek, grunted really. When I was formally introduced, he managed to produce some Greek words he must have learnt by heart welcoming me, wishing my trip had not been too tiresome. I replied. He looked at me blankly, either he was not expecting me to reply or he didn't understand a word I said, or both. Later on, he tried to come by where we were sitting at the banquet and started to produce random lines of the Psalter in an appalling Greek, with a very funny accent. I giggled at his efforts as I looked at some people of my legation. He didn't like that. He shouted something at me in his language, everybody became silent, and left with an angry look on his face. I guess I put my foot in it, completely. I didn't mean to laugh *at* him, I just found it funny, like when back home we had people reciting plays with funny accents. He didn't get it. And then he took his particular revenge for it. After a few hours of celebrations, everybody suddenly stood up and Maria took me gently by the hand, smiling as always, and took me to another chamber. I asked the monk Vasilii to come with me, not to leave me alone. "In this, I cannot help you, dear. It is your duty, but think that is also God's will," he said, and left me at the door of the chamber, where Maria and some of my ladies were waiting to undress me. When Ioannis was going to get inside the chamber to help me undress and put aside the ceremony clothes and prepare me to bed, my husband's men, who were marauding at the door, made a huge fuss. According to them no man was allowed that night in the chamber except my husband. It was not until Vasilii came to explain that Ioannis was not a danger, at all, that they broke out laughing and let it rest. They had been laughing at Ioannis since we arrived because he has no beard and he is always with us. Apparently here eunuchs are as unknown as personal hygiene.

I remember hearing jokes in the corridors of the palace about how my mother's skills were always better displayed in the sleeping chamber than in any other room in the palace. I didn't know what they meant when I was little. I gradually became aware of what they meant. I became increasingly worried after reading the books that Father Vasilii gave me about having inherited some particular skill that maybe I shouldn't have and would condemn me forever. I was trembling when they all left. He came in, quite tipsy but not as drunk as he would other times. He was ruthless, and as long as I live I will remember distinctly the smell of his breath on my face, a mix of alcohol, fermented fish and rotten teeth, as he was pushing his way through. He obviously knew much better than me what he was doing. He grunted a little bit louder at the end, and stayed there for a few moments. He then sat down, arranged his clothes, spit on the floor, and left. I heard the laughter and the cries of the men waiting at the door. I could not stop looking at the wooden beams above me, I didn't dare to move. Maria came back immediately, took the sheet below me, and touched me for the first time. She caressed my hair. I burst into tears. I hated them all, my brother, my husband, even the stupid monk. I couldn't help thinking: "What a piece of crap, having been born in the purple chamber, daughter and sister of Roman emperors to end up like this! All these years of waiting for this."

After a few days we started our way to the city where I was going to live, Kiev. These people must have thought it was something spectacular because everybody was making a huge fuss about it. Part of my people left then and returned to Byzantion, how I wished I could have gone with them. Vasilii stayed, of course. He was not only my confessor but also our translator, and he had some orders to fulfill from the Patriarch. A couple of my ladies and a bunch of servants also stayed behind, but not many stayed behind after the first winter. Ioannis was beaten up one night by these thugs and we had to take him to the Greek quarter for weeks to recover in the house of one of our merchants who could eventually put him in a boat back home. I cried for one whole day when I said goodbye to him. He had been with me since the day Mother had left, always protecting me, always caring for me, always teaching me new things, but he certainly deserved something better than this in his old age.

My husband's visits continued once we were already established in Kiev, which, by the way was nothing special. I never understood what these people saw in this godforsaken place. Any provincial city of the Empire would be so far better by comparison. At least, they probably had sanitation and pavements, which these people clearly can live without. Everything is made of wood, the streets are constantly muddy and it stinks, like them. I have been told that at the end of winter or beginning of the spring, when the snows melt and the river runs quick, and before the summer heat and the midges make life unbearable, Kiev is a nice place. Whatever!

The worst part of arriving to Kiev was that the place was swarming with wives, lovers, and children of my husband. Not very different from our own court, really, but at least there we did husbands and wives consecutively, not simultaneously. I spoke to Vasilii, who apparently had a word with Anastasii the Chersonite, someone whom my husband trusted since the siege of Cherson. I said I was not going to share the palace with former wives. I couldn't care less about sharing him, but not the palace, well, whatever this shed is. The first one at least had to go. I told him to explain to him that in our religion, the one he has just adopted after making such a show of throwing down the river his pagan gods, wives are taken one after another, and then usually only after one has died. "If he wants to have lovers, let him have them, but they are not to sit at the same table with me," I cried.

After a little bit of haggling and many letters to Byzantion and back, and the intervention of Anastasii and other churchmen, the first one is finally out. She and all the children.

Easter, year 6496

Anastasii has come to see me this morning. I have told him again that these wooden houses where we have been lodged are far from what was arranged. He has asked me to be a little bit more patient. For a start, my husband is going to make the whole of the city Christianize, *en masse.* "And couldn't he make them work in my new lodgings instead?" I don't think he thought I was being serious. I was. Maria keeps coming after me. Sometimes some of my ladies laugh at her servile attitude. I have told them to stop doing that, she means well. The other day she came limping and I tried to ask what was the matter. She doesn't understand, of course. I called one of Anastasii's men to act as translator. She said it was nothing. I pointed to her foot. She insisted it was nothing. I told her that if she refused to tell me, I didn't want her around me. Finally she sat on the floor and started to disentangle the mess of dirty clothes tied together with a thin rope she uses as shoes. The stench almost made me faint. I think it must be the pregnancy, I am so sensitive to these things now. When she finished, we could see the black foot and the purulent blisters around her toe, it was a horrible sight. Some of my ladies ran out of the room trying not to vomit. I clenched the monk's arm: "Ask her what happened." Maria didn't know. The monk said it was quite normal, in the mud any nail or piece of wood could have gone through the rags. I asked for the Greek physician who had come with me. Even he made a grimace of disgust when he saw her, and covered his nose. "Cure her," I said. "With all due respect, Your Highness, she is just a servant," he replied. "She is not just a servant," I said, "she is *my* servant, and in this Godforsaken place she seems to be the only one who is truly committed to please me, so cure her. Or shall I remind you how Our Lord washed the feet of the Apostles before the Last Supper? Do you think, physician, you are more important than Our Lord?" The physician was not impressed, but the monk was.

Pentecost, year 6496

Today there was a spectacular celebration. We all went to the top of the hill to see the massive Christening ceremony, people were getting immersed into the water, with their children and some of them with their horses while Anastasii and other churchmen were trying to keep some order and tried to stop people from getting horses and other animals inside. Everybody was in the street; it was like a market day. As we were ascending the hill, I could see the stalls with animal skins, jewellery, honey, candles, and pots. Apparently my husband has given them little option for changing religion: it was Christianity or Christianity. The water was coming down quickly and some people were being carried away by its current. The children were splashing around, and I doubt very few really knew what it was for, or about, apart from having a bath now that the winter was over. I thought that at least it served for washing them a little, which will surely please Our Lord. All, except the children, kept their clothes on, clearly not getting the message, but it was a wonderful spring day, everybody was happy. Even my husband was happy. At one point, he touched my incipient belly and said: "Next one will be he." I smiled back at him, for the first time in all these months, I actually smiled back at him.

One day in autumn, year 6496

The baby was born dead. It was a full baby, but when it came out it didn't breathe. Everybody tried to make him cry, I tried, but he didn't. It was a he. I held him in my arms for hours, crying bitterly over my bad luck, although I was exhausted. Finally Maria came to the bed, as she had done on the night when the poor little thing was probably conceived, and with tears in her eyes she said: "Tsaritsa, let go."

That was not the worst part. When I woke up the physician came and told me that I will not have children ever. They had to take everything out so I wasn't contaminated by the dead baby.

I have been in bed since. I don't want to go anywhere, I don't want to eat, I don't want to be here, I just don't want to be.

A week before Christmas, year 6496

I have now woken up and eaten something, but I don't leave my room. My confessor comes and gives me communion daily, to see if I will be brought back to life with the help of the Lord and the Theotokos. He doesn't understand how pointless my life is now, all of it.

This evening he has finally come to see me. He sat down on the bed where I was lying, took my hands and said: "δισσὰς χλαίνας ἐποίσεν τῷ ἀνδρὶ αὐτῆς, ἐκ δὲ βύσσου καὶ πορφύρας ἑαυτῇ ἐνδύματα. περίβλεπτος δε γίνεται ἐν πύλαις ὁ ἀνὴρ αὐτῆς, ἡνίκα ἂν καθίσῃ ἐν συνεδρίῳ μετὰ τῶν γερόντων κατοίκων τῆς γῆς."[3] "How do you know that?" I asked. "Book of Proverbs," he said. "Yes, I know, but how do *you* know?" "A Greek nun taught me that some time ago. It doesn't matter. Anna, I already have children, more than I care to count, actually. But what you know, nobody in my land does. I need you to help me make this a great city, like your city. We will build a great Church, over the top of the hill, so everybody will see it from every part of the city. We will build it in stone, like yours, with cupolas and frescoes. And a new palace for you, for us. I will call artisans from your land, it will be grand, but please try to recover." I looked at him, he was different, he was determined, he was actually . . . caring? "I want to have it consecrated to the Mother of God." "Fine, as you wish, but please leave the bed. It is going to be my first Christmas and Anastasii and the others are all nervous and asking me things I don't know about." He paused for a minute and looked at me again: "Anna, don't tell your brother this, I would have helped him anyway, but I didn't bring you here to give me more children over whom I will have to divide my land one day, I brought you because I want people to respect me like they respect him. Be my *tsaritsa*, help me build a new kingdom."

Notes

1 Although the day of Anna Porphyrogenita's marriage is not attested in the sources, it would have taken place after the baptism of Prince Vladimir. Baptisms of the newly converted usually took place on key dates of the Church calendar, and it seems plausible that it would have happened around epiphany 988 (first or second Sunday after Christmas 987). It is likely that the Church authorities who baptised Vladimir were travelling with Anna and her entourage.
2 Their mother was empress Theophano and their father Romanos II, who died when Basilii was only five years old. Upon his death, she married Nikephoros II Phokas while serving as regent. Rumour had it that she plotted with Nikephoros's nephew, John I Tzimiskes, to have her husband killed. After being acclaimed emperor, but before the ceremony of coronation, John had to choose between marrying the highly unpopular Theophano or being crowned by the Patriarch. He chose the second and sent Theophano into exile to the island of Prinkipo.
3 Proverbs 31, 22–23: "She makes coverings for her bed; she is clothed in fine linen and purple. Her husband is respected at the city gate, where he takes his seat among the elders of the land."

For additional information

Franklin, Simon and Jonathan Shepard. *The Emergence of the Rus 750–1200*. London: Longman, 1996.
Gonneau, Pierre and Aleksandr Lavorv. *Des Rhôs à la Russie: histoire de l'Europe orientale (v. 730–1689)*. Paris: Presses universitaires de France, 2012.
Herrin, Judith. *Women in Purple: Rulers of Medieval Byzantium*. London: Weidenfeld and Nicholson, 2001.
Raffensperger, Christian. *Reimagining Europe: Kievan Rus' in the Medieval World*. Cambridge, MA: Harvard University Press, 2012.
Stephenson, Paul. *The Legend of Basil the Bulgar-Slayer*. Cambridge: Cambridge University Press, 2003.
Traimond, Véra. *Architecture de la Russie Ancienne, vol. 1: X-XV siècles*. Paris: Hermann, 2003.
Vodoff, Vladimir. *Naissance de la chrétienté russe: la conversion du prince Vladimir de Kiev (988) et ses consequences (XIe-XIIIe siècles)*. Paris: Fayard, 1988.

18

"THE JOURNEYS OF MY SOUL IN THIS LAND OF CANAAN" BY YITSHAK BEN SIROTA

Isaiah Gruber

Yitshak ben Sirota is an imagined Jew (composite historical figure) of eleventh-century East-
ern Europe. His own travels and the stories he hears from others cover Rus', Poland, Byzan-
tium, and Western Europe. Yitshak's imagined autobiographical account corresponds closely
with extant documentary evidence and provides information and perspective on the contem-
porary interactions of men and women, Jews and Christians, masters and slaves, and other
groups. In high and late medieval Hebrew literature the Biblical term "Canaan" designated
the Slavic lands (just as "Ashkenaz" denoted the German lands). Yitshak employs this and
other contemporary terminology, and his "Canaanites" are therefore Slavs. More specifically,
by "Greek Canaan" he means the East Slavic territories where the population followed the
Greek (Orthodox Christian) rite.

Like many medieval travelogues and other writings, Yitshak's tale intermingles a record
of events and peregrinations with assorted explanations and interjections. As a human nar-
rator, Yitshak necessarily speaks from his own perspective and with imperfect knowledge. His
notions of relevance and significance may sometimes differ from those of a modern reader.
However, his portrayals are based on real stories and are consistent with actual historical pos-
sibility. The glossary and endnotes (supplied by a later editor, perhaps the same individual
who translated the text from the original Hebrew) provide a guide for readers who may not
grasp all of Yitshak's idioms and allusions or who wish to consult extant historical documents
in order to verify the essential aspects of his story.[1] The abbreviation "R." means "Rabbi."

* * *

I do not know the land of my birth. I have been told that my ancestors went
down from the true land of Canaan, a place very distant from here. To reach it you
must travel many days beyond the great city of Qostantina [Constantinople]. There
the Holy One of Yisrael [Israel] spoke in days long past to our fathers Abraham,
Isaac, and Jacob, as is written in the Torah of Moses. There also King David ruled
from Yerushalayim [Jerusalem], the holy and chosen city. For this reason Jews and
Christians and other peoples go up every year to Yerushalayim in great numbers

from all the countries of the Greek Land [Byzantium] and many far corners of the world.[2] Our rabbis say that all our people shall return to that place – may it be His will that the Redeemer come to Zion speedily and soon and in our days, amen![3] In these days we sojourn in another land of Canaan, among the tribes of Gentiles who call themselves in their own language Polanim [Poles] and Rusim [people of Rus'] and other such names. Many of my fellow Jews of this exile no longer speak our own ancient tongue but converse only in the language of Canaan.

My father died during war, and my mother perished while giving birth to my younger brother Yosef. I heard these things, and did not see them with my own eyes, for I was very small. We grew up in the care of relatives in the region of Primut (this is the name I remember hearing). I do not know where this land may be, but a certain man once told me that it is the very same city that the Canaanites call Pshemysl or Premyshl [now Przemyśl in Poland].[4] If that is so, then the news that has just reached us is so urgent that I must depart at once, as I shall explain. But first I must tell the story of my childhood. Our relatives cared for us until a time of crisis arose in their land. When bandits broke through, they slaughtered many people and burned the houses. All of us were killed or carried off into slavery – may the Almighty see our distress and rescue us! I and my brother were thrown into a field with our hands bound together. We would have died there, but the Almighty had mercy on us. The man of Canaan called Matviy, a seller of grain to my uncle Shmuel, saw us and his heart took pity upon us. As my uncle was carried away, he begged Matviy to rescue us two boys, promising to repay him well upon his return. Whether this Canaanite believed that my uncle would escape or be ransomed, or whether he rescued us out of kindness or due to his past relations with my family, I cannot say. I awoke in strange surroundings, in a hut with a warm fire and unknown people and images of idolatry on the walls.

We stayed many days in the house of the Canaanite, until I had nearly forgotten my own family. One day I went out to the fields with Matviy, but my brother did not come with us. Woe upon woe befell us! Marauders came again and struck the farmer and his fellow men of Canaan and me too with their spears and poles. I saw blood flowing into the plowed earth. One of the raiders lifted me up from the ground and threw me across his horse. I have never seen my brother or that Canaanite man who rescued us or any of my relatives again, even from that time until this very day.

I, Yitshak ben Sirota, was taken as a slave to the great city of Qostantina, which lies at the mouth of the Two Great Seas [the Mediterranean/Aegean/Marmara and the Black]. A Christian servant of the emperor bought me for ten nomismata, the usual price at the central market. So many women and children were sold that I could not count them all, for this city has a large trade and great profit in the sale of human beings from all the nations of the world. I served my master for three years. He was not an evil man. He beat me once or twice, but not like the other masters – as is well known, many slaves today are maimed and killed by their lords. I worked in his household and did not starve. However, my master forced me to bow down with him before images of idolatry, which is strictly forbidden to all Jews. May God forgive me, even as the prophet Elisha absolved Naaman the Syrian for the same sin [2 Kings 5]!

I thought often of my brother and my relatives and wondered if they were alive, slaves like me, or dead. I hoped that if my brother had been brought here I might find him. One day when I had been sent to the market I saw the slaves being sold as usual and began to cry, thinking of my family. Hardly realizing what I was doing, I whispered one of the prayers I still remembered from the home of my relatives: *Barukh atah Adonai shomea tefilah* [Blessed are You, Lord, who hears prayer].[5] It so happened that a Jewish slave trader was standing near me, bidding or selling, and heard my words. This man asked me who I was and where I came from. When he heard that I had been captured in the land of Greek Canaan, he asked after my master and sent an emissary back with me to the household, having instructed him carefully beforehand. The agent of this slave trader presented a gift to my master and made a speech with many fine words. He then offered to buy me for a high price. My master was loathe to part with me, but in the end he pressed his lead seal onto the bill of sale that had been prepared in advance on the paper of the Arabs, and I was exchanged for fourteen nomismata.

FIGURE 18.1 "Yitshak rejoins his people." Illustration by Sonya Dimand.

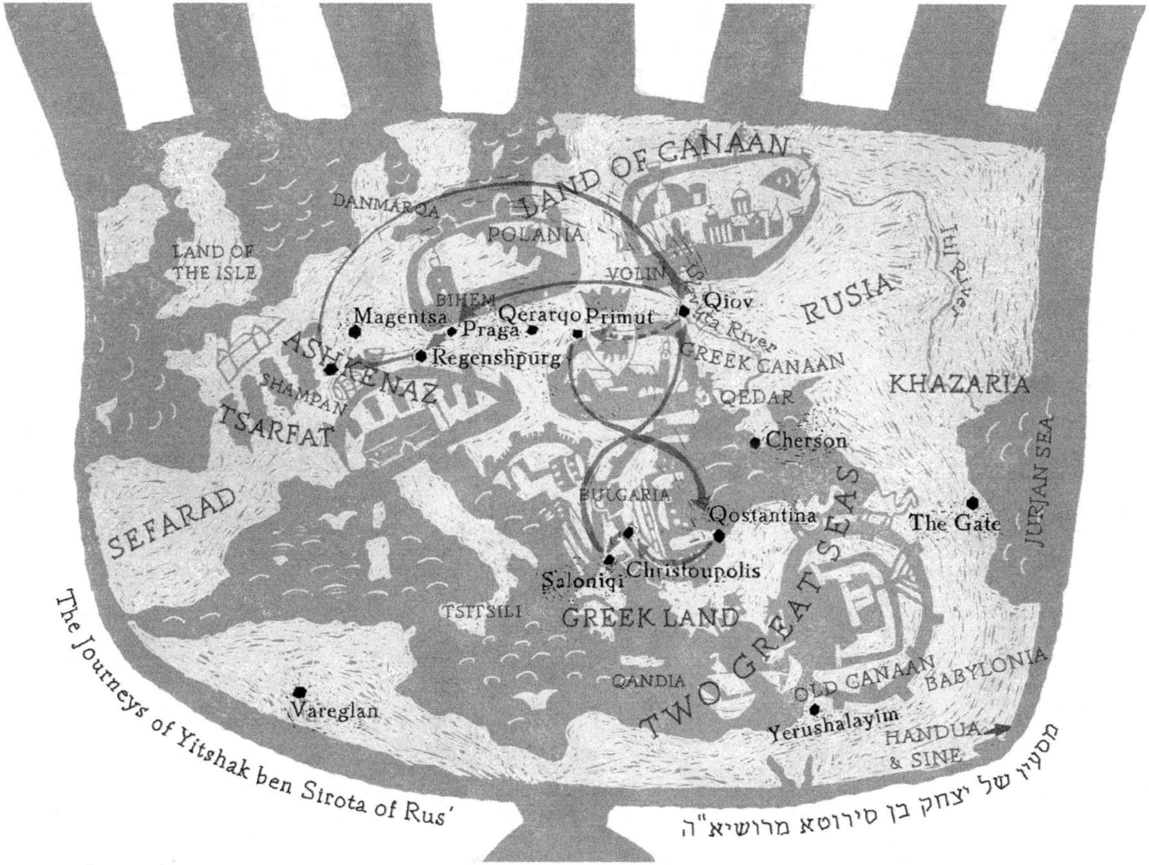

MAP 18.1 "Yitshak's travels." Cartographic illustration by Sonya Dimand.

The Jewish trader who bought me acted not out of charity but rather from a shrewd calculation: knowing that our communities of the exile show care to all fellow Jews in distress whenever they can,[6] he wanted to sell me for a high ransom. Yet he made me swear that I had not been converted to Christianity, otherwise he might lose his investment. We joined a great caravan of Jewish merchants, some of whom were headed for the eastern lands, called Handua [India] and Sine [China], by way of The Gate [Derbent]. They carried with them furs and caviar and other valuable goods from the land of Canaan and many other lands besides. Other merchants travel in the opposite direction, passing by Qandia [Crete] and Tsitsili [Sicily] and going across the desert as far as Vareglan [Ouargla] and beyond. But my master set me apart from his other slaves, and we set our course by the western road along the sea. One Sabbath we camped in a valley near Christoupolis [now Kavala in northern Greece]. These men arranged all the carriages and equipment in a circle and called it an *eruv* according to the Jewish law. I heard Hebrew prayers again for the first time in many years, and I did not understand them all. These traders who travel to and fro across the world from East to West follow the traditions of our ancestors, but some say they create their own *halakhah* and do not consult the rabbis.[7] I saw with my own eyes that they did whatever seemed good to them but also observed some rituals strictly. Their men had intercourse with any of the slave women they chose, but they made them immerse for purity just like Jewish women.[8] Some women immersed while clothed, and this was permitted if their garments were loose.[9]

After fifteen days we arrived in Saloniqi [Thessaloniki, Salonica],[10] which is a city where many Jews live, as well as Greeks and Canaanites and other peoples. The Jews of this place have much strife among themselves, for a part of them adhere to the law of the rabbis while another part are Karaites, whom the rabbis call heretics. The holiday of Shavuot [Pentecost or the Feast of Weeks] was approaching, and a great dissention arose among the Jews of the city about the proper date of the festival.[11] The Karaites sent their agents out to convince all the Jews to observe the festival according to their calculations, while the rabbis denounced them in the synagogues with much vehemence, holding to their own calendar. The rabbis and heads of the synagogues read letters from the great academies of Babylonia [the Abbasid caliphate] proving the error of the heretics, but the latter had their own book of interpretations from Babylonia that they said was older. They also denounced the rabbis to the Christians, accusing them of many crimes, and because of this a heavy fine was levied against the Jewish community. At one of these meetings some elders from the land of Rusia [Rus'] in Canaan, from the city of Qiov [Kiev], were present. They raised a collection for me and purchased my freedom from the Jewish slave trader for twenty silver coins. Praise be to the exalted King!

When the merchants of Qiov returned to their own city, I went with them, and thus I came again to the land of Canaan. We drove our carts through the Jewish Gates,[12] and I saw wooden churches and a synagogue along the banks of the river called Slavuta [Dniepr]. The people of this land wear boots of leather and felt, which can be obtained from excellent craftsmen. They are descended from Tiras son of Yafeth mentioned in the book of Genesis, or some say Ashkenaz son of Gomer the brother of Tiras.[13] The king of the Rusim at this time was Iaroslav, the one they call great in wisdom.[14] In those days monks began to live in the Caves [the Kievan Pecherskii Monastery], and they soon became a great company.

I have lived in this city from then until now, for I was blessed to find a position in the house of bar Kybr.[15] The clan of this elder is descended from the tribe of the Khazars who previously ruled over a great territory extending from this land of Qiov to the Jurjan [Caspian] sea in the east. In our days those who believe in Muhammad's laws dwell there on the river Itil [Volga] and beyond. I learned to arrange the affairs of a trading house, and they taught me the writing of our tongue and that of the Canaanites. The elder bar Kybr called me Sirota, the orphan, and all knew me by this name. When the cantor asked me to read a section of the weekly *parashah* in the community gathering, he called me up to the *bimah* (whether by intention or misunderstanding) as Yitshak ben Sirota.[16] It has been my name ever since, though some call me Ayziq, which is another way to pronounce the same name.[17]

The Christians of Rusia are very pious according to their own faith, although many of the people are completely ignorant of the traditions decreed by the councils of their lawmakers.[18] They have many strange beliefs and others that are completely in accord with the Law of Moses and the Prophets. Many of our people do not know this, but they honor the same writings as we do and even read the words of the Holy Torah rendered into their own tongue. But they call this the Old Law, and change many meanings by substituting a New Law. Some of their preachers accuse us of horrible crimes and incite the unlearned against us. One of their monks, Feodosii by name, came several times at night to provoke us, shouting that all Jews are accursed and deserving of eternal punishment. Some of the people spit as we pass and deride us. Nonetheless, a few of their scholars respect our learning, and they even have books in the language of Sclavonia – which is to say, the speech of Canaan – that contain some words of Hebrew writing. I heard that they were written by Jewish translators in the kingdom of Bulgaria, in the southern lands. When I met the priest called Luka, he would ask me questions about these words of our tongue. He wrote down the meanings I told him in a little scroll, and added new ones from our conversations. However, it is dangerous for Christian scholars to show too much interest in our books. One monk studied the writings of the Hebrew Bible well and did not hide it, and so they called him possessed by an evil spirit.[19]

In those days the Christians did not attack us with violence and plunder and burn our property. This was before the calamity that arose after the monk Evstratii of the Caves was taken captive by Cumans. Word reached Qiov that he had been taken across Qedar [the Pontic steppe in Ukraine] and sold to a Jew in Cherson [Chersonesus Taurica, Korsun]. Now this Evstratii loved to abstain from food and drink; such was his special custom already in Qiov. The Christians said that he told all the slaves of the Jew to fast likewise until they all died. He did this in order to cause the Jew to suffer the loss of a great sum of money that he had paid for these slaves. This story circulated and spread, and soon men with bitterness of spirit proclaimed that the Jew had crucified Evstratii by nailing him to a cross just like Christ.[20] A mob gathered and committed violence against all Jews they found in the streets. They stole and destroyed our property too, and we narrowly escaped with our lives. The rioters beat and killed Christians as well; they were like wild animals who know not what they do.[21]

The loss suffered by the house of bar Kybr at this time was substantial. Our elder decided to raise money from his associates and send fifteen of his men on a trading journey to the western lands. He concluded agreements for the delayed purchase of clothing and merchandise, which our rabbis have permitted, judging that such arrangements do not violate the prohibition against taking interest from a brother Yisraeli.[22] We set out in the spring and passed through many countries, Volin [Volhynia] and Polania [Poland] and Bihem [Bohemia] and Ashkenaz [the German lands] and Tsarfat [France]. In all these lands Jews live in exile. I regret only that I never saw the great kingdom of Sefarad [Spain and Portugal], which is ruled by the servants of Muhammad, for the Jews of this land have acquired great fame through their learning and poetry.[23]

Now Rusia is a great kingdom and a land of forests where animals of fur called sable and marten and others are plentiful. But the lands to the west are not so, and their inhabitants desire these goods. The Christians of these lands follow a different law than those of Rusia, and are very adamant on this point, though I did not comprehend their quarrels clearly. But know that they despise the Christians of Greece and those of Rusia, which are of the same law, as well as all pagans, Muslims, and Jews.

I have time to tell of only a few of our adventures. In the city of Praga [Prague], which lies beyond Qerarqo [Kraków], we heard the mournful poetry of Menachem bar Makhir and the story of how he had to forbid the Jews of that place from baking their food together in the same oven with the forbidden meat of Gentiles. In Regenshpurg [Regensburg] we tasted wine with little strength, so that one did not dilute it like the wine of Rusia, which is extremely intoxicating and dangerous to drink without dilution (we have been accustomed to add three parts of water to every part of wine). Moreover, they use bigger cups than we do. The people of this country prefer large goblets, and the local Jews have adopted this custom also – though of course they do not drink wine made by Gentile hands. In Rusia the Christians will not drink our wine either, nor our mead and beer, for their elders have made a law forbidding it. Now if any Jew drink the beer of Rusia, he is suspected of wanting to convert, for the Christians use beer in their rituals. But the Rusim suspect us so much that even water touched by a Jew they must first purify. The Gentiles of Ashkenaz were not so strict in this regard. Yet they have the same harsh rules punishing any of their communities who might dare to eat our unleavened bread on Pesach [Passover] or venture to pray with us at any time.

In the land of Tsarfat, in a country with many vineyards called Shampan [Champagne], we met a young rabbi who questioned us at length regarding the dress of women in the lands of Canaan. This was a certain R. Yosef ben Shimon, who was composing his own commentary on the book of Isaiah. He argued forcefully that some of the words of the prophet referred to the kind of cloaks worn by women in our land. R. Yosef said that necklaces of beautiful and expensive beads – like those fashioned and coveted by the women of Canaan – had also been mentioned by the prophet of ancient days.[24] One youth of our company doubted that the prophet Isaiah had known so well the fashions of our own land of Canaan, but the elders bid him keep silent.

We returned home more than a year later, arriving before the Day of Atonement.[25] I took the share of profits assigned to me and did not argue, though quarrels broke out among some of the company regarding the distribution of goods. In those days Zimri abducted Reuven's slave girl, who was also his concubine. He hid for some days with Gentiles and then fled to Bihem. Slaves are very plentiful here, for so many of the people sell their sons and daughters. This is how their land came to be called Canaan, for *Canaan was the slave of Shem*, as it is written: *A slave of slaves he shall be to his brothers* [Genesis 9:25–26].[26] Though the people of the land are forbidden from selling slaves to Jews, few of them follow this ruling, and there are many ways to circumvent the law. Shimon, then, took money from Reuven and pursued Zimri; however, he did not find him. Reuven, however, claimed that Shimon had acted on his own accord, stealing money from him and writing a false power of attorney. The judges said they had never heard of such a case of perfidy as this whole affair.

The journeys of my soul in this land of Canaan have not attained to the measure of the years of the sojourning of my fathers in that land of Canaan. Why do I write, when no one can live without seeing both good and evil? Did not the Preacher say: *A time to weep, and a time to laugh* [Ecclesiastes 3:4]? Now that I am growing old, I have heard the most remarkable news of my life. Not ten days have passed since a man arrived with a letter to be read out in all the communities of the lands of the East, by the authority of the great sage Rabbi Yehudah ben Meir the Kohen of Magentsa [Mainz]. As he read the notice, I felt my heart quiver and quake. I seemed to hear the story of an orphan brought up by relatives, entrusted to the care of a Gentile, captured in Premush (so it was written, for I checked with my own eyes), sold into slavery, and spied by a witness in Qostantina. The authors of this letter sought to find that young child from the days of the turmoil, who might yet live. This orphan, they said, had a brother who was spared and later took a wife in the land of Prague, which is Bihem. That brother died, and now the Law prescribes that his widow must marry her husband's brother or obtain the release of *chalitsah*. Else they must prove that the brother has died.

I must go and marry her or renounce her! If indeed I am the one whom they seek. Yet who can doubt it? I will live in this faith. My brother lives – rather, he did live – he had a wife – and I may yet see my relatives in this age, to mourn with them and laugh with them.

And today due to our sins we are in the year one thousand and fifty and six since the destruction of the Temple. I, Shlomo called Sirota, copied this writing of my grandfather Yitshak of Rusia (may the memory of the righteous be for a blessing), who recorded the journeys of his soul in the land of Canaan for a memory and a remembrance. He did not write all his travels; for I was told that in latter days he sailed even to the very edge of the world, to Danmarqa [Denmark]. When I copied out this writing, I altered only some difficult words that are not understood in our days here in the Land of the Isle [England].[27] The One who makes *shalom* in the heavens, he will make *shalom* for Yisrael and for the whole world, amen![28]

Glossary

bimah – A platform and lectern in a Jewish synagogue from which the Torah, blessings, and other texts are read publicly.

chalitsah – Rabbinic release from the obligation of levirate marriage (marriage of a widow to her late husband's brother if they had no children). The ancient custom for preserving a family line is prescribed in Deuteronomy 25:5–10 (cf. Genesis 38, Ruth 4). The Biblical text speaks of brothers "dwelling together," but medieval rabbis applied the principle of levirate marriage more broadly, with the result that Jewish widows could not legally remarry in the absence of *chalitsah* and/or definitive proof of the death of their brothers-in-law.

eruv – A special boundary created for religious reasons, within which certain actions are considered permissible on Shabbat.

halakhah – Rabbinic Jewish law. The term literally means the "[way of] walking"; i.e., the correct lifestyle.

kohen – A descendant of the line of Biblical Aaron (often translated as "priest"). This position had great significance in the days of the Temple and has continued to carry some liturgical and symbolic importance through medieval and modern times.

parashah – A division of the Torah (Pentateuch) usually consisting of a few chapters read aloud in the synagogue on Shabbat.

Shabbat – The Jewish Sabbath; the seventh day of the week and a day of rest (on which work is forbidden). The Shabbat begins on Friday evening and lasts until Saturday evening.

shalom – Holistic goodness and completeness. Often translated as "peace."

Torah – The Pentateuch (Five Books of Moses). The term literally means "instruction" and can also be used in broader senses; e.g., Jewish religious teaching generally.

Notes

1 Most of the relevant sources have recently been collected and prepared for publication (in the original languages and English translation) in: Alexander Kulik, *Jews in Old Rus': A Documentary History* [in process]. Citations below of Kulik section numbers refer to this compilation (for which I served as general editor). For the term "Greek Canaan," see Kulik §II.5.1.1.B.

2 The eleventh-century Persian poet and traveler Nasir ibn Khusraw reported: "From all the lands of the Greeks, too, and from other countries, the Christians and Jews come up to Jerusalem in great numbers in order to make their visitation of the Church and the Synagogue that is there" (Joshua Starr, *The Jews in the Byzantine Empire, 641–1204* [New York: Franklin, 1939], 197 [No. 142]).

3 This frequently attested invocation derives from Isaiah 59:20 and subsequent religious poetry. It expresses widespread Messianic expectations, including a return of Jews to the Land of Israel.

4 This story of the orphan brothers, including several details that follow below, was recorded in the work of R. Yehudah ben Meir ha-Kohen of Mainz (first half of the eleventh century) and preserved in later quotations by R. Eliezer ben Yoel ha-Levi of Bonn (late twelfth to early thirteenth century) and R. Yitshak ben Moshe of Vienna (first half of the thirteenth century). These texts mention the city of "Primut," which has been speculatively equated with Przemyśl, called Peremyshl in Russian. (Kulik §II.5.1.1; cf. Starr, *Jews*, 192–194 [No. 136].)

5 This is a line from the traditional Amidah prayer.

6 Appeals for mutual aid among scattered Jewish communities were common during the Middle Ages (see, for example, Kulik §II.2.1, §II.3.1). In fact, though this might seem to contradict some of his other purported activities (see later in the story text), Hegumen Feodosii of the Kiev Caves Monastery (mid-eleventh century; or else a later pseudo-Feodosii) also instructed Christians to help Jews in need: "Be merciful with charity not only to those of your own faith, but also [to those] of other [faiths]. If you see [someone] naked or hungry or [cold] in winter or gripped by distress, even if this is a Jew, or Saracen, or [Muslim Volga] Bulgar, or heretic, or Latin, or [someone] from [among] all the pagans – show mercy to everyone and deliver them from distress, as you are able, and you will not be deprived of [your] reward from God" (Kulik §I.3.1.2).

7 In his travelogue (ca. 1175), R. Petachyah ben Yaakov of Regensburg reported meeting non-Rabbinic Jews in the Pontic steppe (or possibly Crimea) who had never seen or heard of the Talmud and had their own unique customs (Kulik §II.5.9). According to his vita, the ninth-century Slavic missionary Cyril (Constantine) studied Hebrew with non-Rabbinic Jews in Chersonesus Taurica (see Starr, *Jews*, 122 [No. 55]).

8 According to Rabbinic law, women must immerse after menstruation before engaging in sex with their husbands (see: Leviticus 15:19–24, 18:19, 20:18; Talmudic tractate Niddah). R. Eliezer ben Yoel ha-Levi of Bonn (late twelfth to early thirteenth century) ruled that the same laws of purification applied also to non-Jewish female slaves treated as concubines by Jewish men; i.e., these women also had to immerse for purification (Kulik §II.A.2.7).

9 R. Eliezer ben Nathan of Mainz (early to mid-twelfth century) judged that women could lawfully immerse while clothed if wearing "loose clothing . . . similar to the clothing still worn by the women of the land of Canaan [i.e., the Slavic territories]" (Kulik §II.A.2.4.1).

10 As Yitshak states, this city was home to multiple ethnicities and languages. The famous Slavic missionaries Cyril (Constantine) and Methodius (ninth century), who seem to have invented the Slavic alphabet and literature, hailed originally from Thessaloniki.

11 This festival occurs seven weeks after Passover, i.e., in May or June. The proper method of calculating the date of Shavuot has been controversial since ancient times and formed one of the bitterest points of contention between Karaite and Rabbinic Jews through the medieval period.

12 The Jewish Gates of Kiev are mentioned in the Kievan Chronicle (ca. 1200) under the years 6654 and 6659 from the Creation of the world (i.e., ca. 1146 and 1151; Kulik §I.1.2.2, §I.1.2.3).

13 In commenting on Genesis 10:3, R. Saadiah ben Yosef al-Fayyumi of Sura (first half of the tenth century) claimed that the Slavs descended from Ashkenaz (Kulik §II.A.1.2). In commenting on 1 Chronicles 1:1–5, the Book of Josippon (mid-tenth century) named Tiras as ancestor of the Rus' (Kulik §II.4.1). R. Yitshak of Chernigov (mid-thirteenth century) followed the second of these interpretations (Kulik §II.6.2.1). The Rus' Primary Chronicle (early twelfth century) agreed that the Rus' people descended from Biblical Japheth (the progenitor of both Tiras and Ashkenaz), but without providing further details about the lineage (see Samuel Cross and Olgerd Sherbowitz-Wetzor, trans., *The Russian Primary Chronicle: Laurentian Text* [Cambridge, MA: Mediaeval Academy of America, 1953], 52).

14 Grand Prince Iaroslav I the Wise of Kiev ruled 1016–1054. *Melekh* ("king") is the normal Hebrew word for a ruler of this type (including steppe khagans).

15 Bar Kybr is one of the names attested in the Kievan Letter, a tenth-century Hebrew document that seems to indicate a contemporary Jewish (and Khazar) presence in Kiev (Kulik §II.2.1).

16 In the synagogue readers are generally called up to the lectern according to a traditional Hebrew name form (*X ben Y*). Sirota is possibly one of the names attested in the tenth-century Kievan Letter (Kulik §II.2.1). According to R. Eliezer ben Yitshak of Prague (second half of the twelfth century), the Jewish communities of Poland, Rus', and Hungary had relatively little religious learning but still selected and paid knowledgeable men to serve as cantors and teachers (Kulik §II.5.11.1).

17 A thirteenth-century seal matrix from the Grodno region bears an inscription in Hebrew letters reading "Yitshak Ayzi[q]" – i.e., the Hebrew and local versions of the name Isaac (Kulik §II.8.3).
18 R. Eliezer ben Nathan of Mainz (early to mid-twelfth century) ruled that Jews could rent houses to the "lax" Christians of the German lands – but not to the "pious" Christians of Rus' and Greece, since the latter would put images of idolatry on the walls and gates of the property (Kulik §II.5.6.5). Most historians believe that the common people of Rus' continued to practice forms of paganism long after the official adoption of Christianity (ca. 988).
19 The stories of the monks Feodosii and Nikita (second half of the eleventh century) – the latter of whom purportedly had misadventures related to "Jewish books" – are recorded in the Kiev Caves Paterikon (Kulik §I.2.1.4; Muriel Heppell, trans., *The Paterik of the Kievan Caves Monastery* [Cambridge, MA: Ukrainian Research Institute of Harvard University, 1989], 73, 143–145).
20 This story about Evstratii the Faster comes from the Kiev Caves Paterikon and apparently dates from the late eleventh century (Kulik §I.2.1.2; Heppell, *Paterik*, 123–125).
21 Such a riot against Jews and others is recorded in the Rus' Primary Chronicle (early twelfth century) under the year 6621 from the Creation of the world (i.e., 1113), although the motivation may have been different than described by Yitshak (Kulik §I.1.1.2).
22 R. Eliezer ben Nathan of Mainz (early to mid-twelfth century) made a ruling to this effect with explicit reference to commercial travel to Rus' (Kulik §II.5.6.1). The Biblical prohibition against taking interest from a fellow citizen of Israel is found in Exodus 22:22–27, Leviticus 25:35–38, and Deuteronomy 23:19–20/20–21; cf. Ezekiel 18:5–18, where the practice is categorized together with very severe sins.
23 The Jews of the Iberian peninsula experienced a "Golden Age" under Muslim rule in the tenth and eleventh centuries.
24 In his commentary on the prophet Isaiah, R. Yosef ben Shimon Kara of Troyes (late eleventh to early twelfth century) interpreted obscure Hebrew words in the Biblical text with reference to the dress and ornaments worn by women in the Slavic territories (Kulik §II.A.2.3). Three known manuscripts of his composition refer to the Slavic necklace beads as "red and green" or "green and red," and this is how most people interpret his saying. However, five other manuscripts of the work switch the order of two Hebrew letters, thus reading "expensive" (יקרות) instead of "green" (ירקות). Moreover, the East Slavic word for "beautiful" (красьныи) came to mean "red" at least by the fifteenth century and possibly earlier (P.Ia. Chernykh, *Istoriko-etimologicheskii slovar' sovremennogo russkogo iazyka* [Moscow: Russkii iazyk, 2001], 1.440). As a result, today we cannot know whether R. Yosef intended to speak of "red and green" beads or "beautiful and expensive" ones, as linguistic confusion may have affected the transmission of either or both accounts (his and Yitshak's), or perhaps even their original conversation. Note that medieval Rabbinic literature includes numerous Slavic linguistic glosses, generally described as words of "the language of Canaan" (see Kulik §II.B).
25 The Jewish Day of Atonement (Yom Kippur) occurs on 10 Tishrei according to the Hebrew calendar, a date that can fall in either September or October. See Leviticus 16.
26 The same explanation appears in the travelogue (1173) of R. Binyamin ben Yonah of Tudela (Kulik §II.7.1).
27 Jews from Rus' are attested in England in the twelfth and thirteenth centuries – including a "Ysaac de Russie" (Kulik §II.6). Our Yitshak's descendant may therefore be counted among these immigrants or their progeny. R. Meir ben Barukh of Rothenburg (second half of the thirteenth century) uses the term "the Land of the Isle" in a responsum concerning the conditions under which a wife must follow her husband to a "different land." That same text also mentions the land of Canaan (i.e., the Slavic territories), France, and the German lands (Kulik §II.A.2.11). Note that copyists of medieval manuscripts frequently modified their texts both intentionally and unintentionally.
28 This closing invocation derives from the last line of the traditional Kaddish prayer.

Suggestions for further reading

Cohen, Mark. *The Voice of the Poor in the Middle Ages: An Anthology of Documents from the Cairo Geniza*. Princeton: Princeton University Press, 2005.

Golb, Norman, and Omeljan Pritsak. *Khazarian Hebrew Documents of the Tenth Century*. Ithaca: Cornell University Press, 1982.

Heppell, Muriel. *The Paterik of the Kievan Caves Monastery*. Cambridge, MA: Ukrainian Research Institute of Harvard University, 1989.

Kulik, Alexander. *Jews in Old Rus': A Documentary History* [in process].

Rotman, Youval. *Byzantine Slavery and the Mediterranean World*. Trans. Jane Marie Todd. Cambridge, MA: Harvard University Press, 2009.

19

AGENT OF CHANGE

Evpraksia Vsevolodovna between emperor and papacy

Christian Raffensperger

Evpraksia Vsevolodovna was one of the most well-known Rusian (meaning – of the medieval kingdom of Rus') women in eleventh-century Europe, but her name does not bring much recognition even among twenty-first-century scholars. The difference between the two groups is profound when we acknowledge that the goal of medievalists is to understand the medieval European world as it was, or as close as we can come, given the problems with source preservation, bias, etc. Many modern historians of medieval Europe have elided history, leaving out much of Eastern Europe from their narratives, which is one of the reasons for a volume such as this. This exclusion of half of medieval Europe, deliberate or otherwise, includes figures from Eastern Europe who play a role in the rest of the medieval world. Evpraksia Vsevolodovna is one of those figures, someone who plays a large role in the medieval world, is present in medieval sources, but is often absent in modern secondary sources.

Evpraksia was the daughter of Vsevolod Iaroslavich (ruler of Kiev and all Rus' from 1078–1093), and thus the sister of Volodimer Monomakh (son of Vsevolod Iaroslavich and the ruler of Kiev and all Rus' from 1125 to 1132). She was a very important person, simply by her birth, but even more than that, she is important for historians as she is one of the most well-documented Rusian women of the eleventh century, which, admittedly, is not saying much! Evpraksia is mentioned not just once, but twice in the Povest' vremennykh let *(PVL), the main source for eleventh- and early twelfth-century internal Rusian affairs, where she is mentioned by name and is recorded both entering a nunnery and at her death where she was buried in the Caves Monastery, the oldest and holiest monastery in Rus', where she also had her own chapel erected. In comparison with the other women of eleventh-century Rus', she is virtually a rockstar, with these qualifications. However, it is in the Latin sources that Evpraksia is most well-known. She marries twice into the German Empire, and works with the papacy and thus a whole host of Latin sources mention her. She has her own decrees in the German Empire, she is in attendance at papal conferences, and she moves around a great deal in medieval Europe. Yet, despite all of this information about her, she is still largely absent from secondary sources on Rus', the German Empire, or the papacy.*

Evpraksia lived an extraordinary life in the eleventh century. Before moving on to her portrait, though, some of the historical details of that life need to be described. In 1082, Evpraksia goes to the German Empire with a large entourage filled with gold, jewels, and clothes, carried on horses and camels. She was going to marry Henry III "the Long," the Margrave of the Saxon Nordmark. The marriage was, most likely, a political arrangement negotiated between Henry IV, the German Emperor (emperor from 1084–1106), and Vsevolod Iaroslavich, the Rusian ruler and Evpraksia's father. The marriage does not last long, however, and there are no children, before Henry III dies in approximately 1088. Evpraksia's journey is not done, however, as the next year she marries the recently widowed Henry IV himself, making her the German Empress. This is just the beginning of her career in medieval European politics, however, as she splits from him in the early 1090s to join the side of the papacy opposing Henry IV in what is known as the Investiture Controversy. As part of that she travels around medieval Western Europe making speeches and talking about the travails she went through during her time with Henry IV, culminating in her speaking at the papal council of Piacenza in 1095. After that, mentions of her in Latin sources begin to decrease though she still appears in 1096 and 1097 in the Italian peninsula in particular and afterward it is noted that she returned to Rus', via Hungary. The PVL then picks her up for the first time to tell us that she became a nun in 1106, confirmed in Latin documents, and died in 1109.

Evpraksia writes home – 1093

The portrait of Evpraksia on display here is not an autobiography or journal, or third-person narration, but instead a pair of letters that Evpraksia could have written to her family in Rus'. I have then annotated these letters as if they were historical documents to provide context for the reader about the events that Evpraksia is discussing. These letters each draw upon real events and real people and utilize information from the copious source base about Evpraksia. Further, I would even suggest that she was literate and could have written such letters herself. S. P. Rozanov certainly thought she was literate when he wrote about her in the early twentieth century, indicating that she received training at the Quedlinburg nunnery, run by Henry IV's own sister Adelheid. This idea is not that far-fetched either when we see evidence of her aunt Anna Iaroslavna's (Queen of France, 1051–1060, Regent 1060–ca. 1066) literacy, however minimal, in the Capetian kingdom, and we have plentiful primary source evidence that Evpraksia herself addressed councils of bishops and even the papal council at Piacenza in 1095. The sources themselves tell us that she "read," though modern historians of the German Empire have suggested that such was impossible.

This first letter could have been written by Evpraksia in 1093 around the time she broke with her husband Henry IV to join the party of the papacy. It contains information about her circumstances, people she meets, modes of travel, and many other minutiae of life that we can access through a compilation of sources, even if we do not have them specifically in regard to Evpraksia herself.

* * *

To my dear father Vsevolod Iaroslavich, ruler of Kiev and all the Rus' lands,

I write to you to report that I received your message and I have made arrangements to do as you wish. I have cultivated a relationship with the Countess

Mathilda who is a strong advocate for the Roman Pope Urban II. She is a strong-willed woman who has been perfectly willing to correspond with me, and with whom I have now met several times. In fact, I suspect that she views me as something of a granddaughter, given the difference in our ages and her relationship to my husband. When I told her that I wanted to get away from Henry and come to support her and the pope, she was overjoyed and has planned a rather elaborate escape involving guards, horses, and a midnight ride. In truth I worry that it is more elaborate than necessary, but I am committed at this point to following where she leads.

Once I am with her, she is to take me to see Duke Welf. He is the other main supporter of Pope Urban II, but his importance is largely due to his family. He is my age and though married to Countess Mathilda, she speaks mockingly of him, when she speaks of him at all. His importance in this venture is largely financial, as he and his father rule a large territory, but he will have writers from the pope who are going to craft a story to explain to people how my leaving my husband will help the papacy. Countess Mathilda has instructed me to "be brave" so I cannot imagine it will be a happy story. I will send on information about what the story is, when I know more.

Though I am fulfilling your instructions and understand the need, I regret the necessity, as Henry is by and large a good man who has taken care of me since the death of my first husband. I hold affection for him and know that this betrayal will hurt him a great deal. But it is incredibly important that Pope Urban II sent the holy relics to Kiev. I am only sorry that I am not able to see them, they sound magnificent and further connect our kingdom to the glory of Christ as shown by his saints on earth.

Since I last wrote, events have slowly deteriorated here in the empire. Henry had been counting on the fact that our marriage would change something in regard to Pope Clement III's plan to work with our Church in Kiev.[1] Honestly, though I am aware of the politics involved, I see no reason that this should not work. Could you not have done something to convince Metropolitan Ioann II? Or failing that, to have appointed someone in his stead who might have had the interests of the kingdom more in mind, such as another Ilarion? I know from my sister's letter that there are good men in the Caves Monastery who would willingly work to better Rus'.[2] Henry's disappointment at the failure of this alliance has driven him apart from me, and thus your new plan comes at an auspicious time. Especially so, as his armies were defeated last year by Countess Mathilda, which you may remember me writing about at the time. Henry was furious about this, and still bears her immense ill will.

This is a time of many disappointments for my husband as he is unhappy about the deterioration in his relationship with the basileus Alexius as well. The recent letters that he has received from the basileus have been cold and formal, and have hinted that he now favors the papal side rather than Henry. This shift is troubling, as when we married, Henry and Alexius were working together against the former Roman pope, Gregory VII and his cat's paw Robert

Guiscard. It now seems that Pope Gregory's death has also led to the death of this alliance, both Gregory's and Guiscard's and that between my husband and the basileus.

Though I know that you were unwilling to share all of your reasoning with me, I must confess that I suspect that these disappointments of Henry's are related to our family's change in strategy. The shift in politics is something that you and mother trained me to watch before you sent me here, and I have been, I believe, a faithful observer, sending back reports with the merchants whom you have selected as trustworthy. It would be beneficial for our family if I was able to see more of the larger picture that you are working toward, and it might improve the information that I am able to give you in regard to the political currents here. With the death of my aunts, and the problematic fates of my cousins, there are not many good options for us in Christendom now. Please trust my intelligence, faith, and loyalty to my family.

I am sorry to hear that your ill health continues. I have offered my prayers that you be healed and will live a long life and continue to rule wisely.

Please give my deepest affections to my mother, and please read, or have Rostislav read, this letter to her so that she knows that I am all right. I miss her counsel, especially at this time in my life.

Your faithful daughter,
Evpraksia

This letter of Evpraksia's notes the current conditions and portrays her as a both a devoted daughter and a diplomatic operative for her Volodimerovichi family while in the German Empire. Though a simple letter, and not an official report, it conveys important information to her family, though it would not have reached her father who died in April 1093, and informs them of what she was planning to do.

Evpraksia writes home – 1096

This second letter could have been written home in 1096, after the papal council at Piacenza, and after the tide had particularly turned against Henry IV. In it, Evpraksia notes not only the life that she has led during that time, but the changed relationship with her correspondent, in this case her brother Volodimer Monomakh.

To my dear brother Volodimer Vsevolodich,

I apologize that it has been so long since I have written home. I can imagine that it was frustrating to you not to hear from me, Volodya, but I have been quite busy as I will relate, and I only received your own message recently. The merchant Abraham was upset as he had to travel down from Mainz toward Rome to find me, but he faithfully delivered his message, which I promised to report.[3]

My last letter home was written just before I received news of father's death. I was very sorry to hear of his passing, though I know that he is resting now with Christ in heaven, and is relieved of his illness. I hope that my mother, about whom I have had no news in years, is well. Please write to me of her when you are able, and pass on my love to her.

As you read my last letter you know the plan that I shared with father, and despite my misgivings it worked very well, and the Countess Mathilda took me away to her castle at Canossa. There we met with her former husband, Duke Welf – the two separated last year but there had always been bad blood between them as I told father. Duke Welf and the scribes working for Pope Urban II created a truly awful story about why I had left Henry. I know that you heard some of it from your letter, and I beg you to believe me that it was all a creation of these scribes.[4] They said that it was, in part, the same story that was used earlier against Henry by his first wife and that would make it more believable to the audience. I emphasize that not a single word of it was true. Henry has always been kind to me, even if there is only that between us. Regardless of the truth of the writings, I read them as I was instructed. First to a council of bishops in Swabia the year after father's death and then at the pope's own council in Piacenza last year. In both cases, the bishops were visibly swayed by my words and the accusations against Henry rang true in their minds, if not in my heart, and they began to abandon Henry and work with Pope Urban II.

Pope Urban II himself is a rather incredible figure. I have met him several times now, and though Countess Mathilda is quite fond of him, I cannot say that I share that feeling. Despite that, I have to tell you that he is the most organized and efficient of men in determining what will happen when and who will do it. He never seems to have a thought without a plan for accomplishing it. I do not know what, if anything, he intends for our family, but I encourage you to be wary of entering into any agreements with him and do not oppose him if possible. Though it might seem impudent, I would even suggest that you share my warning with our cousin in Kiev. He can bring downfall on all of us and so should know what to avoid. I leave it in your hands to do what you think is best.[5]

At the council of Piacenza, I met our cousin Philip [King of France, 1059–1108], the son of Aunt Anna. He is quite a dashing man and incredibly charming. Of course, it is this same charm that brought him to Piacenza, as Pope Urban II was quite displeased with him for his marital problems. The two of them seemed to have come to an agreement, though I do not know how long it will last. Philip told me that he had exchanged letters with our cousin Edgar, the son of Aunt Agafia. Philip was attempting, fruitlessly I believe, to support him in his claim against the usurper William the Bastard who took Edgar's birthright in England.[6] Philip would welcome further contact if we could arrange something and he has plenty of nobles who need marital alliances of their own. I know my nieces will need husbands eventually and it would not hurt to curry favor with this cousin Philip.

Now that I have done what father asked, what turned out to be his last wish of me, and left Henry to support Pope Urban II, I would like to have the freedom to make a choice of my own and to come home. I believe that I have served our family well and truly during my marriage to both my first Henry and to my second. I left my husband when father asked me to, and helped to bring his son Conrad along with me to support the Roman pope. I am still married to Henry, and so I may not marry again. I have the means of support still, but they are dwindling as are my relationships here when those I once was very close to have turned to others. The things I have done and the people I have consorted with during this time were not good ones, not even the ones who were supposed to be closest to God, and I am tired of this world of constant maneuvering for advantage while pretending to be pious and Christ-loving. I beg leave of you, in father's place, to allow me to come home.

Until I hear from you again, I shall endeavor my best to work on behalf of our family as I have for this last decade and more. But please know that my heart is in Rus', and that the tales father told of the arrival of the relics of St. Nicholas, and Ianka's example of devotion fill me with more joy than anything that I see before me here.[7]

Your sister,
Evpraksia

This letter, like the one before it, is not a real historical document, but one filled with historical accuracy. Evpraksia's rich life is on display here in these letters in her own words and her allusions to the events of her day and her activities in medieval Europe. Through this technique of using fiction to portray fact, we can reach a broader audience of those interested in attempting to study and understand how medieval Eastern Europe worked, and maybe even felt, to those who lived there and then.

Notes

1 The letter of anti-pope Clement III to Metropolitan Ioann II of Kiev is not extant, but we do have the reply of Ioann II, which is highly dismissive of the Latin church, even polemical, and directs future correspondence to the patriarch in Constantinople. The Rusian policy of engagement with the rest of Christendom was not reflected by the Byzantine-appointed metropolitans who were typically not Slavs, or Slavic speakers, and whose loyalty was firmly based in Constantinople.
2 Evpraksia's sister Ianka was a well-known nun in Rus' with connections to the Rusian Church hierarchy.
3 I know of no actual evidence for how messages were relayed between family members in medieval Europe, but one way that they could have been was through merchants traveling regular routes between cities. In this case, I have highlighted the important and well-documented route of Jewish merchants from Mainz to Kiev.
4 The story that the papal polemicists created was one that labeled Henry IV as a Nicoletian, a sect known from the Book of Revelation to participate in all variety of sexual acts, including orgies. This was a standard slander for these polemicists who used it earlier against Henry IV as well when he was in conflict with his first wife, Bertha.
5 Ruling at the time in Kiev was Sviatopolk Iziaslavich who was a rival of Evpraksia's brother Volodimer Monomakh. The Iziaslavichi and Volodimer would continue to engage in con-

flict with one another for quite some time, and thus it was a bold move for Evpraksia to suggest that one family might help the other.

6 Edgar was the son of Edward "the Exile," son of Edmund II "Ironside" and Agafia Volodimerovna. Sometime after Edmund's death upon his return to England, Edgar began a campaign against William the Conqueror, which involved some amount of coordination with Philip, who shared his distaste for William.

7 Ianka Vsevolodovna helped to bring back a metropolitan to Rus' from Constantinople and receives two mentions in the *PVL*, the same number as Evpraksia – both of whom, incidentally, are second only to the Regent Ol'ga in quantity of times mentioned in the *PVL*.

Suggestions for further reading

Raffensperger, Christian. "Evpraksia Vsevolodovna between East and West." *Russian History/ Histoire Russe* 30, no. 1–2 (2003): 23–34.

Raffensperger, Christian. "The Missing Rusian Women: The Case of Evpraksia Vsevolodovna." In *Putting Together the Fragments: Writing Medieval Women's Lives.* Edited by Amy Livingstone and Charlotte Newman Goldy, 69–84. New York: Palgrave, 2012.

Robinson, I. S. *Henry IV of Germany, 1056–1106.* Cambridge: Cambridge University Press, 1999.

The Russian Primary Chronicle: Laurentian Text, Edited and translated by Samuel Hazzard Cross and Olgerd P. Sherbowitz-Wetzor. Cambridge, MA: The Mediaeval Academy of America, 1953.

20

FOTII, A RUS' PILGRIM TO CONSTANTINOPLE

Monica White

Rus had close ties to Byzantium from at least the eighth century, when adventurous Vikings began collecting slaves, fur, and other forest products to sell in the rich markets of Constantinople. Despite the length and danger of the journey, this trade was extremely lucrative and continued into the late Middle Ages. Following the official conversion of Rus to Orthodox Christianity in the late tenth century, the north-south traffic expanded to include people on church business, including bishops, monks, and pilgrims. Constantinople had long attracted pilgrims from all over Christendom thanks to its vast collection of relics – fragments of the bodies of saints or objects touched by holy people, such as clothing worn by the Virgin Mary (known in the East as the Mother of God). These items, which were believed to effect cures and bring the faithful into the presence of the divine, were highly prized. Constantinople had the best collection in the world of both saintly and Christological relics (the True Cross, Crown of Thorns, etc.). Thus, Christians from Rus, both lay and ecclesiastic, travelled to Constantinople to venerate relics starting in at least the early twelfth century, when the oldest surviving pilgrimage account (khozhdenie) *was written, and probably earlier.*

A rich pilgrimage literature survives from Rus and early Muscovy, which provides a great deal of important information about the treasures of Constantinople and pilgrims' religious experiences. It says very little, however, about most other aspects of pilgrims' journeys: their companions, accommodation, other business in Constantinople, etc. This is because the authors of the accounts assumed that their readers were interested only in the relics, and would either already know or not care about other details. This is, of course, not the case for modern historians, who find the omission of so much information regrettable. The following account has therefore been conceived as a "photographic negative," which relates the experiences of a pilgrim other than the veneration of relics.

Our pilgrim, a monk named Fotii, visited Constantinople in 1277, a time of turmoil in Eastern Europe. Rus had endured destructive invasions by the Mongols in the 1230s, although four decades later the newer cities of the northeast, such as Fotii's native Tver, were prospering through trade. Constantinople, which was conquered by Catholic ("Latin") crusaders in 1204, had been retaken in 1261 by the Greek Orthodox emperor Michael VIII, who was still ruling during Fotii's sojourn. However, Michael was forced to agree to a widely reviled and short-lived union of the churches (known as the Union of Lyon) in 1274 to stave off another crusade. The traditional trade in northern products such as fur and slaves was as lively as ever, but the Venetians and Genoese were rapidly establishing trading colonies around the Black Sea, cutting off older Byzantine trade centers.

In the account below, unfamiliar terms and the historical accuracy or significance of certain remarks are explained in the endnotes. Supplementary information which Fotii would not have included is given in square brackets. The text in italics is taken from primary sources (actual pilgrimage accounts and a late medieval Greek-Slavonic phrase book), with references in the endnotes. Works cited in abbreviated form in the endnotes can be found in the Suggestions for further reading at the end of the chapter. The manuscript containing Fotii's account is imagined, like many others, to have suffered damage and is missing the sections describing Fotii's tour of the relics of Constantinople and his journey back to Tver.

* * *

An Account of a Journey to Constantinople by the Lowly Fotii,
Monk of the Monastery of the Dormition in Tver.

Lord, give your blessing, Father. Although I am most unworthy to write this account, being poorly educated and with little knowledge of grammar, nevertheless the pious brothers of our holy Monastery of the Dormition entreated me with many pleas to describe my experiences in the God-guarded city of Constantinople. For the sake of their instruction, so that my journey may be of some use to them and future monks, I have agreed, sinner though I am. It is indeed beneficial for the soul to learn about the wonders of the imperial city: the churches filled with relics, the monasteries where God is worshipped day and night, the splendor of the emperor and his court. The Greeks [Byzantines] are not without sin and have suffered and continue to suffer at the hands of the wicked Latins, but Constantinople is the source of all wisdom and holiness as the seat of the holy Orthodox Church, and we look to it for our salvation.

Understanding this, our blessed prince Sviatoslav [Iaroslavich] and his pious wife, Evfimiia, were inspired by God to hire masters from the Greeks to decorate our monastery's Gate-Church of the Nativity of Christ. The same prince built this church to commemorate the birth of his first son, named Iaroslav for his grandfather [Iaroslav Iaroslavich], the founder of our monastery, and in holy baptism George. Such generosity has never been seen in the Land beyond the Forest! Although our monastery is new, we are thrice-blessed by the patronage of our pious princes. As it is written: "So the last will be first, and the first will be last."[1]

Our Christ-loving Hegumen [Abbot] Ignatii, a most pious man with knowledge of Greek who came to our monastery at the time of its foundation from the holy Caves Monastery in Kiev, agreed to undertake the journey to Constantinople on the prince's behalf. *He brought with him his chaplain, servants, an archpriest, and a protodeacon, and other priests and deacons.*[2] In addition to them was the icon-painter Sofronii, three novices, and myself, although I was most unworthy. However, my menial skills were of some use to the blessed father: having been trained in my youth to reckon with sums in my family's fur trading business, I was asked to manage the monastery's accounts after I donned the monastic habit. (Through the generosity of the princes and the faithful, the monastery has acquired many lands, villages, and treasures to the glory of God.) I was therefore put in charge of the funds for the journey.

Our party set off in three boats in the year 6785, on the holy feast of the Resurrection of Christ [28 March, 1277], since most of the ice on the Volga had melted. Accompanying us was the young Michael [Iaroslavich], [half-]brother of our pious prince, whom we were taking as a hostage to the Horde.[3] For the first three weeks, we travelled down the Volga past many fine and prosperous towns. In many places, by the grace of God, the local bishop or hegumen came out to meet us and offered us lodgings for the night. But when we crossed into the Bulgar lands we became *despondent and dejected about the journey, for the countryside was completely deserted. There was nothing to see, no villages or people, only beasts: elk, bears, and similar animals.*[4] After almost a week, on the feast of the holy great martyr George [23 April], we began to pass white hills around an arm of the Volga [the Akhtuba]. *It was there that we first noticed Tatars [Mongols], and from there on fear began to take hold of us as we entered the land of the infidel.*[5] Finally, on the Sunday of the Samaritan Woman [2 May], we docked at the great city of Sarai.

In Sarai we stayed as guests of the most pious bishop Feognost. Although the Tatars are pagans and infidels, nevertheless they fear and respect the holy Orthodox Church and have allowed an episcopal see to be established in their capital by the most blessed metropolitan of Kiev. In fact, there are many Christians in Sarai: Rus princes and their envoys, Rus and Greek merchants, even Armenians. Bishop Feognost has therefore learned Greek, although he is a Rus from Rostov. Wicked Latins also live in the city because they have a trading colony there, although they do not have their own bishop and sometimes visit the Orthodox Church.

While we were waiting for our audience with the khan, our Christ-loving hegumen had many discussions with Bishop Feognost about the union with the Latins that the emperor of the Greeks had recently concluded. Bishop Feognost informed us that the emperor had appointed a new patriarch who agreed with this most sinful betrayal of the holy Orthodox Church, causing much strife in Constantinople. We were greatly troubled to hear this news, for how can the emperor and the patriarch perform their duties on behalf of all Orthodox Christians if they are in league with the wicked Latins? We considered returning to Rus, not wanting to be tainted by heresy, but did not want to abandon our mission on behalf of our most pious prince. We resolved to continue our journey and, with the help of God, discover what we could about the situation in order to inform our brothers in Rus.

After ten days we were summoned to the court of the khan. Our Christ-loving hegumen prayed fervently for and blessed the young Michael, that he might be a bringer of peace and remain safe in the care of the khan's wives. Their great number means that there are many children at the court, and Michael soon found a group of companions. After shedding many tears over the boy, whom we had come to love like a younger brother, the khan's officials placed us with a group of slave merchants who agreed to escort us to Tana, for we did not know the overland route. Thanks to their guides and horses, we reached Tana on the feast of Boris and Gleb [20 May]. There, we found accommodation in the merchants' quarter with fur traders from Rus thanks to my family's connections. After celebrating Trinity Sunday [23 May] in Tana, the merchants helped us arrange passage to Cherson on a ship carrying furs and slaves.

With God helping us, the voyage to Cherson was smooth and lasted only one week. After arriving, the merchants showed us to the Rus colony, where we found accommodation with the local priest, Father Dmitrii. His family had fled from Kiev after its destruction by the godless Tatars and found refuge in Cherson, where they worked as fishermen. Father Dmitrii can speak both the Rus language and Greek and was ordained by the Greeks, but serves the Rus colony. He had in his possession a precious item which he saw fit to give to us, unworthy though we are: a wondrous book left by a previous group of pilgrims on their return journey. This book consists of words and phrases in the Rus language, organized by subject, with accompanying translations into Greek. The Greek words are rendered in our Cyrillic alphabet to make them easier to read. The brothers and I spent several afternoons earnestly studying to prepare for our arrival in Constantinople, and prayed to God for help with the fiendishly difficult language of the Greeks!

We admired the orderly streets and courtyards of Cherson and were astonished at the sight of their cathedrals. They are not built in the form of a cube topped by domes, as is our practice in Rus, but rather as a long box with a peaked roof, and on top of it a smaller one, and no domes at all. There are windows down both sides of the upper floor, which let in copious amounts of light. The structure is surrounded by a maze of porticos, and Father Dmitrii explained that this provides shade during the long southern summers. We wandered awestruck around the complex of the Cathedral of Sts Peter and Paul before entering and beholding an even greater wonder: mosaics covering the walls and ceiling, depicting perfect likenesses of the saints and images from the lives of our Savior and his most blessed Mother. None of us had ever seen anything like this in Rus, and we were speechless at the brilliance of the sun shining on the glass tesserae. Even the floors were covered in the most sumptuous designs, with peacocks, griffins, and floral ornaments. We did not believe Father Dmitrii when he told us that there were even more amazing mosaics in Constantinople, although he was correct. Instead of staying for vespers, sinner that I am, I rushed to the artisans' quarter to enquire about the cost of hiring mosaicists instead of fresco painters for our pious prince. It would have been better for me to concentrate on the psalter! The cost of mosaicists is nearly ten times as much because of the need to import glass-making materials and equipment. It is far better for me to venerate these images at length so as to call them to mind later in my prayers, for they were made to glorify God.

Although the cathedrals of Cherson are magnificent, we were greatly saddened to see that the rest of the city had fallen on hard times. Its trade has been severely curtailed by the raids of the godless Tatars in nearby areas and – oh the outrage! – the new trading colonies of the wicked Latins, who have insinuated themselves with the infidels [Mongols] to secure advantages at the expense of the Greeks. Thus, Cherson's spacious markets were mostly abandoned and many of its fine stone churches were in a poor state of repair. Most of the people make their living from fishing, farming, or crafts and petty trade.

After we had been in Cherson a week, we met a group of pilgrims from Novgorod, prosperous laypeople who were planning to visit Constantinople, the Holy Mountain [Mt Athos] and the Holy Land. Together, we negotiated a good price on a merchant ship to Constantinople. While we waited for the ship to sail, we visited the Church of St Basil, where the thrice-blessed prince Vladimir was baptized in ancient times, and the Church of the Holy Mother of God which he founded after he married the Greek princess.[6] In both churches we found a great deal of graffiti left by previous pilgrims from Rus seeking the blessing and protection of the pious couple. The Novgorodians added their names and the date, but Father Ignatii did not allow us to, saying it was better for us to speak to God through our prayers by staying in the churches for all-night vigils. The Church of the Mother of God has precious relics which we spent many hours venerating: a toenail of St Clement and a tooth of St Phoebus, which the Greeks managed to keep secretly when the great Vladimir took the rest of their bodies to Kiev. Great indeed is the wisdom of the Lord, for Father Dmitrii told us that his parents witnessed the destruction of Kiev and the burning of the Tithe Church, where the relics were kept, when the godless Tatars invaded our land.

Having prayed earnestly to the great and blessed prince for protection on our journey, we set sail for Constantinople the next day, the feast of the holy great martyr Theodore the General [8 June]. God granted us fair weather for the first two days, but thereafter the sea became stormy. The other brothers and I, being inexperienced on the open sea, could not move for seasickness nor eat even a morsel of food, and huddled miserably on one side of the ship. But as dawn broke on the eighth day, the clouds parted and we saw the sun sparkling on golden domes in the far distance. I thought first that I had died and gone to heaven, and then that it was some kind of devilish mirage. But the sailors assured us that it was the God-guarded city of Constantinople. Even in my wildest dreams I could not have imagined its beauty! The giant walls, with their elegant turrets, seemed to have been made as a necklace for the city by a race of giants, and beyond them the domes on the churches formed a veritable forest. We docked at the harbor of Theodosios, which was thronged with ships of every description as people in their thousands raced hither and thither.

Father Ignatii had sent word of our arrival to the Pantokrator Monastery, where a community of Rus monks lives. Several of them were from the blessed Caves Monastery in Kiev and had known Father Ignatii in his youth, so we planned to lodge with them. We questioned the sailors carefully about how to find the monastery, but

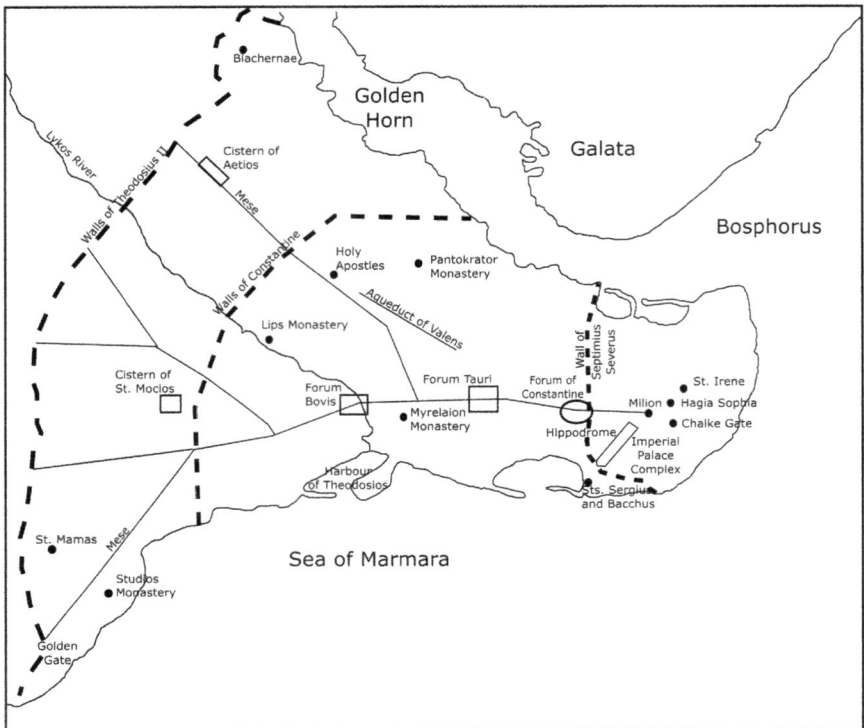

MAP 20.1 Map of Constantinople, courtesy of Christian Raffensperger

we soon became hopelessly lost and wandered the city for hours, unable to communicate with anyone. Although we were fainting from exhaustion, we could not stop marveling at the magnificent churches, palaces, and markets. Eventually, by the grace of God, a pair of Rus merchants overheard and took pity on us. They escorted us to the monastery and warned us that *entering Constantinople is like entering a great forest; it is impossible to get around without a good guide.*[7] But when we arrived we found all the monks sleeping, having spent the entire night in prayer, so we rested outside the gates until evening.

When they opened the gates, we were greeted with much rejoicing by the monks and the most blessed Hegumen Porfirii and given places to sleep in the brothers' cells. My cellmate was a novice named Constantine from Crete who was very kind to me, saying *"You are always welcome. May my cell be like your cell, and your cell like my cell. And we are your brothers. Our hegumen is a good man and the brothers are good, and there are many brothers. Our monastery is beautiful and there is much singing, and they sing beautifully."* Then he asked me *when I arrived, on what day and at what time, and where I had been, in which country and in which city, and why I had come, whether on my own business or sent by someone, and whether I planned to stay long.*[8] One of the Rus brothers interpreted for me, but I added these phrases to our book and committed them to memory.

The next day we went to the Church of St Sophia, that is to say to the Church of the Divine Wisdom. When we came to the great doors . . . [manuscript lacuna] *. . . wonders which we have seen; others we did not see. It is impossible to go to all the holy monasteries or holy relics, or to recount them. Still, there are thousands upon thousands of relics of saints and many wonders which it is impossible to describe.*[9] In the evenings and on days when we were not visiting churches we worked alongside the brothers. I worked with Constantine in the kitchen, learning many Greek phrases: *fetch water; what are you cooking?; prepare food suitable for a fast day; set the table; lay out the bread; prepare the wine; everything is ready; call the brothers; eat, brothers, holy fathers, and don't wonder at what God has given.*[10] All of these I added to our book and tried to remember, though I fear I would never have learned the Greek tongue even if I had stayed until the end of time.

Soon after our arrival, we discovered to our horror that what Father Ignatii had heard was true: I mean that the emperor and patriarch had made a devilish pact with the wicked Latins and stained the purity of the holy Orthodox Church. The situation in the city was confusing, with some saying that the emperor was planning to hold a synod to anathematize the pretender in Thessaly, who opposed the union. Others said that the pretender would retaliate by holding his own synod to anathematize the emperor, the patriarch, and the pope.[11]

Now, our brothers in the monastery, both Greek and Rus, were of the strictest Orthodoxy, maintaining the laws of the holy fathers and keeping all the fasts. Although the monastery was an imperial foundation, the brothers refused to have anything to do with the apostasy of the emperor and the patriarch, and the latter did not dare oppose them. But some difficulties arose in connection with the wedding of the princess Irene to the Bulgarian prince Ivan, which took place two weeks after our arrival.[12] The monastery was supposed to send a representative or risk the patriarch's disfavor and possible persecution. Hoping for divine guidance, the blessed fathers Ignatii and Porfirii prayed all night in the cathedral. During the night, while prostrating himself before the icon of the Mother of God, Father Ignatii had a vision of St Luke painting a portrait of our most holy Lady in our own Monastery of the Dormition in Tver.

Taking this as a sign about the purpose of our journey, Father Ignatii decided that we would attend the wedding, and we set out the next day for the Blachernai Palace. I soon lost my companions in the crowd, and stepped up onto the base of a pillar to try to see them. Instead, I caught a glimpse of the imperial family as they entered, resplendent in the most luxuriously embroidered golden robes imaginable and wearing golden crowns. As the ceremony started, however, I was rudely knocked off the pillar by some of the imperial guards and sent sprawling on the stone floor. Some monks rushed to my aid, and I could tell from their speech that they were Bulgarians. To my astonishment, they told me that they were fresco painters from the entourage of Prince Ivan, having trained in the Zograf Monastary on the Holy Mountain and travelled with him to Constantinople to serve as advisors and interpreters.[13] When I eventually found Father Ignatii and introduced them, the blessed father saw in our meeting the fulfillment of his vision and gave thanks to God.

The fresco painters' names were Kirill and Mavrikii. They were brothers from Plovdiv who had learned Greek during their time on the Holy Mountain as well as some Rus from the monks of the holy Monastery of St Panteleimon. They welcomed the opportunity to go to Rus with us since the situation in Plovdiv was chaotic, with the city being conquered first by Latins, then by Greeks, then again by Bulgarians. Negotiations took some time, since Prince Ivan was occupied with his new bride and dealings with the emperor. However, after another month we were able to make all the necessary agreements and prepare to return to Rus. All of the monks prayed fervently throughout the night that we might have a smooth journey and in the morning accompanied us to the harbor with weeping and wailing. I embraced Constantine like a brother and wept bitterly, since he had been such a dear friend to me. Soon, however, it was time to embark on a merchant ship . . . [manuscript breaks off].

Notes

1 Matthew 20:16. The "Land beyond the Forest" refers to the area of northeast Rus around Moscow, as opposed to the older cities in the south around Kiev. Iaroslav Iaroslavich ruled Tver from 1247 to 1271 and was succeeded by his son Sviatoslav Iaroslavich, who ruled until the early 1280s. Sviatoslav's younger half-brother Michael went on to rule Tver from 1282 to 1318.
2 *RTC*, 395.
3 Michael was about six years old at this time. He was being taken to Sarai, the capital of the Qipchaq Khanate, the subdivision of the Mongol empire which controlled Rus. Michael's stay as a hostage was probably meant to guarantee that Sviatoslav would fulfill a duty, such as tax collection, on behalf of Khan Mengü-Timür.
4 *RTC*, 78. The Bulgars were a Turkic people whose homeland on the upper Volga was devastated by the Mongols in 1236.
5 *RTC*, 82, 84.
6 Prince Vladimir of Kiev oversaw the official conversion of Rus to Christianity in c. 988. According to *The Primary Chronicle*, he attacked Cherson and demanded to marry Anna, sister of the Byzantine emperor Basil II. Basil agreed, on the condition that Vladimir convert to Christianity (*RPC*, 111–113).
7 *RTC*, 44.
8 Vasmer, *Ein russisch-byzantinisches Gesprächbuch*, 19, 83, 84.
9 *RTC*, 92, 164.
10 Vasmer, *Ein russisch-byzantinisches Gesprächbuch*, 98, 99.
11 The "pretender in Thessaly" is John the Bastard, ruler of one of the many small successor states which emerged after the end of the Latin occupation. The synod in Constantinople took place on 16 July 1277, and John's counter-synod in December.
12 Michael VIII married his daughter Irene to Ivan III Asen as part of his support of Ivan to become the ruler of Bulgaria.
13 Zograf was the Bulgarian monastery on Mt Athos, and St Panteleimon was the Rus one.

Suggestions for further reading

Jordan, Robert, "*Pantokrator: Typikon* of Emperor John II Komnenos for the Monastery of Christ *Pantokrator* in Constantinople", in *Byzantine Monastic Foundation Documents: A Complete Translation of the Surviving Founders' Typika and Testaments*, ed. by John Thomas and Angela Constantinides Hero. Washington, DC: Dumbarton Oaks, 2000, 725–781.

RTC: Majeska, George, *Russian Travelers to Constantinople in the Fourteenth and Fifteenth Centuries*. Washington, DC: Dumbarton Oaks, 1984.

Martin, Janet. *Medieval Russia 980–1584*, 2nd ed. Cambridge: Cambridge University Press, 2007.

Nicol, Donald. *The Last Centuries of Byzantium 1261–1453*, 2nd ed. Cambridge: Cambridge University Press, 2002.

RPC: The Russian Primary Chronicle Laurentian Text, trans. and ed. Samuel Hazzard Cross and Olgerd P. Sherbowitz-Wetzor. Cambridge, MA: Mediaeval Academy of America, 1973.

PORTRAITS OF EASTERN EUROPE

Conclusion – pulling back the curtain

Christian Raffensperger

History and imagination

Though the lives portrayed in this volume can best be described as "imagined," they are real representations of our modern understanding of the past. The scholars who have created these portraits researched the context for each life that they imagined and they created a realistic, if not real, portrait of what life was like for a Scandinavian trader, a princess in Rus', or a Serbian monk. The readings that they have provided at the end of their portraits give you a sample of what you too can use to investigate the lives of these medieval individuals. For more information on these individuals, and more resources to investigate their lives, you can utilize the companion website to the project – www.routledge.com/cw/ostrowski.

The discussion that I would like to have here, though, is one about history and how history is created. Once upon a time (typically we generalize this to the nineteenth century, but it happens still today), historians viewed history as a collection of "facts" that could be learned from primary sources (documents written at or around the time of the events that they describe). Those facts could then be assembled to present an accurate representation of what life was like in whatever period of history was under investigation. Developments in historiography over the course of the twentieth century called the basic fundamentals of this process into question – they problematized not only primary sources and their purpose but the existence of objective "facts" in the first place. This culminated in the postmodern movement in history, which has become most identified with these views and which has shaped the current generation of historians to a great degree, this historian included. One historian has suggested that, for historians, postmodernism "is the prioritization of language over experience, leading to outright skepticism as to the human capacity to observe and interpret the external world, and especially the human world."[1] What to do with this problem and this shift has provoked multiple responses among historians, but the way that I have dealt with this is to incorporate these ideas into an overarching context for the historical progression. Just as we stress context for the development of historical ideas in the classroom, we must rely as well on the understanding that the historical profession evolves and changes over time. Postmodernism, and the questioning of the observable, provable nature of historical fact, is just one of those schools of thought that has adapted to help historians study history.

The problematic nature of history and "fact" has provoked much discussion in college classrooms as students, who learned history as a series of names and dates to be tested on in high school, transitioned to a history curriculum where history, the pre-modern world in particular, is much more amorphous and full of "probablys," "maybes," and "could have beens," as well as deep discussions of what the primary sources say and what they mean. This volume plays a role in the larger discussion of what historians do, by asking historians to do something that seems outside the bounds of their normal work: to take their academic research, their immense knowledge of primary sources and secondary scholarship, and then to write something that adds in a dose of imagination to bring to life the historical actors that they are portraying. The part we play in this discussion, however, is the reality that this is actually not abnormal to the life of a historian. We often, it turns out, use our imagination to fill in the numerous gaps between the bits of information provided by the primary sources; typically we just call it conjecture. Depending upon the historian, this can be indicated in an academic text by saying clearly that "one can conjecture that" or rather more obtusely but much more commonly with the phrase "must have been." "Must have been" phrases are a historian's rhetorical device that translates into layman's language as "I don't have evidence for this, but I think it happened this way." Though historians writing history, not imagined lives, are definitely writing non-fiction, they (we) are using our own knowledge of the life and times (contextual information), combined with the primary sources, and topped with a dash of imagination/conjecture to create the historical picture that we present in our monographs and articles.

I share these thoughts not as a way to undermine history, or historians' credibility, but to explain how history and historians work, to fulfill the title of this conclusion by "pulling back the curtain" somewhat on the process of writing this volume and being a historian in general. It will also, I hope, add to the discussion about what historians do, how they work, and what tools are in their toolbox. These are tools that historians in training can also utilize as they develop their historical skills.

Translation and reality

There is a base problem with teaching medieval history, of anywhere, to undergraduates and that is that the students typically lack the language experience to read sources in the original languages. It is the rare college freshman these days who comes in with either Greek or Latin, much less Old East Slavic! To remedy this, many of the sources have been translated into English, and it is those translations that are typically listed in the suggested readings section of each portrait. However, here I would like to move beyond the translation of texts to address a greater, and even more difficult, issue: the translation of concepts and ideas.

As editors of this volume, Donald Ostrowski and I made a decision to allow the authors to utilize their own translations of terms, names, and concepts, rather than impose a uniform set upon them. The goal of this was to reflect the scholarly diversity inherent in how academics from a variety of places, studying different areas, think and write about the same topics. Sometimes these differences have at their root a basic disagreement over meaning, while at other times they are simply expressing different scholarly traditions of translation. Here, I will talk in some detail about one example – the title of the ruler of Rus' – to give examples of these differences as contained in the portraits in this volume.

There are several portraits in this volume that deal with Rus', and Rusians (the inhabitants of Rus'), whether from the earliest days of the Scandinavian explorations, the marriages of princesses and ruling of queens and kings, or their ecclesiastical history. The title of ruler in Rus' in the language of the time (Old East Slavic) was *kniaz'*. Kniaz' derives from the root *kuningaz, sharing that root with words in Old Norse (*konungr*), German (*konung*), Anglo-Saxon (*cyning*), and even English (king). How that word is translated and what that word means are separate, but deeply interrelated, conversations. The word means, at its root, ruler. And that is certainly one way that it can be translated. I typically translate it as that, as I have in my portrait here. However, the typical translation into English is "prince" as you will see in other portraits relating to Rus' here. To take the conversation a step further, I have argued elsewhere that the title should be translated not as prince, but as "king."[2]

How can one word come to be translated as ruler, prince, and king (which is not to mention those who translate it as "duke")? That gets us into the question of what the word means. In medieval Europe of the tenth through thirteenth centuries, there was a great deal of interaction between Rus' and the rest of Europe. The local, Rusian, sources describe the ruler of Rus' and the rulers of the various cities of Rus' with the same title, kniaz'. When those rulers interacted with the rest of Europe, they appeared in sources written in other languages – and were called konungr in Old Norse and rex in Latin. This gives us some sense of a contemporary equivalency of titles, as perceived by the neighbors of Rus'.

Over the course of the thirteenth, fourteenth, and fifteenth centuries there was a growing disconnect between the new power center of northeastern Rus' – Muscovy – and the rest of Europe. When British traders arrived in Moscow in the sixteenth century, they found a court ruled by a tsar' and staffed by multiple kniazia (plural of kniaz') who were members of the same family as the tsar' but were his subordinates. They translated this model of rulership onto their own and the ruler at the top became a king, or sometimes emperor, and the kniazia became dukes, and later princes. The use of these translations into English became common over the centuries of diplomatic interaction between the Anglophone world and the Russian one, such that when historians began writing about the medieval history of Eastern Europe they had at hand easy translations for titles such as kniaz'.

Where the problem arises is that though the translation of kniaz' as duke or prince is accurate for the sixteenth century, or perhaps a couple of centuries earlier, and certainly through to the present, it is not the correct translation for the tenth, eleventh, and twelfth centuries. Scholars, though, have followed good practice and cited existing examples of translation to prove their point, thus creating even more examples of kniaz' being translated as prince. It is in this way that one word can be translated in many different ways, though each translation expresses a slightly different concept. Translating kniaz' as king is different from translating it as prince. The resulting impression of Rus' is also different.

Keeping all of this in mind, and part of the lesson of pulling back the curtain, it is important to consider the historical context not just for people and events, but words. Words and meanings too have their time and their place, as can be drawn from multiple modern examples, the most well-known being "awesome." The King James Bible can use "awesome" to describe God's might, but this is a different meaning than that used by Bart Simpson, or most anyone in the twenty-first century. Like so many things in history, context is everything.

What is medieval Europe?

A casual perusal of the keywords "medieval Europe" in any college library catalog will turn up from dozens to hundreds to thousands of books with "medieval Europe" in the title. The vast majority of those books will be found to deal with only a small portion of medieval Europe, perhaps with a focus on England, France, and the papacy and their interactions with one another; the Vikings' attacks on them; and their attacks on the Middle East. But despite the fact that the books have "medieval Europe" in the title, they leave out more than half of the continent.

On the other hand, works that deal with the medieval history of the rest of Europe, Poland, Hungary, Ukraine, Russia, and the Balkans, often exist inside national silos rather than as part of a broader horizontal framework of medieval history. And, I have found, it is quite impossible to write a book about this part of medieval Europe and call it *X in medieval Europe*. Reviewers and publishers tend to have strong objections along the lines of, "but you do not deal with *all* of medieval Europe, just the East." If you have read the portraits in this volume, you will certainly understand the irony in such a complaint, having seen the impressive breadth of medieval European history just in this limited area that we have covered.

All of this is part of my goal to "pull back the curtain" on some of the editorial discussions and scholarly debates that went into the making of this volume. Students of history are historians in training, and they need to know that history is not cut and dried facts, but a process of understanding and creation of understandings of the past that fit the sources we have and our interpretations of them. A big part of this is scholarly discussions of frames of understanding; thus, "what is medieval Europe?" is actually a big question with multiple potential answers. For our purposes, though, I would like to talk particularly about only part of medieval Europe, the part we put into the title – medieval Eastern Europe.

What is "Eastern Europe"?

Though popular culture and the news media use certain terms, like Eastern Europe, readily, they are more problematic among academics as well as among people who live in, or near, those areas.[3] Eastern Europe is a particularly fraught concept in modern politics, stemming most recently from the Cold War, but historically there have been concepts of Eastern Europe stretching back to the early modern period. From the Cold War period, Eastern Europe retained a legacy of Soviet influence – being non-Western in many ways including economically, culturally, and socially. The newly non-Communist states in that territory post-1991 worked diligently to define their future as explicitly *not* Eastern Europe. This new geopolitical reality led to an increasing use of new terminology to describe many of these areas. The term "Central Europe" in particular became quite popular, and has remained so, as a way for formerly Eastern European states such as Hungary, Poland, and the Czech Republic, to shed their identity as "Eastern" and become not quite Western, but something other than "Eastern."[4] Other scholars have not quite left behind "East" and adopted instead the term "East-Central Europe." This is most popular with scholars working on southeastern Europe who also would like their polities to no longer be "Eastern" but recognize that it is not Western, or even quite Central Europe.[5] Left out of all of these formulations is a rather large part of Europe – Ukraine, Belarus, and Russia – which is rather the point in many cases. "Eastern" became identified with Russian, and with Russian and Soviet dominance, and thus there was a desire to break away from that influence and connection. However, if one follows this breakdown and accepts all of the labels, a progressive gradation of Europe has been created from the West (England and France), Central Europe (Germany, Poland, Hungary), East-Central Europe (Bulgaria, Romania, the Balkans), and then Eastern Europe (Russia and Ukraine). This seems overly complicated and overly divided for a relatively small continent.[6]

The real problem for our purposes as historians comes when these modern political rationales for territorial divisions are then read back into the past to create a medieval Central Europe, medieval East-Central Europe, etc. And this is where we return to a discussion of our volume. As I argued in my *Reimagining Europe: Kievan Rus' in the Medieval World*, there was not a medieval Eastern Europe in the tenth through twelfth centuries. Rather, Rus' (which was not Russia, or Ukraine read back into time, but a medieval polity in its own right) was integrated with the rest of medieval Europe via dynastic marriages, religious connections, trade connections, and so on.[7] This is an important concept to take as a starting point, and can be expanded to other areas. Medieval Europe was deeply interconnected from Scandinavia in the north to the Italian peninsula in the south; from Byzantium in the east to France in the west.[8] Falsely dividing medieval Europe into regions, as is being done regarding modern Europe, does not serve to increase our understanding of what happened and why.

That said, given the above material about not being able to simply call this volume *Portraits of Medieval Europe* and exclude the western part of Europe, we had to make a terminological choice. In this volume are portraits that deal with people from Scandinavia, the Baltic, eastern Europe, central Europe, and southeastern Europe including Byzantium. Stringing these together creates a rather unwieldy title that not only does not fit on a book jacket, but also is more confusing than enlightening. To avoid that, but also to ideally not increase confusion, we opted simply for medieval Eastern Europe. In my mind this best expressed the information that we wanted to convey to you – our audience. This book *is* about medieval Europe, even if the focus is on the eastern part of medieval Europe, broadly construed.

Ideally, this discussion of the choices made regarding terminology have explained rather than complicated the matter at hand. Beyond that, I hope that it has pulled back the curtain on some of the methodological issues that go into the construction of academic debates and the eventual publication process of academic work.

Notes

1 John Tosh, with Seán Lang, *The Pursuit of History: Aims, Methods and New Directions in the Study of Modern History* (London: Pearson, 2006 [Fourth Edition]), 194. There is much more here about postmodernism and its impact on history and historians as well, for those interested.

2 Christian Raffensperger, *The Kingdom of Rus'* (Kalamazoo, MI: ARC Medieval Press, 2017). There is a full discussion of the problems with translation and titulature here, which have only been very briefly summarized in this conclusion.

3 To add a wrinkle to this conversation for those especially interested – Eastern Europe with a capital "E" refers to the idea of Eastern Europe, and particularly the stereotyped ideas that are discussed above; while eastern Europe with a lowercase "e" refers to the geographic direction. In my recent work, I attempt to use the latter, eastern Europe, rather than the former, Eastern Europe, to describe the region with which I am working. That said, it is not easily possible to use a lowercase letter in the title to a book, which might have obviated the need for this digression.

4 There is an excellent discussion of the idea of Central Europe, as well as a justification of it, in Nora Berend, Przemysław Urbańczyk and Przemysław Wiszewski, *Central Europe in the High Middle Ages: Bohemia, Hungary and Poland, c. 900–c. 1300* (Cambridge: Cambridge University Press, 2013), ch. 1.

5 See Florin Curta, ed., *East Central Europe and Eastern Europe in the Early Middle Ages* (Ann Arbor, MI: University of Michigan Press, 2005).

6 And truth be told, Europe's claim to the title of "continent" largely rests on the Greco-Roman associations of our modern academic systems of classification.

7 Christian Raffensperger, *Reimagining Europe: Kievan Rus' in the Medieval World* (Cambridge, MA: Harvard University Press, 2012).

8 Though one should also note that there was no Byzantium or France in the Middle Ages. These modern labels are, again, anachronisms. Byzantium was the Roman Empire and was called such by its emperors and people, even if they spoke Greek. France was the kingdom of the Franks for much of medieval history, rather than a modern nation read back into the past. The same is true for polities throughout Europe. Thus, though the maps in this book are useful tools, even they bear some hint of this commonly accepted anachronism.

INDEX

Gračanica 118
Great Britain 8
Greece 7–8, 170, 172, 176n18
Gregory, slaveowner 138
Gregory, son of Paul 105
Gregory, son of Stephen 102
Gregory VII, pope 105, 180–1
Gregory IX, pope 41, 133
Gregory of Nazianzus 51
Gruber, Isaiah xiii, 3, 166
Güyük, son of Ögödei 71, 72, 78n14

Haithabu 153–4
Halecki, Oscar 8
Halyč-Volynia 50, 52, 53, 56
Häme 40–9
Harqasun 72
Hedeby 153
Helen, daughter of John Asen II 98n24
Helen, queen of Hungary 111–14, 117
Henry, brother of Vladislav 127
Henry, of Lower Silesia 132
Henry, priest 3, 33, 36, 38n9
Henry III "the Long" 179
Henry IV, Holy Roman Emperor 6,
    179–82, 183n4
Henry Dandolo, doge of Venice 101
Henry the Bearded 135
Henry Zdík, bishop of Moravia 5, 123–7
Hercegovina (Hum) 8, 106
Hermann, bishop of Tartu 34, 37
Holmes, Sherlock 2
Homer 81
Hrvatin, count 105–6
Hryhoryj, ascetic 52–7
Hungary 4, 5, 7–8, 56, 69, 72, 76, 95,
    98n23, 102, 104–5, 108, 111–12, 113–15,
    129–36, 138, 140, 142, 175n16, 179, 197,
    198; Hungarians (Majarat) 62, 72–5, 76,
    78n16, 132
Huru Arkapoika 44

Ianka Vsevolodovna, sister of Evpraksia
    183n2, 184n7
Iaropolk Iziaslavich 17
Iaropolk Volodimirovich 21
Iaroslav, kniaz' of Torzhok 29
Iaroslav Iaroslavich, kniaz' of Tver' 192n1
Iaroslav Sviatoslavich, grandson Iaroslav
    Iaroslavich 186
Iaroslav Volodimirovich 34–8
Iaroslav Volodimirovich (the Wise) 171,
    175n14
Ibn Fadlan 151
Iceland 8

Ignatii, hegumen 186, 189–91
Igor' Sviatoslavich 62, 64–7
Ilarion, metropolitan 180
India (Handua) 170
Ingjeld 152–3
Innocent, pope 125, 127
Investiture Controversy 6
Ioann II, metropolitan of Kiev 180, 183n1
Ioannis, eunuch 160–2
Ioann the Bulgarian Exarch 51
Iran 68, 76
Ireland 8
Irene, daghter of Michael VIII 191, 192n12
Irene (Eirene) Doukaina 81, 84, 86
Irene-Yolanda of Montferrat 119
Isaac, biblical 166
Isaac Angelos 67
Isoaho, Mari xiii, 4, 40
Israel (Yisrael) 166, 173
Italy 8, 107
Iugra 25
Iurii Dologrukii 62
Iurii Oleksinich 24
Iurii Vsevolodovich 38
Iziaslav Mstislavich 21

Jacob, biblical 166
Jadwiga, queen of Poland 143–4
Jakusz (Janusz) of Boturzyn, master chef 144
James Tiepolo 107
Jan Długosz 5, 143, 144
Japheth, biblical 175n13
Jarl Igor 153–5
Jazdów 55, 56
Jebe 68–70, 73, 75
Jerusalem (Yerushalayim) 95–6, 98n15,
    98n17, 98n27, 124–5, 166, 174n2
Jin Empire 68, 73, 76
Joachim I, Bulgarian patriarch 92, 97n1,
    97n4
Joachim Gútkeled, bán of Slovenia 103
Jochi 68–70, 72, 78n15
Jochi, Ulus of (Qipchaq Khanate) 4, 110
Jogaila (Jagailo, Władysław-Jagełło),
    Lithuanian Grand Duke 57
John I Angelos 110, 113
John I Tzimiskes 165n2
John III Vatatzes 98n20, 98n24, 99n 28,
    111, 113
John Asen II, Bulgarian emperor 92, 97n2,
    97n8, 98n13, 98n22, 98n23, 98n24, 98n28
John (Ivan) Asen III, Bulgarian emperor
    191, 192n12
John Chrysostom 51
John Climacus 51

11211815R10085